24 �ₚ
4

CHURCH-LIFE AND CHURCH-ORDER
DURING THE FIRST FOUR CENTURIES

JAMES VERNON BARTLET

[Frontispiece

CHURCH-LIFE

AND

CHURCH-ORDER

DURING THE FIRST FOUR CENTURIES

WITH SPECIAL REFERENCE TO
THE EARLY EASTERN CHURCH-ORDERS

THE BIRKBECK LECTURES
DELIVERED AT TRINITY COLLEGE CAMBRIDGE
IN 1924 BY THE LATE
JAMES VERNON BARTLET
M.A., OXON.; HON. D.D., ST. ANDREWS

AND EDITED BY
CECIL JOHN CADOUX

with a Foreword by Dr. W. B. Selbie,
and a Memoir by the Editor

BASIL BLACKWELL : OXFORD
1943

Made and Printed in Great Britain
by Hazell, Watson & Viney Ltd.
London and
Aylesbury

TABLE OF CONTENTS

vi

character of the earliest Church-order; growth of the
theory of a Divinely-ordained constitution; tension
between the legal and the evangelic spirit; some survival
of spiritual freedom, notwithstanding; nature of the
influences moulding Church-order; local conditions
affecting Church-order; those involving separation of
agape and eucharist, and a great expansion of the official
ministry; varieties of racial and cultural psychology;
the place of the sacramental principle; the eucharist as the
sacrament of unity; its influence in the growth of the
monarchical episcopate; yet growth in numbers restores
functions to the presbyters; distinction between bishop
and presbyters not at first sharp, especially at Alexandria; contrast between earlier and later theory of
Church-order; questions raised by the contrast; liberty
of spirit and prophecy now virtually excluded; the
silent protest of monasticism; spiritual dualism between
clergy and laity; consequent defect in true "organization", and lowering of the Church's vitality and power;
causes favouring the change; summary description of
the change; the root-principle of a genuinely-catholic
Church-order.

FOREWORD

by the Rev. W. B. Selbie, M.A., D.D.,
Principal-Emeritus of
Mansfield College, Oxford.

The making of this book has been a labour of love. If this
brief foreword which I have been asked to write can in any way
serve to commend it, I shall be glad indeed. It is, I think, a
not-unworthy memorial of one who was in many ways a really-
remarkable character. I first met Vernon Bartlet in the autumn
of 1882; and from that time onwards we were close friends.
For many years we were colleagues in the work of Mansfield
College, where I always found him a most loyal and devoted
helper. He was a man whom to know was to respect, admire,
and love. A great Christian, his religion dominated his whole
life, and determined all his relations with his fellows. He
lived, if ever man did, "as ever in his great Taskmaster's eye".
If there was at times a touch of austerity about him, it was due
to his deep seriousness and utter sincerity. He had been brought
up in a harshly-Calvinistic atmosphere; but he thought and
felt his way out of it into a larger and serener faith. This
experience gave him a deep sympathy with all who were perplexed with religious difficulties and a real understanding of
their needs. He spared no pains in order to help them; and in
this way he ministered most usefully to many generations of
younger men. He had a very large charity, and could make
allowance for human frailty: but he would suffer no toning-
down of the ethical implications of the Christian Gospel. His
religion was very real; and he made it real to others because,
like Chaucer's parson, he wrought as well as taught. And he
carried his charity into things ecclesiastical. Though a
Puritan and a Free-Churchman, he was never intolerant. He
had many friends in all the Churches; and he worked hard
for a better understanding and for friendlier relations between
them. He had no illusions about corporate reunion; but one
of the most cherished objects of his life was to further that
unity of spirit which makes all true Christians one in Christ.
Bartlet was a scholar to his finger-tips, but no mere dry-as-

dust. He carried his learning lightly, and never lost sight of its possible practical applications. His main interest was the origin and expansion of the Christian Church. He was as much at home in the field of New-Testament study as in that of Church-History, as witness his admirable commentary on the Gospel of St. Mark. As a scholar he was exact and cautious to a degree; but he never lost sight of the wood for the trees. If he seemed sometimes to halt between two opinions, this was only because he wanted to be sure of his ground. He had no hesitation about the verdict, where all the evidence pointed that way. But he was very impatient with hasty generalizations and with theories not sufficiently grounded in facts. As he once said to me, he did not like half-cooked food. In this respect he was a true disciple of Dr. Sanday, "my revered teacher who taught me to verify my references". It seems to some of his friends unfortunate that much of Bartlet's best work is buried in encyclopaedias. But he himself would not have felt it so. In writing for them he felt that he was writing for serious students present and future, and that they deserved the best that he could give them. The number and variety of such articles may be seen from the bibliography at the close of this volume so carefully compiled by Dr. Cadoux.

When Bartlet died, it was hoped that he had left material for other books, for, as Dr. Fairbairn once said, there were many books in Bartlet. Materials were certainly there in abundance, but in such a condition that no use could be made of them. The only fragment that could be rescued from the chaos was the manuscript of the Birkbeck lectures on Church-life and Church-order in the first four centuries. These lectures have now been revised and edited by Dr. Cadoux, than whom no one could be more fitted for the task. They form a striking and valuable contribution to our knowledge of an obscure and difficult subject; and they illustrate very well Bartlet's mind and his method in the treatment of Church-history. He was always sensible of the dangers of organization, knowing that, while the Spirit may create the institution, the institution tends to quench the Spirit: and he found ample confirmation of this tendency in the period under survey.

To Dr. Cadoux also we owe the biographical sketch: and we must be grateful to him for the way in which he has accomplished a difficult and sometimes-delicate task. There was nothing spectacular about Bartlet's life, no moving adventures

such as make the work of a biographer easy. All his days were
spent in the comparative seclusion of the Oxford that he loved
and in the humdrum work of teaching and College-admini-
stration.   But the man himself was greater than anything he
did: and his brief life-story will be welcomed by many who
loved and honoured him, not merely for his works' sake, but
for himself.

W. B. S.

BIOGRAPHICAL MEMOIR

JAMES VERNON BARTLET was born at Scarborough on the 15th of August, 1863. He was the second child and only son of the Revd. George Donald Bartlet and his wife Susan Robe, née McNellan.

His father, the son of an elder of the United Presbyterian Church, hailed from a farming home in the Glen of Dyce near Aberdeen. He received his education at the Old Grammar School and at Marischal College, Aberdeen, and duly graduated. Notwithstanding an early bent for the ministry, he spent most of his active life as a teacher. He became a master in the academy at Alloa near Stirling, and later town-missionary and prison-chaplain there. During the vacations he took the divinity-course at the United Presbyterian Hall, Edinburgh. After completing this, he became (about 1853) master of the academy at Blandford in Dorsetshire. The London Presbytery ordained him in 1857; and two years later he married Miss Susan Robe McNellan, of Alloa. Their first child—born in 1860—was a daughter, Jane Susan, who is still living. In 1862 he opened a private school of his own at Scarborough; and it was here that his son James Vernon was born the next year.

Early in 1864 Mr. Bartlet was appointed headmaster and Chaplain of Mill Hill School near Hendon; and he moved south with his family to take up his new duties at the commencement of the second half-year. The fortunes of the school had fallen to a very low ebb; and he set himself strenuously to revive them. He succeeded in doubling the number of pupils; but the long-standing financial difficulties of the school were even so not surmounted. At one stage he offered to buy the school from the governing committee; but the project fell through owing to the inability of the parties to agree on the price. Finally, at the end of 1868, the school was actually closed down for a time; and the engagements with the headmaster and the staff were terminated. Mr. Bartlet then established a private school of his own at Solsgirth House, South Grove, Highgate, next door but one to the Highgate Congregational Church. He became increasingly associated with Congregationalism, accepting as he did the Congregational view of the relations of Church and State: and during his residence in Highgate, he often attended the London Congregational Board. It was at his school at Solsgirth House that his son James Vernon received his early education. In 1877 he was transferred to Highgate School, where he remained for five years, until he was able in October 1882 to proceed to Oxford with a scholarship at Exeter College.

From an array of certificates and school-prizes, it is clear that he was a diligent and successful student. A collection of drawings in pencil, crayons, and water-colours, shows that he possessed in boyhood considerable artistic gift. But he distinguished himself chiefly in historical, classical, and scriptural studies—the best educational prelude to his later work. He was also a keen cricketer, played for both school and college, and kept up his facility at the game until he was well on in middle life. He became a life-member of the Oxford University Cricket Club, and always took a great interest in county-cricket. In his later years he was a vigorous tennis-player.

At Oxford he secured in 1884 a first class in Classical Moderations, and in 1886 a second class in the final Honour-School of Literae Humaniores. He then set himself to prepare for the Honour-School of Theology.

His parents belonged to the strictest sect of Scottish Calvinists—rigid as regards their supposed orthodoxy, fundamentalist as regards the Bible, and ultra-puritanical as regards Christian living. Such opinions, indeed, were by no means incompatible with a very genuine and profound religious faith and a high standard of Christian character; and it is clear that Bartlet appropriated from the ethos of his home and early training all that these could impart in the form of genuine piety and lovable uprightness. But it was a type of religion which carried certain grave drawbacks with it—in the form of an unduly-negative attitude to innocent pleasures and to mundane affairs generally. When he moved from the sheltered atmosphere of his home to the freer conditions of life in Oxford, his suspicious apprehensiveness of all worldly corruptions was at first accentuated. But during his days at Exeter College, he began to feel the hard impossibilities involved in the forms of Christian belief traditionally supplied to him: and as a theological student under great scholars like William Sanday and Edwin Hatch, who represented the claims of the "historical method" in biblical and theological study, he began to undergo a gradual and far-reaching change in his religious attitude. Along with this intellectual and theological enlargement there went a corresponding enlargement of his general sympathy and tolerance, while his fundamental Christian loyalty and his habitual gentleness and courtesy remained unimpaired.

It was at the commencement of Michaelmas Term 1886, the very time when Bartlet was commencing his University-studies in theology, that Dr. Andrew Martin Fairbairn, the late Principal of Airedale College, Bradford, began work as Principal of a new theological College now to be opened in Oxford, though not yet built. After long deliberation, it had been decided to transfer the Springhill College for the training of students for the Congregational Ministry from Birmingham to Oxford. The scheme was not only approved and generously supported by Congregationalists all over the country, but was broadmindedly welcomed and encouraged by such distinguished Oxonians as Drs. William Sanday, Edwin Hatch, Benjamin Jowett, and James Bryce. The two national Universities, after having been long reserved exclusively to Anglicans, had in 1871 been legally opened to Nonconformists; and the men just mentioned felt that it would best serve the interests of Free-Church students and of the University of Oxford as well, if these students had their own collegiate centre in the city. Not only would they be thereby protected from the danger of shedding their religious loyalties under the powerful influence of an otherwise-alien atmosphere; but with a College of their own they might even be able to contribute in a useful way to the vigour and freshness of theological study in the University.[1] Mansfield College, as the new institution was named, did not for many years stand in any official relation to the University, and does so now in only a restricted way. But all its members were from the first members of the University also, either as having belonged as Arts-students to one or other of its constituent Colleges, or as having joined for the purpose the Non-Collegiate body now known as "St. Catherine's Society". Although the new Mansfield College-buildings were not opened until October 1889, Dr. Fairbairn conducted classes in a room at 90, High Street; and teachers like Drs. Sanday,

---

[1] Describing the low state of religion in Oxford in the sixties, Dr. L. E. Elliott-Binns writes: "Nonconformity had not yet come in to strengthen the Evangelical side, nor Mansfield, under the massive learning of Fairbairn, to be an intellectual stronghold" (*Religion in the Victorian Era*, p. 323). See also below, pp. xlii–xliv.

Hatch, Driver, and Cheyne allowed their names to appear on the printed list of Mansfield's tutors and lecturers.

It was apparently in January 1887, when he was already nearly half-way through his work for the Honour-School in Theology, and when "Mansfield College" had lived through its first term, that Bartlet came into touch with its great Principal and began to attend his lectures, though not yet formally admitted to it as a student, and still studying under the teachers assigned to him by Exeter College. He was already in the enjoyment of a circle of intimate Free-Church friends, through "The Oxford University Nonconformists' Union", whereof Robert F. Horton, then a Fellow of New College, was a leading spirit, and W. B. Selbie of Brasenose a member. The latter was one of the very first men to put himself under Dr. Fairbairn's training, when he began his work in October 1886: and in June 1887 Bartlet, besides securing First Class Honours in the School of Theology, was formally accepted by the Board of Mansfield College as a student there.

It was as a pupil of Dr. Fairbairn that he gradually and happily emerged, through what must have been painful as well as long-drawn-out struggles, and (it must be added) to the lasting regret of both his parents, from the grim obscurantism in which he had been trained, into a serene and open-eyed faith. Firmly grounded in a devout and filial trust in God as Father through the revelation of Him given to us in Jesus Christ, his religion no longer stood in need of evading or defying the clamorous demands of history and of reason. It had for many been becoming increasingly difficult to harmonize the traditional forms of orthodoxy with the claims of literary and historical evidence and of full intellectual integrity. Notwithstanding the suspicion with which in consequence these claims were regarded by the older and more-conservative adherents of the faith, the moral necessity of coming to terms with them weighed more and more heavily on many Christian hearts; and Mansfield College stood from the first for a full recognition of the duty of meeting them frankly. Dr. Fairbairn himself did not succeed in achieving any great new theological construction in line with his avowed ideal: but by the way in which he combined candid methods of enquiry and bold principles of investigation and discussion with a profoundly-religious spirit, and set an example of reconstructive theological effort, he did much to prepare the way for others to

2

follow later and on ampler lines. One result of his efforts was that he exercised an enormous influence on the men who came year after year under his care. Among those who never ceased to feel themselves deeply in his debt, Bartlet was one of the most emphatic and articulate. He loved to sing Fairbairn's praises, and to exalt him halo-crowned before the wondering gaze of successive generations of alumni of Mansfield. He was in his element at the College-jubilee a few years ago, when he solemnly outlined to a gathering of its past and present members the precise theological position which to-day seemed to him to be, as he said, "echt fairbairnisch".

Of the early days when he himself was eagerly drinking in fresh and stimulating truth from the revered teacher's lips, there still remains—oddly surviving out of unmeasured masses of discarded paper—a venerable scrap, never henceforth to be looked upon by the eyes of Mansfield's sons without astonishment, reverence, and gratitude. It is a single sheet, printed in squares in the fashion of a school-register, filled up in the hand-writing of Norman H. Smith (the first Bursar of the College), and recording the attendances at Fairbairn's lectures in November and December 1888. Among the twelve names are those of J. V. Bartlet, C. Silvester Horne, J. H. Jowett, W. B. Selbie, H. T. Andrews, and Percy Alden. There are entries for only four dates; and only one absence is noted: possibly the zeal and regularity of the scholars were such that it was soon felt unnecessary to carry the record further.

Having already passed the Honour-School in Theology, Bartlet occupied himself during the latter part of his student-ship under Fairbairn in preparing to compete for the Senior Hall-Houghton Greek Testament Prize. This he won in the summer of 1889. Passing now finally out of the status pupil-laris, he was appointed a tutor of Mansfield College, and took up residence in the Tower of the newly-opened buildings, along with his friend and co-tutor, W. B. Selbie. The two men had been much thrown together during the past three years, both as students of Dr. Fairbairn and as fellow-members of "The Oxford University Nonconformists' Union". They now lived together for a year as colleagues in the teaching-work of the College: and the friendship thus cemented between them lasted on to the end of Bartlet's life. Besides being tutor, he was the first Librarian of the College, and held the office for some years. In this capacity the main responsibility for arranging and cataloguing the books transferred to Mansfield Library from Springhill College, Birmingham, lay in his hands. It was not long before he began to appear in print. His earliest discoverable articles were published in 'The Expository Times' for July 1890; and in the same month there appeared an important treatise, on the title-page of which indeed his name did not figure, but in the preparation of which he had taken a significant part. This was the Hibbert Lectures on 'The Influence of Greek Ideas and Usages upon the Christian Church', delivered in 1888 by Dr. Edwin Hatch. The lecturer's death in November 1889 had prevented him from personally superintending the publication of his lectures; and the task of editing them was undertaken by Dr. Fairbairn. The spade-work, however, was done by Bartlet; and it received generous recognition in the editor's preface.

In the autumn of 1890 his regular co-operation with Selbie came to an end for some years, on the latter's acceptance of the pastorate of Highgate Congregational Church (where he had his late colleague's parents as members of his flock). Bartlet stayed on at Mansfield as Senior Tutor in Residence for the next ten years.

It must have been about this time that he became a member of the Taylerian Society. This was a circle which had originally been founded in connexion with the Unitarian College at Manchester. When Manchester College was transferred to Oxford in 1889, the Taylerian Society was enlarged so as to include scholars of every variety of theological persuasion resident in Oxford. It was however felt that a still-further change in name and organ-ization was called for. In May 1891, accordingly, the Society was dissolved: and a new body with an enlarged membership, to be known as "The Society of Historical Theology", was founded to take its place. Of this Society, then, Bartlet was a constant member from its inception until his death. More than that, he was in 1894 appointed its Secretary along with the Rev. H. Rashdall. In later years, his co-Secretary was Canon B. H. Streeter: but Bartlet himself was the working partner throughout. As time passed, and the attending members were constantly if only gradually changing, a growing proportion of influence fell to those who remained permanently in Oxford—and not unnaturally to the repeatedly re-elected Secretaries. Thus it was that Bartlet came to occupy a position of quasi-paternal control, which was the more willingly accorded to him by the Society in view of his catholic policy and irenic manner.

He and those most closely in touch with him felt very strongly the value of the friendly discussion—between men of widely-differing theological and ecclesiastical views—not so much of the doctrinal issues on which they differed, as of the historical questions in which as scholars they were all alike interested. The membership of the Society of Historical Theology was therefore catholic in its range, including (besides a solid nucleus of liberal Anglicans and Free-Churchmen) representatives of the Oxford-Movement, members of the Roman Church, Unitarians, Jews, and a few laymen. A price indeed had to be paid for the joyful harmony regularly characterizing the discussions: the topics treated were limited to matters of mainly-historical interest. Once or twice the question was raised as to whether the Society might not safely venture on further and more-contentious questions. But Bartlet and others felt sure that such an extension would gravely imperil the success thus far attending the Society's activities: as he once urged in conversation, if members with strong ecclesiastical predilections were to "find the atmosphere too bracing", they would be likely to stay away. Despite, however, this confinement of the field, he was convinced that the custom of amicably discussing purely-historical questions with men of a widely-different outlook from one's own, had great value in preparing the way for deeper sympathy and fuller co-operation on larger issues. The social and academic discipline of respecting the conscientious opinions of those from whom one differs is the best possible preparation for an atmosphere of closer Christian unity.

The Society's membership was not confined to persons resident in Oxford or even in Britain. It has always been glad to receive into its ranks distinguished foreign scholars, and when opportunity served, to listen to papers from them. The fraternity is loved and valued by those privileged to belong to it; and all such acknowledge a great debt of gratitude to the man who gave himself so zealously to the practical establishment of its traditions. He was honoured by being called to the Presidential Chair for the Session 1934–5; and he did not vacate the Secretaryship until October 1936.

Two other important events in Bartlet's career took place in 1894. One was the publication of his first book, 'Early Church

History'—a volume that so far retained its value that as late as 1925 a re-issue of it in fresh type and setting was called for. It must have been within a few years after 1894 that Dr. Fairbairn is reported to have said, "Bartlet has written only one book; but there are many books in Bartlet". The other event was the commencement of Dr. Sanday's Seminar on the Synoptic Gospels. Dr. Sanday was at this time Lady Margaret Professor of Divinity; and the Seminar met at his lodgings in Christ Church three times a term. Bartlet was a regular member of it from its commencement until Dr. Sanday vacated his Chair in 1919. In view of the comparative infrequency of the meetings and the leisureliness of the procedure, the achievements came to light only very slowly. But the Seminar more than justified its existence by the production in 1911 of the 'Studies in the Synoptic Problem'—a series of essays by members of the Seminar (Bartlet among them), which became something of a landmark in the discussion of the important problem with which it dealt. But over and above this literary product, no inconsiderable value belonged to the imponderable effects of the gathering, in bringing New-Testament scholars together in an atmosphere such as only the personality and spirit of one like Sanday could create.

In later years, Bartlet spoke of William Sanday and Charles Gore (Principal of Pusey House from 1884 to 1893) as "the two noblest sons of the Anglican communion" whom he had been privileged to know as his friends "over the greater part of a life-time".[1]

Yet another theological group to which Bartlet belonged was the St. Hilary Essay Society. This had been in existence for some years, and early in 1895 was on the point of extinction. Bartlet had served it at various times as Treasurer, Secretary, and twice as President. When the time for dissolution came, it was decided to devote the Society's small cash-balance towards the cost of a photograph. A copy of the group is before me as I write. Six members are there, furnished with bowler-hats and walking-sticks as if for a ramble, and grouped on and around a seat apparently in the University Parks. Bartlet, with his heavy drooping moustache, sits at one end of it, his bowler on the ground beside him. With him are his Old-Testament colleague, G. Buchanan Gray, also A. E. Taylor

[1] In *The Hibbert Journal*, vol. xxx, p. 459 (Apl. 1932).

and his brother E. W. Taylor, David Russell Scott (now of Edinburgh), and E. T. Campagnac.

In 1898 Bartlet visited Italy in company with two or three friends.

To one who studied under him during the last years of the century, when he was still housed in the Tower at Mansfield, Bartlet appeared to be "a man already old, who had never been young".[1] Such an impression is intelligible enough in view of the gravity of his aspect, the deep seriousness of his attitude to life, the habitual dignity and occasional obscurity of his speech, and his life-long inability to read fiction.   These characteristics were largely the result of the atmosphere of his home and the predominantly-academic character of his personal associations.   But, as the informant just quoted has been at pains to tell us, nearly thirty years later Bartlet seemed to him "a much younger man".[2] He never lost his religious seriousness or the solemnity of his utterance: but his constant contact with younger minds, the width of his interests, his long-sustained participation in cricket and tennis, and especially the equability and cheerfulness which marked his bearing from middle-age onwards, both fostered and reflected the development of a broader mind and a more-youthful spirit.

In 1899 appeared his first—and indeed his only—big book —'The Apostolic Age: its life, doctrine, worship and polity'. It was, significantly enough, dedicated "To my Parents, my first teachers in religion: to Drs. A. M. Fairbairn and W. Sanday, my earliest masters in theology".   In later years he modified the opinions expressed therein on one or two controversial topics: but the book has been recognized as a standard treatise on its subject, and it marks the particular field in which, notwithstanding his wide studies in Church-History generally, he always felt his chief interest to lie.

The following year, having now been Senior Tutor for nearly a decade, he was appointed by the College-Council Professor of Church-History (January 1900).   Later the same year he married Miss Elizabeth Gibson of Norwich, the wedding taking place there on the 15th of September.   The couple lived first in a house in Bevington Road, Oxford: but did not remain there very long.   In the course of 1901 they moved to 35, Museum Road; and this house, so familiar to many of his friends,

---

[1] H. Wheeler Robinson in *Mansfield College Magazine*, Jan. 1941, p. 638.
[2] H. Wheeler Robinson, as before, p. 639.

remained his regular home until the end of his days. It was there that his elder son George Vernon was born on the 2nd of February, 1902. Very shortly after this, he took into his home his aged parents, now impoverished by the "Liberator"-crash: and they both spent the last years of their lives under his roof. Not only does this fact say much for his own filial loyalty and for the graciousness of his wife; but a trustworthy tradition bears specific witness to the patience and charity with which he ministered to his parents' needs in the evening of their days.

A second son, Edward McNellan, was born on the 10th of September, 1903: but a cloud of sorrow now began to lower upon the household. On the 20th of March, 1904, the baby died—to be followed to the grave three months later by his mother, who passed away on the 30th of June. The inscription on their tombstone in Wolvercote Cemetery ran: "Living unto God. Amavimus, amamus, amabimus".

It was indeed but a poor comfort for such domestic sorrow, though academically a very great distinction, when on the 29th of March of that same year the University of St. Andrews conferred on Bartlet the degree of Doctor of Divinity. The diploma describes him as a "virum . . . tum vita moribusque integerrimum, tum in Evangelio praedicando diligentem, et in literis sacris colendis spectatum et cognitum". It was, rather strangely, the only doctorate ever offered to him.

He remained for over two years a widower: and on the 12th of September, 1906—nearly five months after his father's death at the age of 83—he married again. His second wife was Miss Sarah Burgess, the daughter of the Congregational Minister of Little Baddow in Essex. There were no children by the second marriage: but Mrs. Bartlet bestowed all a mother's care on her stepson; and between herself and her husband there prevailed to the end that love, companionship, and mutual service which made their home-life a thing of beauty and of peace. His house was for many years the constant resort of an innumerable array of friends, who came either to discuss problems with him in his study or to partake of Mrs. Bartlet's hospitality in his drawing-room.

During all these years of his Professorship, Dr. Bartlet was busy with his regular duties as a Professor at Mansfield College, as well as in other ways. For several years he taught Church-history to the students of Manchester College. Of his work as an author, the bibliography printed at the close of this volume will speak in detail. There were, besides, certain additional undertakings in which he was long engaged and which may fitly be mentioned at this point.

For the space of forty years—from September 1892 to October 1932—he was Secretary of the local branch of the British and Foreign Bible Society. The branch elected him President at its annual meeting in December 1932—an office which he did not resign until October 1939.

Another interest was his attendance at the International Congregational Councils, which are held approximately every ten years, and alternately in England and America. The first of the series was held in London in July 1891. Dr. Fairbairn and the Rev. R. F. Horton represented Mansfield College: and at the suggestion of the former, Vernon Bartlet and W. B. Selbie attended as onlookers. The Second was held in September 1899 at Boston in Massachusetts; and Fairbairn, Selbie, and Bartlet were among the hundred-and-thirty-odd who went thither as delegates from Great Britain. Bartlet contributed a short address on 'The Living Christ' in the discussion that followed Principal Alfred Cave's paper on that subject. The Third Council took place at Edinburgh in June-July 1908. Bartlet and Selbie were again among the delegates; and Bartlet read a paper on 'Is the Congregational Ministry Apostolic?' The Fourth Council was held in 1920 at Boston in Massachusetts: Bartlet did not attend it, as he was that year attending the preliminary meeting (at Geneva) for the World-Conference on Faith and Order. The Fifth International Conference took place at Bournemouth in July 1930; and he and Selbie were once more delegates, and both gave addresses on 'The Living Church'.

For many years Bartlet did work for the University of Wales. A theological degree had been established by this University in 1895–6, the syllabus for which was for the most part drafted by Dr. Fairbairn. Bartlet was one of the examiners year by year from 1909 to 1920 inclusive, regularly attending in this connexion the meetings of the Theological Board at Shrewsbury. In 1923–4 he took part in a visitation of the Theological Colleges associated with the University, "when" (the University Registrar writes) "very important questions of policy were under consideration, including the position of St. David's College, Lampeter, the establishment of Schools of Theology at Bangor and at Cardiff by the co-operation of the University

Colleges of Bangor and Cardiff respectively with the Theological Colleges at these centres, and the reform of the B.D. curriculum. The recommendations of the Visitors included also a scheme for the recognition by the University of theological teachers and the establishment of a Diploma in Theology for non-graduate students. In the preparation of the reports of the Visitors Professor Vernon Bartlet took a great part". He was again examiner in Church-history for Wales from 1925 to 1930 inclusive. At Oxford he was among the first Free-Churchmen who were allowed to examine in "Holy Scripture" (long an indispensable accompaniment of "Responsions"), discharging this office in December 1918 and June 1919.

In the Easter vacation of 1909 Dr. Fairbairn's long and distinguished career as the first Principal of Mansfield College came to an end. He retired, covered with years and honour, to his home at Lossiemouth in Scotland: and the Rev. W. B. Selbie—Dr. Bartlet's former fellow-student and colleague, and now minister of Emmanuel Church, Cambridge—was appointed to succeed him. The two men thoroughly understood one another: and no friction ever marred the happy co-operation with which for the next nineteen years they carried on the work of their great teacher. The third in the team of colleagues was Dr. G. Buchanan Gray, a student of Dr. Fairbairn's slightly junior to them, and a brilliant Old-Testament scholar. These three men were the "pillar-apostles" of the place, until the sudden death of Dr. Gray in 1922 tragically "broke their fair companionship".

Dr. Alexander Mackennal, a prominent Congregational minister, a friend of the College from its inception, a member of its governing Council, and the successor of Dr. R. W. Dale as chairman thereof, had died in June 1904. Steps were taken to raise a memorial fund in order to keep on record the honour in which he was held: and in June 1909 the Council of the College decided to devote the money raised to the part-endowment of the chair of Church-History at Mansfield, and to associate his name with it. Bartlet thus became the first "Mackennal Professor of Church-History". (In this connexion it should perhaps be explained that, in the Congregational colleges, the senior teachers had come to be called "Professors": thus the term has only denominational validity, and, in the case of Mansfield College, indicates no official relationship to the University of Oxford).

An opportunity for a fresh form of service to his brethren in the ministry was opened up to Dr. Bartlet in the summer of 1911, when the movement which soon came to be known as "The Swanwick Free-Church Fellowship" started on its way. It was inaugurated by a group of mostly-younger Free-Church ministers (several of them old Mansfield men), who felt that the whole standard of Christian life and thought, as they knew it in themselves and in their Church-work, needed to be overhauled and reinvigorated through a fresh apprehension of Christian truth and a new self-dedication to the loyalties which that truth evoked. A conference—the first of a long series—was held at The Hayes, Swanwick, Derbyshire, in September 1911. Time would fail me to tell of the leaders of that and subsequent gatherings, or to describe the tone of the fellowship, the character of the proceedings, the thrill of the awakened vision, the vast range of the activities undertaken, the buzz and hum of questing minds, the tense atmosphere of the devotions. The organization has lasted on into our own day, battered by the vicissitudes of history, reduced in numbers, and altered in some of the forms of its undertakings, but still an inspiration to those who belong to it, and indirectly through them to others.

Though a good deal over the average age of its members, Bartlet was in The Swanwick Free-Church Fellowship from the beginning, and was a regular member of its Committee. When, after the first few years, women were admitted as members, Mrs. Bartlet also joined, and has ever since taken a keen part in its life. Bartlet's main share of the work consisted partly in his assistance in committee-discussions, partly in the composition of valuable memoranda on theological and other questions, and partly in his contributions to debates, both public and private. I have no doubt he had a hand in a comprehensive scheme, drawn up in the early days of the Fellowship, wherein its whole energies were to be ambitiously harnessed in two great groups of "commissions"—one group (A) parcelling out the entire universe of Christian doctrine on a classified scheme, and the other (B) directed to the special study of all the various types of personnel with which the Christian churches had to deal. I remember that, when these plans were first submitted to the brotherhood for consideration, Dr. Bartlet had occasion to rise and explain that a certain item of doctrine which some member thought had possibly been omitted was duly covered by a particular section of one of the

A-commissions, inasmuch as that section was to "deal with God, Man, the World, and their relations"!

The rise and prosperity of The Swanwick Free-Church Fellowship prompted the formation of a similar movement in the Church of England. Between the Free-Church and the nascent Anglican Fellowship there existed very close and friendly relations. In all such fraternal associations between Christians of differing denominations, Dr. Bartlet always delighted to participate. In a very striking way he combined a strong Congregational and Free-Church loyalty with a genuinely-oecumenical sympathy. During these years of which we are now treating—as indeed generally throughout his life—he was busy vindicating the great things for which the Puritan tradition stood. The article on 'Congregationalism' which he contributed to the eleventh edition of 'The Encyclopaedia Britannica' (1910) has long been recognized as a classic exposition of its theme. A piece of work much to his mind fell to him in the autumn of 1912, when meetings were held at Mansfield College in commemoration of the two thousand nonconforming clergy who had been ejected from the Church of England in 1662—two hundred and fifty years before. A large body of Free Churchmen joined in these celebrations; and the occasion received a good press. Bartlet's personal share in the proceedings was to conduct a party of visitors round the College, and show them the portraits of Puritan leaders with which its walls are hung, giving a little explanatory account of each leader portrayed. He also delivered an address on the occasion entitled 'Lest we forget' and subsequently printed in 'The Oxford and District Free Churchman'. He had also to deal with a little sectarian criticism of the celebrations which appeared in the press. In November 1913 he attended the Triennial Conference of the Liberation Society held at Holborn Hall in London, and read a paper there on 'The Moral Aspect of Disendowment'. This, along with an essay by Dr. T. Bennett on 'The Legal Aspect of Disendowment', was published as a booklet, and went into a second edition.

The outbreak of the Great War (1914–1918) was to him as to others a profoundly-disturbing shock. His sensitive spirit, his antipathy to all forms of violence and cruelty, and his deep respect for conscience, brought him into very close sympathy with his numerous pacifist friends: yet he never took the pacifist position. The high-handed wickedness of Germany in

Belgium seemed to him then—as the analogous procedure of the Nazi-Government seems to most now—not only to need curbing by force of arms, but to justify the individual Christian in himself participating to the full in the work of curbing it. It was not without sharp inward tension that he took up this position from the outset; for he felt the force of the Christian objections to participation in war, and met them only by a somewhat-subtle doctrine of relativity. His personal charity, however, coupled with a sense of the real complexity of the problem and a very-characteristic reverence for conscience, gave him more sympathy with conscientious pacifists than was felt by many who agreed with him on the practical issue. War or no war, conscience must have its rights, or the future of Christian progress is blotted out. To a colleague who argued for the right of the State to suppress conscientious objectors on the ground that they threatened its existence, he replied with a pained look, "I do not doubt your personal ethos, Robinson; but you seem to me to be sitting on the safety-valve of progress".[1]

During the War Bartlet continued his normal activities in home and College, since a small number of men remained under training throughout. On the 2nd of May, 1915, his mother passed away at the ripe age of ninety. Immediately after the conclusion of the Armistice in November 1918, he went to France as one of the delegates of the National Council of the British Evangelical Free Churches to visit the Protestant Churches of France. The party's tour included an inspection of the battlefields; and Bartlet gave some account of his visit in an article in 'The British Weekly' shortly after his return.

In 1917, despite War-conditions, he produced what bids fair to rank among his greatest pieces of work. It was a large volume entitled 'Christianity in History: A Study of Religious Development'—the joint work of himself and his old friend of Exeter-days, Dr. A. J. Carlyle. It suffered indeed in outward appearance from the period of its publication: I well remember Dr. Bartlet, having just received his "author's copy", holding a sheet of it up to the light in the Tutors' Room one evening after dinner, and exclaiming as he fingered it, "Gray, Gray, just look at this paper: it's like bread made with potatoes!" But whatever the inferiority of the paper, there was nothing inferior about what was printed on it. The book is neither a history of the Church, nor a history of Christian doctrine: it is

---

[1] H. Wheeler Robinson, in *Mansfield College Magazine*, Jan. 1941, p. 638.

a survey, on unconventional lines, of the character and significance of Christianity during the successive epochs of its history from New Testament times to the present day. It gave no explicit indication as to how the work had been divided between the two authors: but no one who knew the men could be in much doubt as to whose work he was reading in this part of the book and in that. Dr. Carlyle has kindly enabled me to indicate in the bibliography the parts for which his collaborator was mainly responsible. He himself contributed much of what was written on the Middle Ages: but the initiation of the scheme, the treatment of the early centuries, and several of the later chapters, were Bartlet's work. Chronologically, the work is very unevenly distributed—a feature which matters much less than it would in a history proper. The first two parts, dealing with 'The Beginnings' and 'Ancient Christianity', give the most penetrating and sympathetic account I know of the religious movements designated by these titles. In depth of religious understanding and power of interpretation they surpass anything I have met elsewhere. A cheaper edition of the book appeared in 1935; and it deserves to be studied and restudied and studied yet again by all who desire to understand the rise and genius of the Christian religion.

I should like to couple with these remarks about 'Christianity in History' a brief tribute to his next important literary production. This was a revised edition of the Century-Bible commentary on St. Mark, which had been originally written by Dr. S. D. F. Salmond, and which appeared in its revised form in 1922. Though nominally a revision, and as such embodying a good many of Dr. Salmond's sentences, it was to all intents and purposes a new work, showing, in my judgment, very striking insight into the inner meaning of our Lord's ministry, besides furnishing a thoroughly-competent treatment of the literary, historical, and exegetical questions within the spatial limits, and conforming otherwise to the special requirements, of the useful series to which the book belonged. Yet it seems to have attracted comparatively-little notice, perhaps owing to the fact that it was a revision, and one designed moreover for readers with no knowledge of Greek. It deserves to be far more widely known and used.

One of the major interests in Bartlet's life, apart from his professional studies, was the movement for Christian "Reunion". Mention may perhaps be made first of the negotiations commenced in 1919–20 for the amalgamation of (1) the Anglican, (2) the Wesleyan-Methodist, and (3) the already-united Congregational and Presbyterian churches, in the mission-field of Southern India. Practical work on the spot had convinced many of the missionaries and their supporters that a larger measure of organizational unity would be in the interests of the supreme object of all foreign mission-work; and the possibilities, conditions, and obstacles involved were the subject of long-drawn-out negotiations. These, though valuable in enlarging mutual understanding and sympathy, have not yet resulted in the practical achievement of union. Bartlet was one of a small number of Free-Church scholars who were taken into constant consultation by the Free-Church representatives in the field. He was in cordial sympathy with the desire for closer relations between the several bodies, and was prepared to concede the Anglican demand that the reunited body to be set up should be episcopal in constitution and government, so long as the episcopacy in question should be after the pattern of that prevailing in the primitive Church, i.e., pastoral and representative rather than diocesan and monarchical. Congregational and presbyterian forms of government were in this and other ways to be allowed to operate as modifying elements in the newly-established episcopal body. Furthermore, at the initiation of the union, there should be—he urged—no re-ordination of ministers already ordained, but a service in which the representatives of the several bodies concerned should solemnly extend to one another's ministries formal recognition and authorization for the wider mutual and combined ministrations which the united Church would thenceforth undertake. I must not occupy more space here in describing and dwelling upon the many other issues involved and Bartlet's personal part in the discussion: reference to the years 1930, 1932, 1933, and 1940 in the Bibliography will reveal particulars about some of the articles he wrote in connexion with it, while for fuller details the persons more directly responsible for the consideration of the scheme must be consulted. A brief account of it may be seen in 'A Christian Year Book', published in 1941 by the Student Christian Movement Press, pp. 87a, 100f.

If self-restraint in the matter of space is needed in connexion with the South India Scheme of Church-Union, much more is it needed in dealing with the wider schemes for Reunion of

a more-general kind.   A good general account of them is
given in the 'Year Book' just quoted, pp. 82-105.   The
Reunion-Movement, in the sense of a movement for union
between all Christian bodies, really dates from the World
Missionary Conference held at Edinburgh in 1910.   Later the
same year the Protestant Episcopal Church of the United
States passed a resolution for the holding of a "World-Conference on Faith and Order", for the purpose of considering the
possibilities of closer union between the several Christian
denominations throughout the world.   Useful committee-work
was done on both sides of the Atlantic.   In particular, mention
may be made of a conference between fifty-four Anglican and
Free-Church ministers who met at Mansfield College in January 1918, Bartlet of course taking part in the discussions.
A preliminary meeting of the "World-Conference" was held at
Geneva in August 1920, which he attended, accompanied
by his wife and son.   He was in poor health at the time: but he
rose from his bed to deliver a moving appeal for wider sympathy on the part of the Greek and Anglican Churches with
those Christian bodies who revered the oecumenical creeds as
marks of progressive intellectual definition of the implicates
of the faith, without being committed to them in the literal
sense.   He spoke in the light of the 'Appeal to all Christian
People', which had recently been published by the Anglican
Bishops assembled at Lambeth—a document which, in its
breadth of Christian sympathy, constituted a landmark in the
relations between the Church of England and the Free-Churches.
The spirit of his address created a marked impression on the
Conference; but the delivery of it was followed by a sharp
attack of illness for the speaker.

The World-Conference proper was held at Lausanne in
August 1927.   Bartlet was present as one of the Congregational
delegates, and took an important part in the deliberations,
representing the Congregational contribution to the great
problem of the unity of Christendom.   He toiled strenuously
on numerous committees with the object of reaching terms on
which Christians of differing traditions could satisfactorily unite
in voicing their common faith.   A full report of the proceedings
was edited in 1928 by Canon H. N. Bate under the title 'Faith
and Order'.

The Conference had a controversial sequel when in May 1929
the Assembly of the Congregational Union insisted on modi-

fying its proposed response to Lausanne in order to safeguard
the Congregational belief that the Church is constituted by the
gathering-together of believers for worship and service, and is
therefore not dependent for its existence on the presence of any
special ministry, however practically desirable and Divinely
blessed such a ministry may be. This response was eventually
printed, along with those of other denominations, in the volume
entitled 'Convictions' and published in 1934 by the Student
Christian Movement Press.

The activities of the Reunion-Movement did not come to a
full-stop with the Lausanne-Conference of 1927. Various
committees were appointed to continue the discussion of outstanding questions; and it was in order to attend one of these
that Dr. and Mrs. Bartlet went to Mürren in Switzerland in
August 1930. On their return they visited Professor and Frau
Strohl at Strassbourg. A year later he was one of a party of
representative ecclesiastical scholars who were entertained by
Dr. A. C. Headlam at his episcopal palace at Gloucester, and
who produced jointly under the auspices of the World-
Conference the volume on the Doctrine of Grace listed in the
Bibliography under the year 1932 (see below, p. 194). Recur-
rent indisposition interfered considerably with Bartlet's
attendance at this and other World-Conference committees:
and it was a matter of keen regret to him, as to others, when
ill-health made it impossible for him to attend the Second
World-Conference on Faith and Order which was held at
Edinburgh in 1937. Though personally absent, he made
strenuous efforts through the post to secure the holding of a
joint communion-service in some episcopal church for all
attending the Conference—unhappily without success.

Before we leave the subject of Reunion, a few further remarks
may be offered regarding Bartlet's personal attitude to the
problem. He believed that the key to it lay firstly in the
common loyalty felt by all professedly-Christian people to
Jesus Christ as Lord, and secondly in a sincere respect for the
consciences of one's fellow-believers. He was never weary of
emphasizing the importance of this respect for conscience, and
the conclusions that might rightly be based upon it. He saw no
reason why there should not be, pending all settlement of outstanding differences, common participation in the Lord's
Supper on the part of those who shared a common faith in Him.
Seeing as he did the crucial differentia of Christian discipleship,

not in subscription to some hallowed doctrinal formula or ecclesiastical usage, but in the religious attitude of man's inmost soul, he pleaded with those who depended on such formulae and such usages as indispensable, to recognize the essential Churchmanship of brethren who, without disloyalty to Christ, hesitated to commit themselves to a literal acceptance of highly-abstruse metaphysical formulae touching His Person and the inner being of the Deity.   On the other hand, he went further than some of his fellow-Congregationalists were prepared to go, along the road of negotiating a business-agreement between the Free-Church denominations and the Church of England.   In this connexion he was prepared to accept episcopacy as of the bene-esse of the reunited Church, provided that certain constitutional safeguards of a congregational and presbyterian kind were established, and provided the reunited Church were not committed to any specific theory of the episcopate, such as that of Apostolic Succession. The objection that a Church reunited on an episcopal basis would ipso facto involve the virtual unchurching of those Christian individuals and groups which for whatever reason should dissent from its credal or organizational requirements —a flaw which Congregationalism on its present lines is alone calculated to forestall—does not seem to have appealed to him.

While thus ready to be compliant with the conscientious conviction of others that the Church, if reunited at all, must be episcopally governed, he was always vigilant against any additional catholicizing of the Church's ways and teaching. Hence it was that, in the controversy over the revision of the Book of Common Prayer in 1927 and 1928, his pen was busy in the composition of numerous letters, some addressed to private friends, and some addressed to 'The Times', 'The Guardian', and other papers, exposing what he felt to be new elements of a Catholic tendency, particularly in the order of service for Holy Communion, such as—while meeting the particular views of a certain section of the Anglican clergy—would gravely impair the good chances that already existed for closer union in the future between the Church of England and the Free-Churches.

Resuming now our survey of successive episodes of interest in Dr. Bartlet's career, we must record that in 1924, on the invitation of the Council of Trinity College, Cambridge, he delivered the Birkbeck Lectures there—on 'Church-Life and

-Order in the first four centuries'. This contribution to our knowledge of the life of the early Church is described with sufficient fullness in another part of this volume.

The largeheartedness with which, despite his unflinching Protestantism, he was prepared to co-operate with Roman Catholics in sacred things, so far as the ground common to them and to Protestants allowed, is illustrated by his acceptance of an invitation from the local Roman Catholic chaplain to take the chair at one of a short series of "Conferences on the Foundations of Religion" held at the Oxford Town Hall in March 1924. The lectures at these Conferences, which were designed for members of the University, were given by two Dominicans, but were concerned with such matters as do not divide Protestants and Catholics; and the chair was taken by various distinguished Protestant members of the University. It was exactly the kind of co-operation of which Bartlet approved, and he gladly rendered the service asked of him.

In April 1924 there was held at Birmingham the Conference on Christian Politics, Economics, and Citizenship, usually known in abbreviation as "C.O.P.E.C." His particular part in it is indicated in our Bibliography of his work; but apart from his personal participation in the Conference itself, he was involved in sundry meetings in London and elsewhere, both before and after the Conference—either in preparing for or continuing its labours, or in expounding to others its ideals and findings.

The following year came another large-scale effort in Christian co-operation, a further instalment as it were of the same sense of concern as had produced C.O.P.E.C.—the Universal Christian Conference on Life and Work held at Stockholm in August 1925. This is not the place in which to attempt an account of the aims and doings of the Conference. The Rev. Edward Shillito has written a small volume for this purpose entitled 'Life and Work', and published by Messrs. Longmans, Green and Co. in 1926. (See also 'A Christian Year Book', 1941, pp. 109-112.) We must content ourselves with recording that Dr. Bartlet, accompanied by his wife, attended the Conference as one of the representatives of the Congregational Union of England and Wales, travelling to Stockholm via Copenhagen. The only public part he took in this most-interesting gathering appears to have been that he spoke in support of the appointment of a Continuation-Committee. He and

Mrs. Bartlet lunched with the Crown-Prince and -Princess of Sweden in the course of the proceedings, visited various other centres in the country and travelled home via Trondjem, Oslo, Copenhagen, and Berlin—at which last they paid a visit to Dr. Adolf Harnack.

As C.O.P.E.C. had had a successor in Stockholm, so Stockholm had a successor in Oxford. Under the leadership of Dr. J. H. Oldham, a Conference was held at Oxford in July 1937 on 'Church, Community, and State', and eventuated in the production of a series of seven handsome volumes dealing with the several problems suggested by the general title of the Conference. To his great disappointment Bartlet was prevented by ill-health from attending this Conference, as also the Faith-and-Order Conference at Edinburgh the same summer (see above, p. xxxii).

We have touched on the Oxford Conference at this point in order to complete our account of the series of Conferences generally: but we must now return again to a more-orderly time-sequence. A somewhat-unfamiliar task fell to Bartlet in the summer of 1927, when he was asked to speak at the annual prize-distribution at Silcoates School near Wakefield, one of the old-standing Congregational schools of the country. His address to the large Saturday-afternoon gathering of boys and their friends was on the call to ward-off dullness and boredom and on the means of doing so. He also preached to the boys at their School-service next day, and received a number of them into Church-fellowship.

It was the rule at Mansfield College that members of its staff should vacate their chairs on reaching the age of sixty-five (unless for exceptional reasons the Council felt that a year-by-year extension for a very few years more was desirable). Under this rule Dr. Bartlet retired from the Mackennal Chair of Church-History in the summer of 1928. The Old Men's Association at its annual meeting took an affectionate farewell of him in his capacity as a teacher in actual harness, and made him a money-present which enabled him and Mrs. Bartlet to take an enjoyable though unfortunately overtiring holiday in Italy. There was a further manifestation of the esteem in which the old members of the College held him when in 1934 they arranged for a crayon-portrait of him to be drawn by Mr. Francis Dodd, and hung in the College dining-hall.

The termination of Bartlet's appointment as Mackennal

Professor of Church-History by no means involved a complete
severance from Mansfield College. On appearing at the annual
College-dinner in morning-clothes within a few years after his
retirement, and being asked by one of the Old Men why he was
not in war-paint, he replied with his characteristic freshness,
"Because I am no longer a warrior". But although no longer a
warrior, he still filled the rôle of an unofficial guardian-spirit.
Continuing to reside in the immediate neighbourhood of the
College, he hovered about its precincts, befriended its members,
dined in hall as an honorary member of the Senior Common
Room, and even assisted in the teaching when Principal Selbie
was ill.

Nor did the vacation of his chair mean any cessation of his
literary activity. In 1929 there appeared, not indeed his last
valuable contribution to theological literature, but his last
substantial piece of work on Christian doctrine. This consisted of three chapters in the composite volume entitled 'The
Lord of Life: A Fresh Approach to the Incarnation'—a work
which he and eight other members of The Swanwick Free-
Church Fellowship had united to produce. His section included
an historical survey of the whole development of the doctrine of the Person of Christ: and it crystallized conclusions
which had been for many years developing in his mind. He
was himself aware of the importance in the changed orientation
of his Christological views, represented by his contribution to
this book: but I will postpone any attempt to characterize this
orientation further, until a later point in this study.

A piece of work which occupied much of his time during the
last ten years of his life, and which, so far as I know, has never
seen the light in printed form, was a long study of the place of
the Scriptures in the life of the Church during the first several
centuries. This was to form part of a complete survey of the
history of the Church from the point of view of those who
believed Protestantism to be the true representative of the
spiritual religion of the Bible, in distinction from the ritualism
and sacerdotalism of the Roman Church. The whole thing
was to be called 'Les Fruits de la Bible dans l'Histoire', and
was to form the third and last volume of a 'Dictionnaire
Encyclopédique de la Bible'. The editorship was in the
hands of a little group of French Protestant scholars, who
had secured the collaboration of leading Protestant theologians
in several other countries. Bartlet took a deep interest in the

scheme, and wrote a great deal in connexion with his own special contribution to it—which of course had to be translated into French. I think I am right in saying that a great part of his rough notes and manuscripts dealing with religious developments in late Judaism was destined for inclusion as an introduction to his more-specific treatment of the Christian period. However that may be, it is impossible to furnish any very precise information regarding the project as a whole. Progress was apparently slow; and the outbreak of war adversely affected the normal conditions of international collaboration, and eventually brought the negotiations with this country to a standstill. Possibly in brighter days to come, some portion at least of what Bartlet wrote will see the light.

Many years before the end of his life he seemed to begin to feel the envious hand of time. When he had yet many years to go before his retirement, he spoke to a student at the commencement of his course, contrasting their positions as those of men commencing, and approaching the end of, their respective careers. It was as early as July 1925 that he concluded thus a letter to an old student who had sent him a presentation-copy of a book he had produced: "As a man comes within measurable sight of the end of his own activity in the great field of Christian Truth, he has no greater satisfaction than to feel that he has been privileged to help others to enter the same, perhaps at a point further on than he himself entered, helped though he may have been (as was my happy lot) by great workers in the same field. Or, to change the figure, it is good to feel that there are strong runners of one's team who will hand on the torch of Truth, loved and sought, after it has dropped from one's own nerveless hand".

On two or three occasions in the course of his last years at Oxford, he opened out quite spontaneously to old pupils, reflecting on the career which was ere long to terminate, and touching both on its privileges and on its shortcomings, and on what he felt he might still be able to say, were time and strength granted to him. The feeling is accounted for by the enormous fertility of his mind (reflected also in the immeasurable mass of thoughts which throughout his life his prolific brain was always prompting him to commit in some form to paper): it was also doubtless in part due to the growing experience of physical weakness. Conscious for a very long period of being delicate in the chest and throat, he suffered for several years before his death from emphysema (a loss of elasticity in the lungs) and from constant trouble if he ever over-exercised his voice.

It became increasingly clear to his friends that his health was failing: and in October 1939, on the urgent advice of his doctor, he left Oxford, and went to spend the winter on the south-coast at Charmouth in Dorsetshire. From here he kept up a vigorous correspondence with a wide circle of friends, always hoping that eventually he might be able to reside again at Oxford for at least the sunnier part of the year. In April 1940 he went with Mrs. Bartlet to stay at Yelverton, as the guest of his former colleague at Mansfield, Dr. W. H. Cadman. Towards the end of July they both returned to their Oxford home, intending to spend only a few days there for the purpose of dealing with some matters concerning the house. Before the month was out, however, he was in bed, suffering from an attack of influenza. No fear was entertained at first that anything more serious was the matter than one of his numerous temporary set-backs. But unhappily influenzal pneumonia set in and developed rapidly: and a little before midnight on Monday, the 5th of August, he passed quietly away. Had he lived for another ten days, he would have completed his seventy-seventh year.

A memorial service was held in Mansfield College Chapel on the afternoon of Thursday, the 8th of August, conducted by the Principal of the College, Dr. Nathaniel Micklem, with the assistance of the Principal-Emeritus, Dr. W. B. Selbie. Despite the awkwardness of war-time conditions, the season of the year, and the shortness of the notice, a large number of friends gathered to pay the last honours to the dead. Some had travelled from considerable distances for the purpose. There were represented, not only his family, but also his old College (in the person of the Rector of Exeter), his circle of University-friends, the Congregational churches, and in a special measure the Mansfield-constituency. His body was laid thereafter to rest in Wolvercote Cemetery, in the grave of his first wife and their infant son, and alongside that of his parents.

Obituary notices appeared in 'The Oxford Mail' for the 6th of August, 'The Manchester Guardian' for the 7th of August, 'The Times' for the 7th, 9th, and 15th of August, 'The Oxford Times' for the 9th of August, 'The Times Literary Supplement' for the 10th and 17th of August, 'The Christian World' for the 15th of August (from Dr. Selbie, his tribute being reprinted with a few changes in 'The Congregational Year Book' for 1941, pp. 392 f.), 'The British Weekly' for the 15th of August (from Dr. Micklem: also a letter from Dr. Garvie in the issue for the 22nd of August): Dr. Selbie contributed an article on his life-long friend to 'The Congregational Quarterly' for the 1st of October, and Dr. A. J. Carlyle to the issue of the same journal dated the 1st of January 1941. In that of a year later the Editor himself drew an interesting comparison between Bartlet and Hort (pp. 11 f.). 'The Mansfield College Magazine' for the 1st of January, 1941, was mainly devoted to tributes to his memory written by several of his old pupils. Mrs. Bartlet received a great number of private letters of condolence, testifying to the affection and esteem in which her husband was held by his many friends.

His surviving son, Mr. George Vernon Bartlet, died prematurely from heart-trouble a year later, on the 1st of August, 1941, leaving behind him his widow, his little daughter Anne, and his gracious stepmother.

The foregoing fragmentary sketch of Dr. Bartlet's life-history will convey only an imperfect impression of his personality as a whole. Those who knew him well will sense the gaps: those who knew him slightly will be but poorly enlightened. Some attempt must therefore be made, however difficult the task may be, to touch on those outstanding phases of his character, which do not readily lend themselves to inclusion in a chronological outline of the events of his life.

As fundamentally important, and abundantly testified by all who knew him, must be mentioned his deep personal religion. It not only dominated his daily interests, controlled his conduct, and moulded his character; but to all beholders it was quite clearly the master-passion of his life. The stress he always laid in his teaching and writing on the filial spirit, on faith as loyal personal trust, and on religious experience as the essence of the Evangelical tradition, the tone of the prayers he offered in the College-chapel, and the very atmosphere of his presence, all told the same story of one who walked humbly with his God.

"Nor ever narrowness or spite,
      Or villain fancy fleeting by,
      Drew in the expression of an eye,
Where God and Nature met in light".

As will be seen in a moment, his Christological views were of a
kind to cause anxiety to some of his more-stringent friends:
but these views did not interfere with his exaltation of Jesus
Christ as Lord; nay, being certified as they were by his personal
experience, they reflected the more surely the loyalty and
trust which he felt towards the living Saviour.

It is significant that he once confided to an old pupil in
an apparently-casual conversation, that his favourite hymn—
one in which all widely-differing Christians could unite—was

> "Jesus, these eyes have never seen
>   That radiant form of Thine;
> The veil of sense hangs dark between
>   Thy blessed face and mine.
>
> "Yea, though I have not seen, but still
>   Must rest in faith alone,
> I love Thee, dearest Lord, and will,
>   Unseen but not unknown".

It was this deep, living religion that constituted the foundation of all the other aspects of his life and work: and we shall
do well to keep it in mind as we study these in succession.

Firstly, then, in regard to his professional qualifications as
a scholar. Of the range and massiveness of his learning his
published work and the memory of his teaching are sufficient
testimony. A glance round his library revealed an acquain-
tance with and interest in every section of that huge field
known as "Church-history"; and the unnumbered multitude of
his jottings written on the margins of almost every book and
on scraps of paper tucked within it and filling every odd
corner, as well of course as heaps upon heaps of less-disorderly
notes, showed a mind unusually prolific, not by any means in
trifling comments, but (as the contents of the jottings and
notes abundantly show) in penetrating and interpretative
reflections on the themes engaging him. The man thought on
paper; and his thoughts were at once abundant and wise.

He was a convinced champion and exponent of what is
known as "the historic method"—the method he had first
learned from Sanday and Hatch and had pursued with the full
approval of Fairbairn. In essence it means the effort to
discover first what the extant records have to tell us of the
thoughts of those who first penned them, without regard to any

preferences we investigators may have touching what they ought to have meant, and before attempting to assess their religious meaning and value for later generations. In order to use such a method with advantage, a man must be not only widely-read, but conscientiously exact in assessing the evidence he collects, and must continually resist the temptation to "over-run his scent" in the hope of seizing an attractive quarry. But Bartlet had more than the competent critic's power of marshalling and weighing evidence; he possessed in a remark-able degree the gift of sympathetic insight into the minds and feelings of men of the more distant as well as the nearer past. Such a gift, no doubt, has its dangers, as the modern imagina-tion is fatally apt to go astray when playing interpretatively upon the religious phases of the past: it is only when (as was the case with Bartlet) it works in company with a really-thorough knowledge of the actual evidence that it can be trusted. It is the combination of these two qualifications in the author that gives such high value to certain works of his like 'Christianity in History', the Century-Bible Commentary on St. Mark, and his chapters in 'The Lord of Life'.

Much of his work was put into articles written for diction-aries, encyclopaedias, and theological journals, such as are apt to get lost sight of and thus to miss the notice and credit due to them. But enough of his published work became well-known to win him a high reputation as a scholar both in this country as well as in America and on the Continent.

His subject was Church-history. But within that area he rather specialized on the early Patristic period and on the development of thought concerning the Sacraments. As his Birkbeck Lectures show, he held that the characteristics of early Christian worship, when studied in the light of the period in which they were developed and manifested, and not in that of the later mediaeval system, or even of the fourth century, yielded a meaning far more favourable to Free-Church tradi-tions and ideals than had usually been thought to be the case. His keen interest in the Apostolic Age brought the New Testa-ment well into his field; and some of his best work was done on New-Testament problems. Dr. Sanday once remarked that he knew no one so well qualified to carry on his New Testament work as Bartlet. I have already mentioned his commentary on St. Mark and his brilliant exposé of Christian beginnings in 'Christianity in History'. He contributed an

essay on the structure of St. Luke to the Oxford 'Studies in the
Synoptic Problem'.   He also wrote the article on 'Paul' for
'The Encyclopaedia Britannica'; and I would like to say at
this point that he was one of the very few men I have met who
could give a convincing interpretation of the great Apostle's
central teaching.   He produced the Century-Bible commentary
on Acts, published short commentaries on some of the Epistles,
and left behind him lecture-notes on others.   It is a curiosity
of his critical judgment that up to the last he clung to the full
Pauline authorship of the Pastoral Epistles, in the teeth of the
overwhelming linguistic and other arguments against it, and
—what is still more strange—proposed to put all three of them
in the period covered by the Acts of the Apostles, without the
help of any theory of a second imprisonment of their author at
Rome.

I do not remember ever hearing him wax enthusiastic about
the glories and beauties of Oxford: but there can be little doubt
that he gave his heart to the place.   He resided in it almost
continously for nearly fifty-seven years; and as his association
with the University shaped his mental development, so his
familiarity with the city's visible form and surroundings
contributed richly to his inner spirit.   "He became", writes
one who knew him well, "one of the half-dozen or so best-
known figures to Varsity and City alike.   He loved Oxford
above all other earthly things; they became very close to each
other, and neither would have been quite the same without the
other.   The Parks, South Parks Road, and the walk therefrom
to 'Mespot', St. John's Garden, and Christ Church Meadow
were his favourite haunts; and in the portions of those pleas-
aunces most sheltered from the dreaded blasts of Boreas, his
mind was wont to be at its most prolific, and ever and anon its
distillations were committed to his diary and the backs of
envelopes".
Within these beloved precincts of the City, his affections
were centred on Mansfield College: and generous acknowledgement is due to the great service he rendered to it as an institution and to the wider Free-Church interests which it was
founded to serve.   It is with no ungracious desire to revive the
troubles of the past that we bring to mind here the changes
which have taken place in respect of these interests.   But the
simple necessity of historical truth requires us to recall, not

only that the Universities had been an exclusive preserve of the Anglican Church from the days of Charles the Second to 1871, but that there existed in general a great gulf of antipathy between the Church of England and the Free-Churches. In our own day, that mutual estrangement has happily to a very large extent passed away; and where it does survive, it survives mostly in village-areas and usually in the form of legal restrictions to this or that method of co-operation in worship and in the staffing and control of public elementary schools. In the place of bitter antagonism there has come to be not only much personal brotherliness, but also much mutual respect and recognition and a large sense of religious comradeship. So great a change as this was not effected in a single day. It has been a matter of long-drawn-out growth; and it has not even yet run by any means its full course. But in the promoting of it the sons of Mansfield may rightly claim that their College has "laboured more abundantly" than many. When Mansfield was founded, there was—as might have been expected—a good deal of dislike and apprehension felt in certain Oxford-circles, notwithstanding the generous welcome given to the College by a few outstandingly-liberal Anglican scholars. That that unpopularity quickly began to fade, and has by now long vanished completely, is owing in the first place to the courage and eminence of its first Principal, but in the second place and in no mean degree, to those who, having been trained under him and sharing his ideals, carried his work forward as his colleagues and successors. Among these, pride of place belongs unquestionably to three men—Dr. W. B. Selbie, who succeeded Dr. Fairbairn as Principal, Dr. G. Buchanan Gray, the eminent Semitist and Old-Testament Professor, and Dr. Bartlet. These men, working shoulder-to-shoulder over a long stretch of years, gradually won for themselves and their College a warm place in the heart of the University, besides rendering in numerous ways practical assistance to the Congregational churches of the neighbourhood. Accepting without complaint such lingering restrictions as Anglican privilege still placed upon them, but commanding the respect of their contemporaries by the quality of their scholarship and conciliating favour by their personal graciousness, they little-by-little broke down the middle wall of partition, and helped to bring about that happy cordiality between the College and the constituency of the University which has now been long taken by all concerned as a matter of course, and for which subsequent generations can never be too grateful.[1]

In that work of reconciliation Bartlet took a full and indeed a special share. His continuous residence in Oxford was longer than that of either of his colleagues; his subject itself opened up to him the thorniest of all fields of controversy; his full competence as a scholar compelled recognition; and his ideals as a Christian and a controversialist (of which latter we shall say more in a moment) acclimatized the stiffest opponents to the amicable discussion of sharp differences in an atmosphere of mutual regard. At the same time his position as Secretary and informal general-manager of the Society of Historical Theology gave him particularly-abundant opportunities of coming into touch with men of different traditions from his own. Thus it was that he laid Mansfield College, and through it his fellow Free-Churchmen, under a great debt, in the matter of smoother and worthier relations with other Christian bodies alongside of whose work their own work lies.

Such an achievement was, as I have indicated, mainly the fruit of Bartlet's fine scholarship and his profound personal religion. But it also owed much to the broad catholicity of his more-specifically theological attitude. Deep as was his interest in Christian history, especially that of the earlier period, he was still more profoundly concerned—as he admitted to myself and others—with its theological interpretation: and to this task he brought gifts of a high order. Apart from his full knowledge of the historical data, he was helped by the fearless honesty of his thinking and the breadth of his Christian sympathy. There was nothing cloudy or evasive in his arguments, nothing narrow or uncharitable in his judgments. He felt instinctively that, however Christians might need, for subjective reasons, to differ in their doctrinal formulations, they ought to pay more attention to the underlying unity of spirit by which they were bound together. While himself sympathetic to what are known as liberal ways of thinking, he was always striving to explain the liberal to the traditionalist and the traditionalist to the liberal, and pleading that mutual love ought to dominate all controversy between them—sometimes even, in view of special conditions, to the point of involving the exercise of

[1] See the handsome acknowledgement regarding Mansfield made by Dr. C. C. J. Webb in his work, *A Century of Anglican Theology* (Oxford, 1923), pp. 3 f.

some reserve on the part of the liberal. To a progressive friend once chafing in Bartlet's study against the need for exercising caution in publicly expressing his real beliefs, in the same way that a statesman has to adjust his utterances to the political needs of the passing situation, Bartlet replied that he would himself base the need for caution, not on political considerations, but on the principles of the thirteenth chapter of First Corinthians.

He had a theory of his own by the help of which he believed he was able to bridge the gulf of antagonism between differing theological schools. He pleaded for the distinction between what he called "idea" and what he called "conceptions". The "idea" was the deep underlying religious reality common to all believing Christians, apprehensible in experience and imperfectly describable in speech, but not capable of being run into any mould of formal definition. "Conceptions" on the other hand were the formulated doctrines in which men endeavoured —and rightly endeavoured—to expound the significance of the idea. "Conceptions" were quite important: but, unlike the Christian "idea", they were necessarily relative, and therefore unsuitable for authoritative imposition on Christians generally. They were inevitably in large measure determined by the subjective conditions of their framers; and as these conditions were, to some extent at least, special, they seriously limited the universal fitness of the formulations themselves. It was this factor that Bartlet had in mind in using the word "perspective" so frequently as he did.

In the field of Christian doctrine, he was continually drawing attention to the way in which the great "idea" of the Gospel-message, first given to men in Hebraic categories of thought, with consequent stress on the personal, the volitional, the religious, and the ethical, was soon—to a small extent even within the New-Testament period—re-cast in categories furnished by the very different world of Hellenism. Hence there arose in course of time a dominant set of metaphysical conceptions framed on Greek soil, and therefore in part disguising the inner character of the original reality, yet acclaimed to the Church at large as furnishing the one and only form in which Christ's Gospel could rightly be appropriated. Nay more, only too soon they were actually substituted in the mind of Christendom for the idea itself.

The bearing of this contrast or tension upon the great problem of the Person of our Lord was borne in upon his mind with growing insistence in his latest years. Even as early as the production of his share of 'Christianity in History', his dissatis-faction with the Chalcedonian doctrine was apparent: and by the time he was contributing to 'The Lord of Life', his objec-tions to it had still further crystallized. His latest thoughts on the subject are seen in five long private letters written to two friends in 1938–40. Three of these letters he asked to have returned to him, desiring to keep them as records of his own ripest reflections: there is therefore some ground for now treating them as public property, though I may add that I have the explicit permission of both the gentlemen concerned (whose names there is no need to mention) to report upon, and to quote from, what Bartlet wrote to them.

These letters make it clear that he fully realized the gravity of the change involved in this latest development of his theo-logical thought. He felt, however, that he had no option but to come to terms with "what had gradually impressed itself—against both training and personal preference—upon me in my later years with commanding authority as truth".

The evidence of the New Testament, he held, was not strictly uniform in regard to either Christology or eschatology. In the matter of eschatology, the Christian mind had admittedly been led, by experience and reflection in the light of the facts of history, to abandon the primitive eschatology of the earliest period for the more mystical interpretation found in the later Pauline expressions and in the Johannine writings. The principle of *selection* therefore had to be recognized as justified, since—whatever eschatology one might accept—no eschato-logy would synthetize, without undue forcing, *all* the data contained in the New Testament. Now in regard to Christo-logy, there were similarly two types of doctrine distinguishable: and the Christian disciple is here also entitled to make a choice. In the Synoptic Gospels, the Book of Acts, and First Epistle of Peter, and in certain early traditions traceable in Hebrews, we have what might be called the Pneumatic theory of the Person of Christ. We are shown the figure of "the man Christ Jesus", who, by the full indwelling of God's Holy Spirit,

"wrought

With human hands the creed of creeds
In loveliness of perfect deeds,
More strong than all poetic thought".

By filial trust in God as Heavenly Father, and genuine communion with Him through prayer, he reveals within the compass of humanity the full splendour of the Divine love and holiness, and becomes to as many as will receive him the means whereby they too can rise to a share in their true destiny as sons of God, "that he might be the firstborn among many brethren". Involved in the fulfilment of this high redemptive calling as Lord and Saviour, and imprinted in the history of his life as unmistakably as in his unique God-consciousness, there stands his true humanity. He never claims Divine honours or worship such as are paid to the Deity. On the contrary, he experiences not only the physical weakness of man, but also his liability to real temptation, being tempted in all points like as we are, and so able to have a fellow-feeling with our infirmities. Thus his Divinity is a quality completely interpenetrating a personality which is itself truly human in its finitude. According to his own clear declaration, the acid test of genuine discipleship lies, not in any attitude such as might find expression in the cry "Lord! Lord!", but in personal compliance with his teaching and in imitation of his example. It was on behalf of the due recognition of these aspects of the Lord's life that in the earlier centuries the School of Antioch had waged a losing battle against the School of Alexandria. The protest of Nestorius against a view which virtually ignored them failed partly for lack of "the clearer conception of 'personality' which has been one of the distinctive gains of modern thought as compared with ancient or patristic or mediaeval".

Over against this line of interpretation there stands the regnant traditional Christology as settled at the Council of Chalcedon in 451 A.D. According to this Christology the real seat of Jesus' personality is not located in his human life at all, but in the coeternal Divine Logos of God. The movement towards this conclusion begins with the early Christian attempt to account for the redemptive work and power of Christ by means of speculative theories of a non-Hebraic type regarding the metaphysical nature of his person. The attempt shows itself in the ascription of pre-existence to Jesus by Paul, and the envisaging of him as a Divine being who descends from the heavenly sphere in order to participate in human life. It is further developed in the Christology of Hebrews, shaped as it was under the influence of the philosophical tendencies associated with Alexandria, and in that of the Fourth Gospel, shaped as it was in the Hellenic atmosphere of the Province of Asia. Yet not even in these writings is the Person of Jesus carried back into the inmost being of God Himself, nor are the traits of his real humanity ignored. As, however, this alternative line of reflection was further and further pursued, it became increasingly difficult to find a proper place for the real humanity, so clearly attested in our Saviour's actual history. First in certain premature Gnostic theories, then in Clement of Alexandria, later on in Athanasius, Apollinarius, and Cyril, and finally in Leontius of Byzantium, there is clearly discernible a tendency towards a view of Christ's humanity which is essentially "docetic", in that it fails to allow him a full measure of humanity such as we men ourselves possess. True, the failure is unintentional. The bald docetism of the Gnostics is rejected as heretical; so too is Apollinarius' denial that Jesus possessed a human "spirit" or "reasonable soul"; so too is the Monophysites' acknowledgement of only one nature in him. Yet the Chalcedonian Formula, which is recognized on all hands as implying that his human nature was "impersonal", and the abstruse theory of "Enhypostasia" by which Leontius of Byzantium (followed later by John of Damascus) endeavoured to expound the matter, are seen—when viewed in abstraction from their technical terminology—to be constructively or virtually Apollinarian in their refusal to recognize in Jesus a human person, and in the artificial exegesis by which certain pieces of New-Testament evidence (touching, e.g., the limitation of Jesus' human knowledge) have in deference to the resultant doctrine to be explained away.

Bartlet shared with many modern theologians the conviction of the Antiochene School that, if the human realities of our Lord's own life of obedient fellowship with God amid human conditions and temptations were obscured or ignored, however unavowedly, his power for Saviourhood in the lives of his disciples would be gravely impaired—not to mention the violence done to the actual records of Scripture. He did not overlook the difficulties, both for piety and for thought, in the doctrine to which he himself inclined; but he held that for piety they were by no means insuperable, while for thought they were distinctly less than those presented by the traditional doctrine. In any case, he urged that liberty of conscience must be mutually allowed between Christians in the matter of theological construction as in other matters of divergent judgment. For both types of Christology safeguarded what was really essential to faith, namely, "the *unique* vocation, and quality of Sonship, in Jesus as God's true 'image' in human personality, and His Saviourhood and Lordship for humanity, as Head of the Body of spiritually renewed men, who are His 'brethren' in God's true family".

To one of the two correspondents referred to he wrote:

"As regards what you say on Christology in particular, so frankly yet circumspectly in relation to one's speech to others generally—who might misunderstand, and be 'caused to stumble' by half-understanding only—you may perhaps not have read my two essays on this theme in *The Lord of Life*. But if you do so, you will understand more fully how welcome to me is your own attitude to the sense in which *actual Divinity* (I should prefer this to Deity) is to be recognized and confessed in Jesus as the Christ, the Son *par excellence* of God, among the 'many brethren' of the human race whom He raises by his *unique quality* of divine Sonship (as God *fully* incarnate) to the *like* (but not equal) level of personal participation in the 'Life eternal' *proper* only to Deity. This is man's *potential* heritage, in virtue of the immanent presence or 'incarnation' *in principle* of God, as the archetypal and fontal Reason (Nous) in human 'flesh'.

"Here I had long been feeling my way gradually, as did Sanday, my revered and loved master in such matters, as regards the true method of approach to high themes and the timing of one's speech to others . . . (see notably his *Christologies Ancient and Modern*, and his less known but most revealing *Divine Over-ruling*: . .). By the time I wrote in *The Lord of Life* I had become clear that the Christology which placed the 'seat of personality' in Jesus the Christ . . . in his pre-existent nature as *the Logos* rather than in his humanity . . . , as dependent receptivity or capacity for God's own nature . . . , was mistaken. It involved Cyril's own theory of the matter, and Chalcedon so far as it implied it, in virtual Docetism touching Christ's humanity (as Nestorius felt, . . .). But already in what I wrote on the subject in *Christianity in History* . . . it was hinted and implied in germ.

4

"Accordingly I am glad to know that you, along with my old and valued friend, Vernon Storr, hold virtually the same conviction, even as I was greatly reassured, when writing in *The Lord of Life*, to believe that Dr. W. R. Matthews was with me in deciding definitely against Bp. Temple in his persuasive putting of the other alternative in his *Christus Veritas*.[1] (My old pupil Miall Edwards . . . had also reached the same conclusion, along his more purely philosophical lines; see his essay in *The Lord of Life*)".

After expressing his concern lest the prospects of "Reunion"—on the principle of "Unity in diversity"—would be imperilled unless room was found for the theological position which he and others were advocating, Bartlet added towards the close:

"The name 'Modernist' places the emphasis wrongly, as a description of such an attitude . . . as I have (with you) in mind. 'Liberal Evangelical' places it rightly, as bringing out the continuity of the Gospel as primary in idea, while 'Liberal' is only an epithet descriptive of its progressive quality as to 'conceptual forms' ".

It was in keeping, both with his personal bent and with his developed theological views, and in loyalty to the idea of mutual love as the normal relationship between all professing Christians, that—while stoutly fulfilling his rôle as an apologist for Protestantism in general and Congregationalism in particular, and regularly participating all his days in the life of a local Congregational church—he cultivated the friendliest and most intimate relations with those who belonged to other schools of thought within the Church. Although crushingly logical in his apologia for infant-baptism, he stood in the happiest relations with his Baptist students, colleagues, and acquaintances. His friendship with Dr. Gore was but a special example of an array of friendships with Anglican scholars. He was, in fact, in sympathetic touch with a large number of theologians and religious leaders in Britain, on the Continent, and in America. He associated amicably and without any mutual sense of strain with a number of Roman Catholics. One such pronounced him the most Christian controversialist he knew. The gentleness and good feeling with which he put

[1] I have Dean Matthews's permission to quote this passage from Dr. Bartlet's letter.

forward his arguments both powerfully supported his case and winningly disarmed antipathy at one and the same time. All the interest he took and the time and toil that he spent in such schemes as those for the United Church of South India, C.O.P.E.C., the Stockholm Conference, and the "Faith and Order" Movement, were eagerly given out of a great sense of the essential value of the underlying spirit common to all sorts and conditions of Christians and a great concern for their co-operation in the service of the one Kingdom of God.

One of his old students has described him as "a poor teacher in the class-room".[1] There are, however, many different standards by which the excellence or otherwise of a lecturer may be judged; and not all possible types of excellence are mutually compatible. Bartlet usually lectured by dictating to his class continuous and beautifully-worded paragraphs on successive selected phases of the Church-period he happened to be treating. Many have a natural dislike to being "dictated to" in any sense of the word. But those who took pains to preserve what Bartlet dictated to them, and to use it in connexion with their textbook-study, can hardly have failed to find in it much enrichment of mind and clarification of understanding. It was his custom, moreover, to pause ever and anon in his dictating, and comment extempore on what he had been reading about. Some of these interjected remarks were veritable flashes, and stick in the memory, when much of the more formally spoken word has escaped into oblivion. Thus —"That is where Tertullian is so unfair. He pins you to the wall with his logic". Or, after noticing Diocletian's removal of the imperial capital to Nicomedia—"Fancy that! If you had said to Augustus—or even to Trajan, 'The capital of the Empire will be moved from Rome to Nicomedia in Bithynia'" (then rapidly, after an impressive pause), "you would have made him open his eyes". "Thus", he added solemnly in the same connexion, "the incredible becomes the inevitable". But those are probably right who, whatever their appreciation of his lectures, felt that they got most out of him as a teacher in seminars, essay-readings, and tutorials.

For it was in the closer personal contact which these latter made possible that his extraordinary capacity for friendship found larger scope than in his formal lectures. As he acknow-

[1] J. S. Whale in *Mansfield College Magazine*, Jan. 1941, p. 641.

ledged in moving words when replying to the good wishes of the Old Men's Association on his retirement, he longed and tried all his years to win the intimacy and esteem of younger men. Naturally enough, I suppose, he laboured under a sense of having only very partially fulfilled this ambition. There were, of course, those who failed to appreciate his really-great qualities, and felt themselves put off by his solemn and somewhat eccentric manner and at times slightly inquisitorial and grandmotherly tone. While however there was thus among his younger acquaintances a narrow marginal group of such misguided individuals, they pale into comparative insignificance beside the great company of those who, while perhaps irreverently amused now and then by superficial things, sought his company, treasured his friendship, were helped by his words, and as long as they live will hold his memory dear. Not only did he leave his stamp upon successive generations of students; but he retained their circumstances in his memory long after they had left College, and continued in such ways as were open to him to minister to them as a friend. Thus the reach of his influence, often unconsciously exerted and unconsciously received, has been more extensive than can be easily measured or realized. His watchful care over those who were privileged to know him well was not confined to the loftier interests of life, but condescended to things that were lowly. If he thought you were putting on too much weight, or getting too thin in the legs, he would express his concern, and gently urge that remedial measures should be taken. Homœopathic treatment appealed to him, at least for a time; and he used to recommend it to his friends. He was, I am told, liberal with his purse sometimes almost to a fault, in the desire to relieve the financial embarrassment of those who appealed to him for help. Alike in the lesser and in the greater aspects of the welfare of those he loved, he put himself unstintingly at their service. In the case of one unfortunate man—with whose name only those who knew Dr. Bartlet many years ago would now be acquainted—the extent of his voluntary ministrations was such as greatly to astonish many of his friends.

Dr. Bartlet never held a Church-pastorate, nor did he often appear on a public platform. It might easily be said that he was not cut out to be a pastor. There would be some truth in saying so—for a regular pastorate would have greatly limited those scholarly studies for which he was so supremely fitted. Moreover, as years advanced, the academic stamp naturally became more deeply impressed upon his temperament and capabilities. But it would in my judgment be a mistake to suppose that he was constitutionally deficient in the qualifications most essential for pastoral work. His naturally some-what-excitable temperament was kept under firm control. His profound piety, his patience and sweet-temperedness, his love for men, his unfailing courtesy, his capacity both for warm affection and for deep sympathy, his zeal for the Church and his keen interest in its affairs—on the large scale as well as on the small—would all have been valuable assets in the make-up of a good minister. How far his somewhat leisurely and unsystematic habits in matters of business (in the wider sense of the word) reflected a fundamental feature of his character, or were acquired in the course and under the actual conditions of academic life, I do not know: but that seems to me to have been the only serious drawback which might have imperilled his success, had his life been given to the regular work of the pastorate. As it was, he served the churches partly by being a diligent personal member of one, partly by himself frequently conducting services and preaching, not only in his student-days in the villages, but up to within fifteen years of his death both in the villages and in numerous places elsewhere. He took a great interest in and kept close touch with Church-problems, as known to him through the confidence of ministerial and missionary friends. In 1900 he was President of the Congregational County-Union of Berkshire, South Buckinghamshire, and South Oxfordshire. The surviving pencil-draft of a letter he wrote in 1910 to a student whose ordination-service he was prevented from personally attending illustrates what a deep interest he felt in the work of the ministry, and how profound and spiritual was the view he took of it.

His field of sympathy, however, was not limited to the history, theology, and administration of the Church. The Christian love which was his guiding principle as a Churchman, a scholar, and a personal friend, moved him to concern himself with a multiplicity of good causes. The "lame dog" of whatever particular type could always count on his sympathy. On issues where it was not primarily a matter for rendering personal help or relief, he gave the needed service with his pen. Apart from his books and often weighty articles in magazines, he was in the habit of writing frequently to the Press (particularly 'The Times'), when his conscience was roused on some matter of public interest. His concern over the international situation occasionally drove him to action. There remain among his papers a copy or draft of a letter he addressed on the 10th of March, 1918, to Mr. A. J. Balfour as Foreign Secretary, about preparing the way for the League of Nations, and an actual letter addressed to him by Mr. Ramsay Macdonald on the 14th of January, 1935, clearly in reply to one of his, on the subject of disarmament, with particular reference to aerial warfare. It would probably be true to say that his desire to step-in, wherever help of this kind seemed needed, in all probability hampered unduly the fulfilment of certain more-professional tasks for which he had a special and unique aptitude. He had a very keen sense of the gravity and urgency of the social problem, and was often busy with contributions of one kind or another towards its solution. He was, for instance, the initiator and unobtrusive editor of the useful volume entitled 'Property: its duties and rights, . . . ', which was published in 1913.

One particular aspect of social reform on which he concentrated in a somewhat special way was Temperance. Beneath all that he wrote and said so calmly about it, one could discern a controlled but passionate indignation that the fleshly frailty of so many men should be for the sake of financial profit purposely exploited and aggravated by their fellows, to the impoverishment of their substance, the ruin of their physical health, and the corruption of their character. He collected and studied the best literature on the subject he could find, participated in the work of the Oxford Temperance Council, and was ready to defend the cause whenever opportunity offered. In November 1937, for instance, he wrote a long letter to 'The Oxford Times', welcoming and emphasizing a local doctor's recent exposure of the true effects of the consumption of alcohol on the body. He was replied to by someone signing himself "S.C.", who made fun of the length of his letter, and quoted three authorities as controverting the claim that the medical profession now realized the fact that alcohol contained no food or strength-giving qualities. A sentence or two from Bartlet's rejoinder are worth quoting, as aptly illustrating his method of discussion in such cases.

"Sir (he wrote to the Editor), I do not know what value I or your other readers ought to attach to the challenge by S.C. of my letter underlining Dr. Southall's contention. . . . For we do not know who he is, and so can judge of his knowledge of and competence to estimate the scientific evidence on the point only by the specimen of those which his own letter furnishes".

Then, after reducing the three authorities adduced by S.C. to one, and discountenancing that one as disagreeing with the great array of physiologists, he concludes:

"Let S.C., then, extend his study of expert authorities, and on a more representative basis. Let it include the Report of the Medical Advisory Committee of the Central Control Board . . . " (details of three other treatises are then given). "A study of these, I feel confident, will convince him, and any of your readers who want to reach the truth for themselves, that his challenge is not supported by the bulk of scientific opinion on the matter at issue between us".

Unlike his zeal for temperance, his aversion from tobacco, though not without its moral basis, was far more a matter of physical dislike. One mentions the two aversions together, not because he regarded them as at all on the same footing, but because, as social habits, they are often thought of in conjunction. Tobacco-smoke had an unusually-irritant and probably-deleterious effect upon his sensitive breathing-apparatus. But I think I am right in saying that, even had this not been so, he would still have regarded smoking with some disapproval, and not altogether groundlessly: for even a smoker need not hesitate to admit that there is a grain of salutary truth in what Bartlet was once heard to say: "Nothing could very well be more distorted than the smoker's sense of his rights!" But he never carried his dislike of the habit to the point of creating embarrassment for his friends. He was, of course, often in company with men smoking; and mildly-amusing situations sometimes arose as a result. On one occasion he made me feel somewhat of a hypocrite: unaware that, after many years as a non-smoker, I had for some time been in the habit of temperately indulging, he came over and sat by me in a crowded meeting, saying as he did so: "I am coming to sit by you, as you have no bad habits". Most of his acquaintances know that a letter of his to 'The Times' on the subject once drew a disclaimer from his namesake Mr. Vernon Bartlett the journalist.[1]

Adverse comments have been made, by some of Bartlet's best friends, on his style both as a speaker and as a writer. It has been said that as a speaker he was halting, and too fond of long words and elaborate circumlocution to be easily understood. His written sentences, too, were inordinately long and involved, and stuffed with so many parentheses and qualifications that his main drift was often hard to follow. There is force in these criticisms; but they do not give the whole case. The real ground of this impression of wordiness and obscurity was his two-fold habit of dignity and precision in all his use of words. Such was his regard for truth, both in speaking and writing, so anxious was he to give the exact shade of meaning required, that he certainly was apt to get his sentences unduly complicated and involved. This tendency is particularly noticeable in what he wrote during the later years of his life. In editing the Birkbeck lectures printed in this volume, I have had again and again to remove, for the sake of brevity, balance, and clarity, parenthetical clauses which he had inserted for the sake of completely expressing his meaning, but which the reader might well be expected to take for granted. The same feature of style is visible in his long explanatory letters to his friends. These, I am told, he would often carefully draft and re-draft before settling finally on their wording. He always declared that he was a slow worker: if so, the amount of good matter he managed, even in the course of so long a life, to get down on paper is truly amazing.

But the literary flaw now in question must not be over-estimated. Solemn though his speech often was, lacking as he was said to be in small-talk, and long as his words frequently were, he was anything but an uninteresting talker. On the contrary, his stately sentences and dignified diction, when applied to quite-ordinary affairs of life, were often highly

[1] In *The Times* for 1st April, 1936. In his autobiography Mr. Bartlett writes: "We are an unexpectedly large band, we Vernon Bartletts, or Bartlets. The most famous is the learned doctor who thus unknowingly earned me more money and who has subsequently got me into minor difficulties. When members of my club scowl at me I realise that he has made some public declaration against the disgusting habit of smoking. When clergymen treat me with great deference I suspect that he has written another letter to *The Times* on some religious subject. . . ." (*This is my Life* [1937], p. 63).

amusing; and I have little doubt that the humorous effect he could create in this way was not seldom quite deliberate, though his manner never suggested that he was intentionally joking. Certainly the frequent solemnity of his words did not mean that he could not immensely enjoy the humorous side of things. As for clarity, he was capable—despite the magniloquence of his speech—of being a most incisive and weighty speaker in group-discussions.

Nor are his printed works, for the most part, characterized to any considerable extent by undue wordiness and complexity of construction. I doubt whether the suggestion that such features prevented them from being as widely read as they would otherwise have been, is really sound. Perhaps the defect did not develop noticeably until the later period of his life. His best books and essays are written in a clear, readable, and dignified style, which in some cases conveys a really-extraordinary impression of accuracy and penetration. His personal letters were often couched in the same vein, thus decorating the ordinary communications of life with a quaint but impressive beauty. Here, as a sample, is a message he sent to a man on the occasion of the birth of his first baby:

> "I must send a line of hearty congratulation to Mrs. —— and yourself upon the fresh joy which has broken suddenly (out of sorrow, as the Fourth Gospel so truly represents it) upon you both. My wife and I are rejoicing with you in the gift, and in the deepening of all life which this fresh experience of its solemn mysteries brings with it".

The outer man is a very important facet of personality, if only for the large part it always fills in the associations which the person's name calls up in the minds of his friends when they speak it or hear it spoken. In the good-tempered and therefore well-controlled levity prevalent in the atmosphere of friendship—particularly such friendship as prevailed in the circles in which Bartlet moved—it was inevitable that his striking figure and appearance should occasionally be the butt of mild merriment. One flippant friend might liken him to a Spanish admiral; and another imagine what a splendid Don Quixote he would have made in Christmas charades or amateur theatricals. But all save the most unresponsive and unimpressionable saw in his tall slim figure, his solemn bearded face, his kindly smile, his devout mien, and his stately phrasing, something far greater than matter for idle jesting, however good-humoured such jesting might be. They sensed the presence of a great soul and a worthy friend. They might or might not continue to smile at his surface-eccentricities—his horror of draughts, his dislike of smoking, and so forth—but they failed not to acknowledge the nobility of his character and the power and range of his mind. Few of them would realize what his "often infirmities" must have meant to lim. Long before he began to sicken of the trouble that so hampered him at the end of his life, he was a frequent victim to attacks of influenza and laryngitis, brought on by very slight provocation. None of his friends knew that from boyhood onwards he possessed the sight of only one eye. They might sometimes affect amusement at his valetudinarianism, but the objective grounds for his caution in matters of health were real enough. It was sad to see his stoop getting more pronounced and his physical weaknesses multiplying. And yet amid it all he never got plaintive, nor was he ever heard giving way to self-pity.

But one cannot finish an account of him while dwelling on his physical weaknesses. Memory is called back at the end to the pure and Christlike spirit which "informed his tenement of clay". The fortunes of that spirit are still despite death in the keeping of wiser Hands than ours: and though he is now shrouded from our eyes, we know him to be still yielding his best service to the God beyond Whose care death cannot take him. Pending the future enlargement of our vision, his memory and his work remain to bless us. We rejoice to have known him; we praise God for the work he did; we respond to the aid and stimulus his record imparts to us. There will be many who will always acknowledge their great debt to him for the powerful help he gave them in their struggles and quests after the things that matter most. They will rejoice as they call to mind, not only his personal kindness, but the service he rendered in opening up to them the things of God.

> "And what delights can equal those
>   That stir the spirit's inner deeps,
>   When one that loves but knows not, reaps
> A truth from one that loves and knows?"

C. J. C.

EDITOR'S PREFACE TO THE LECTURES

Dr. Bartlet having bequeathed most of his books to Mansfield College Library, it fell to me as the Librarian—acting with the approval of his executors—to deal, after his death, with the literary contents of his study. Along with his books were found immense quantities of unsorted written matter, in all stages of manageability between solid sets of lecture-notes and backs of envelopes or other scraps scribbled over with scarcely legible pencil-jottings. The task of dealing with this amorphous heap of papers was by no means short or easy. It was divided out between two or three friends, Dr. Selbie kindly undertaking the lion's share. It was obvious that no use at all could be made of the innumerable rough jottings; and there was no option but to destroy them—though, after being obliged to decipher portions of Dr. Bartlet's manuscript notes, it has been with some qualms that I have seen bundle after bundle of these scraps consigned to the waste-paper-basket: for I could not but fear lest some precious units of deep and penetrating Christian thought were being thereby for ever lost to mankind.

Among the material sorted by Dr. Selbie, there was found a large brown-paper parcel containing masses of notes, continuous manuscript, and typescript, all for the most part clearly belonging together. They turned out on examination to be the papers connected with certain lectures which Dr. Bartlet had given at Cambridge in 1924, and which—so Mrs. Bartlet tells me—he had subsequently had put into type and had always intended to publish. The task of doing so must have resembled another task he once told me of, when handing over to me the charge of Mansfield Library years ago—namely, the proper placing of a set of books which, he said, had been put aside in a safe place, "pending the leisure of the Librarian—which never came". Dr. Selbie suggested that the material might well be prepared for publication; and Dr. Bartlet's executors formally requested me to edit them for this purpose. It was thought advisable to prefix a biographical memoir and to append a bibliography: and thus the production of the present volume in our late friend's honour was undertaken.

In May 1923 Dr. Bartlet was appointed by the Council of Trinity College, Cambridge, to the Birkbeck Lectureship in Ecclesiastical History for the following year. The letter of Professor J. J. Thomson conveying the invitation is before me as I write. The call was duly accepted; and in 1924 Dr. Bartlet gave six lectures at Trinity College—on the 9th, 16th, and 23rd of February, the 1st of March, the 20th of October, and the 24th of November. He took as his subject 'Church Life and Order in the first four centuries, with special reference to early Eastern Church Orders'. He evidently lectured from a somewhat roughly-written manuscript, which, so far as one can judge from its present condition, was several times read over afterwards and emended. Presumably it underwent a definite and final revision before almost the whole of it was put into type. A top typescript and three carbon-copies of it were found with the other papers: and one of these typed copies had evidently been subjected by the author to a still-further polishing. It seems clear, however, that the typescript did not exactly correspond with what was actually written for and read at Cambridge. Instead of six main divisions, it contains nine: and at certain points it seems to be incomplete. Moreover, among the more-finished and more-easily legible sheets of manuscript there were found a number of passages of varying length, very relevant to the theme and deserving of inclusion, though they had apparently not been typed with the rest. Several of these I have incorporated at suitable points in the text, indicating however by means of a note wherever I have had to break the sequence of the typed matter in order to do so. Here and there it has been possible to correct undetected slips in the typescript from the corresponding passage in the manuscript.

Along with the loose manuscript sheets there was a fair-sized note-book containing—inter alia—what looked like two separate additional drafts of the first lecture, dealing with certain preliminary questions as well as handling on somewhat different lines the subjects treated in the first section of the typescript. The state of the contents, however, though doubtless crystal-clear to the learned author, wore to the eyes of his humble disciple an appearance of such inextricable complexity, that it was hopeless to try to reconstruct a single complete discourse from them, even had it been possible to tell which of the two drafts (if only two there were) was meant to be the final

one. Valuable therefore as many of the things here written
seemed to be, there was really no option—so far as my immediate
task was concerned—but to discard the greater part of them.
There were, however, certain paragraphs which, although not
subsequently typed, presented important introductory considerations, and in some cases seemed clearly to have been read
—or intended to be read—at Cambridge. These I have
collected into a preliminary chapter, calling it 'Introduction'
(to avoid the need of disturbing Dr. Bartlet's own numbering
of the subsequent chapters), and doing my best to arrange its
component parts in some sort of intelligible order, so that they
might read more or less as a unity.

The task of reducing this heterogeneous collection of writing
to a form fit for public acceptance in print has necessarily
been long and arduous. More than once I have been reminded
of Carlyle's account, in the eleventh chapter of Book I of
'Sartor Resartus', of how he had to deal with the six paper-
bags containing "miscellaneous masses of Sheets, and oftener
Shreds and Snips, written in Professor Teufelsdröckh's scarce
legible *cursiv-schrift*. . . . Daily and nightly does the Editor sit
(with green spectacles) deciphering these unimaginable Documents from their perplexed *cursiv-schrift*; collating them with
the almost unimaginable Volume, which stands in legible
print". But the toil has been the reverse of uninteresting
and unrewarding: and I am confident that it has been well
worth-while getting this series of discourses published,
notwithstanding the labour involved and the occasionally-
disjointed form in which some successive paragraphs have to
appear.

The general theme of the lectures is the interplay of two
distinct elements in the life of the early Church—the inward,
spiritual, and experiential on the one hand, and the external,
formal, and organizational on the other. Dr. Bartlet's thesis
is that, with the lapse of time, valuable and indeed vital aspects
of Christianity connected with the former were lost sight of
and sacrificed, out of regard for the traditional fixity of the
latter. This general idea is, of course, not new. It was, for
instance, advanced and defended by Rudolf Sohm, both in his
'Kirchengeschichte im Grundriss' (1887), and in the first
volume of his 'Kirchenrecht' (1892). What is, so far as
my knowledge goes, new in Dr. Bartlet's work is the elabora-

tion of this thesis with special reference to the contents of the Church-Orders.

The question will doubtless occur to many, whether it is advisable to publish what was written so many years ago.

To this I should answer in the first place that, after the lectures had been delivered, Dr. Bartlet kept the material constantly before him, revising it thoroughly for the purpose of getting it typed, and emending it here and there even after that, with the intention (entertained to the last) of publishing it when he could get time.

Secondly, in order that the contents should not suffer from any failure to take due account of later work, I have endeavoured to bring them where necessary up-to-date, by means of supplementary notes of my own. In discharging this part of my editorial task, I have had the valuable assistance of my friend the Rev. E. C. Ratcliff, M.A., of The Queen's College, Oxford—one who has made the liturgical literature of the early Church a field peculiarly his own. He has been kind enough at my request to look through what I was proposing to publish, and to criticize it, especially from the point of view of the literary problems involved—in regard to which Dr. Bartlet had a good deal to say. The early Church-Orders constitute a very special section of Christian literature—one of great complexity and bewildering difficulty for the student in regard to all questions concerning their literary origin, provenance, and history. One seems at times to be hardly able to turn to a single accessible document without being told on authority that it must be a later and interpolated version of something else. It has therefore been a special boon to have Mr. Ratcliff's help and to be guided in many points by his judgment and suggestions. He does not, of course, accept any responsiblity for Dr. Bartlet's opinions or for mine: but I owe him a great debt of thanks for his willing and generous help.

The third observation I should like to make in answer to the objection that this is work written many years ago, is that— provided care is taken to watch important contributions of later thought—the views of a competent Church-historian like Dr. Bartlet do not depend for their validity on the precise date, earlier or later, within the period of his maturity at which they were first written. The great bulk of the literary materials for his subject were available in 1924—most of it a good many years before that: and the main judgments of an historian possessed of the extraordinary insight with which our friend was endowed are not likely to need serious emendation as a result of the lapse of the few years that have passed since he first put them in writing.

I have already explained that it is impossible at this distance of time, and seeing that Dr. Bartlet is no longer with us, to know for certain how much and precisely what portions of the matter contained in the papers dealt with was actually included in the six lectures given at Cambridge, though from the difference in the numbers indicated above, it seems reasonable to conjecture that not much of the spoken lectures is missing from the written matter. My main task has been to "edit" as much of this written matter as Dr. Bartlet seemed anxious to preserve and as would lend itself to more-or-less connected arrangement. In several places I have had to insert explanatory notes of my own: these I have placed within square brackets, and signalized with my own initials. But beyond that, I have also allowed myself a fairly-free hand in modifying the original wording in the interests of smoothness and clarity, and also in supplementing it with precise references to the documents quoted or referred to, where these were not already given. I have not bothered to put into square brackets any such references, or cross-references to other parts of the book, supplied by myself.

I have felt it to be a rather-delicate task—one of a kind I have not previously had to perform—to cause to be put into print as substantially the work of another words which are not in every detail his ipsissima verba (with stress on the "-issima"). There was, however, no option but to face boldly whatever risk of possible misrepresentation may have been thereby incurred. Some measure of editorial revision was absolutely essential if the lectures were to be published at all: and as Dr. Bartlet was not here to do the revising, someone-else had to undertake it for him. I can however assure the reader that all in the sequel which is not in square brackets represents at least the substance of what Dr. Bartlet wanted to say, and almost entirely in his very own words. The changes and additions I have made to his actual composition (apart from references to literature) are limited to details regarding which I feel sure he would have accepted as at least permissible the wording I have chosen, had it been suggested to him as a slightly-clearer way of expressing his meaning. Unlike that second-century presbyter of whom Tertullian tells us (apparently a Smyrnaean, I regret to say), who confessed that out of love for Paul he had concocted apocryphal 'Acts' about him, and who got unfrocked for his pains, I have forged no pseudonymous paragraphs in honour of my hero, but have modestly limited myself to transcribing, and here and there elucidating, the wise words which he himself had written, but which he had been compelled to leave more or less in the rough.

The thanks of the executors and of the editor are due, and are hereby sincerely accorded, to the Society of Historical Theology, the Council of Mansfield College, and several other friends, whose generosity has made the publication of the book financially possible—also to Dr. W. B. Selbie for having originated the idea of producing it, contributed a Foreword, assisted in the proof-reading, and otherwise guided and encouraged the editor in the execution of his task.

With these brief explanations, "I, Tertius, who edited these lectures, salute you in the Lord".

C. J. C.

INTRODUCTORY[1]

THE title of these lectures[2] has been chosen with a view to suggesting as fully and fitly as may be their actual scope. That scope is at once comprehensive and special. It deals with Christian life as a whole, but primarily in one aspect, that namely of the order or organized forms in which this life found outward and corporate expression. The central aim will be to study and interpret those facts which bear most closely on the mutual relations between life and order, to mark the various views of these relations entertained by Christians at different times and in different places, and to trace the changing emphasis placed upon the one or the other in the course of the Church's development.

"Life" and "order," as applied to the Church, are terms which are capable of a two-fold use, according as they designate facts on the one hand, or ideas on the other. In the former sense, they stand for the inner and outer aspects respectively of corporate Christian experience, its animating spirit and its embodied form, its invisible soul and its expression to the senses, both being necessary to the full enjoyment of the experience in question. In the latter sense, "life" and "order" stand for the ideas entertained regarding the facts themselves —ideas springing out of these facts and in turn reacting upon their development, as the mind strives after the fittest possible conceptual expression of its experience for the purpose of its clearer apprehension and more-effective impartation to others. Such conceptual expression, however, is always relative, and never more than approximately adequate as an embodiment of ideas which have a depth of vital quality and power of potential meaning beyond the reach of any set of formal conceptions.

. . . . .

Among the problems we shall need to face are these. Is there a specifically-Christian idea of the place and nature of

---

[1] [See above, pp. lx f. A pencil-jotting in the notebook referred to in the Preface indicates that Dr. Bartlet meant to begin his first lecture with an allusion to his feelings in speaking in the place where the great scholars Lightfoot and Hort once taught. C.J.C.].

[2] See above, p. lx.

5   I

"order" in religious life; and if so, what is it? How far has the
Church's actual order at different stages been true to type?
How far, too, in trying to do justice to this or that element of
order seemingly most needful to its life at a given time, has it
unduly sacrificed other elements originally latent, if not
patent, in corporate Christianity, and so impaired its own
complete well-being at that time and still more for future
ages?

Included in our survey will occur some account and estimate
of the ancient Church-Orders, or comprehensive bodies of
ordinances for worship and discipline, mostly belonging in
their present form to the fourth century, but all of them
containing earlier matter, which we shall try to distinguish
and trace to its original historical setting.

. . . . .

The discussions[1] of the last generation on Church-order
and Church-institutions have by a vitally-true logic gradually
pushed back the central issues more and more from the formal
to the essential, from method to aim, from rules to principles,
from law to faith, from letter to spirit, from order to life,
from religion viewed from the outside to religion viewed from
within—the realm of human experience. Writing in 1913, my
own Oxford-master in this field, Dr. W. Sanday, said of Dr.
C. H. Turner's picture of the organization of the Church in
' The Cambridge Medieval History '[2] that "this statement is
formed primarily on the fourth century, and the earlier portion is an introduction leading up to this, and subordinated to
it". To my thinking this fact affects, not only the form, but
something of the substance of that massive essay, at least as
regards the atmosphere, so to say, in which the whole, and not
the fourth century only, is viewed. That means that even
primitive Church-life and -usages are viewed too little in their
own proper atmosphere of "the Spirit" as the primary factor in
all things connected with the Church as the Messianic Body of
"the Saints" of which the Christ is the Head, and too much in
that of the fourth century, when "order" was the central
preoccupation and when the idea of "the Spirit," whose prior

[1] [The four weighty paragraphs that follow are transcribed from a couple of
odd pages written over in very light and small pencil-writing, such as one
imagines can hardly have been read from in a public lecture. But they com-
mence immediately below the allusion to Lightfoot and Hort referred to above
on p. 1, n. 1, and therefore look as though designed for oral delivery. I judge
them to be worthy of reproduction.   C.J.C.].

[2] *Camb. Med. Hist.*, vol. i (1924), pp. 143–182.

attribute is liberty or spontaneity, was rather at a discount. Thus the enthusiasm of the first age hardly has justice done to it; and to that extent Dr. Turner's picture is not fully historical, being coloured with a traditional hue, owing to a failure to look at the phenomena of the Apostolic Age with sufficient sympathy to do justice to that Age's positive meaning. A certain fourth-century reserve of attitude, such as that which a Eusebius or an Ambrose would have felt, seems to pervade the earlier exposition of what was really most characteristic of the great Age of the Spirit.

The same applies to Bishop Gore's[1] . . . i.e., it is formed and pivoted on the end of the second century, and tends to judge the value of the first-century facts in this later light. These first-century facts are thus in part obscured, even in relation to the age in which they occurred—apart from any lessons they may have for ages later than the second and the fourth, lessons other and more valuable than those centuries were able to perceive, but which may be perceptible now when once more the Spirit as the Spirit of liberty is blowing through the historic Church of Christ.

The method, then, of these lectures which may, I hope, warrant my reviewing in part ground traversed by others in recent times, especially by the 'Essays on the Early History of the Church and the Ministry', will be one of the closest possible adherence to the genetic or strictly-historical order both of thought and presentation, facing consciously and with as impartial an intent as possible both the inner and the outer sides—the life that craved expression and the outward forms of expression in Church-order from stage to stage, and keeping the two as far as possible in constant correlation. This should enable us to keep in mind at least the co-operation of the two factors of Church-development—life and order—until we reach the fairly-stabilized Church-Orders of a comprehensive kind at the end of the fourth century, and to mark how the relative emphasis on the one or the other of them changes during the process. It is, then, a study in development, a two-fold development throughout, that these lectures will aim at presenting as objectively as the personal factor in their author will allow.[2] An attempt will be made to distinguish more than

[1] [This word is followed by a short blank space, which itself is followed by a few words I cannot satisfactorily decipher: the last seem to read "C.H.T.'s revision". C.J.C.].

[2] See below, p. 5.

is often done between "primitive" and later conceptions and customs, by giving the former a rather more limited definition than is customary, as regards idea even more than of time.[1] Further, not only must "primitive" and "Catholic" be distinguished in a really-historical sense and spirit; but, within both of these, different stages must be discriminated as regards the degree to which the emphasis and elements most characteristic of the one tend to prevail over those of the other, and the most-marked epochs of transition in this respect must be traced.

But above all, the special feature of this survey will be its two-fold scope—the constant reference of the outer order to the inward experimental life of the corporate Christian society, in which Christianity as the religion constituted and inspired by Christ took actual shape during the first four centuries. This will carry our consideration behind organization to the life of the Church, and will involve an attempt to evaluate the theory or interpretation of this distinctive life put forward, by those conscious of it, in such ideas as those of the Spirit, of Divine Grace, and of its nature and modes and conditions of operation.[2] Beyond that, history can hardly go in tracing the secret of Christianity.

.   .   .   .   .

If history teaches anything, it is that all terms have meant different things at different times. For not only words, but also the realities of experience which they represent so imperfectly (because so largely as mere symbols), derive much of their meaning from their historical context, and particularly from its psychological or inner side as human experience. Put the record of past life back into its full original context; and it will stand out anew with vividness and intelligibility, like writing in invisible ink when exposed to the fire. This is true alike of experience itself, and of the images and conceptions in which men's minds preserve and reproduce the abiding ideas implicit in experience. Hence, while there are certain great staple elements of experience and mentality which are common to human life and thought generally, and which mould all

---

[1] [Dr. Bartlet means that, *within* the area commonly treated as "primitive" or "early" Christianity, he proposes to discriminate between what is strictly primitive (in idea even more than chronologically) from subsequent developments which set in at a fairly-early date. A partially-illegible marginal note protests against the method of treating everything prior to the "mediaeval" as being a single "primitive" unity. C.J.C.].

[2] [The last four or five lines have involved rather more editorial conjecture and emendation than usual, as some of the words were undecipherable. C.J.C.].

language on certain broad lines of similarity, so that we can understand roughly what those who spoke them meant, yet there is always an element, larger in fact than even most educated persons realize, in which difference and not identity of meaning is really present. We see this clearly in the familiar fact that a strictly-literal rendering of a passage in a foreign tongue may be less faithful to the original, i.e., to the historically-true sense of what it purports to give us, than one that is free. Real translation must always be a free, paraphrastic, and to that extent an interpretative rendering of the original terms used, and this in proportion to the remoteness, both in space and time, of the conditions of the vital context to which they were related.

It is such interpretative translation, true to the spirit as well as the letter of the historical facts, read as continuously expressive of life, that is here to be essayed. It will involve, of course, an element of subjective construction alike in lecturer and hearers; but that is inevitable. The one safeguard against errors due to this condition of all history worth the name, i.e., to this ideal reconstruction of past human experience in the consciousness of the present, is to face the dangers of the enterprise frankly, and so in a spirit of full responsibility apply all available means of avoiding such errors, up to the limits of one's capacity.

. . . . .

While, however, these lectures will be one sustained attempt at historical"translation", it will be needful in the course of the present lecture to try to lay its foundation securely in the case of a few terms of far-reaching significance. For error or confusion of thought here cannot be made up for by any amount of correctness in minor matters of principle or of detailed fact. . . .

By Church-life, then, we shall mean piety—in the sense of the Latin word "pietas"—the dutiful attitude in the first place to God, and in the second to men, as seen in the light of His gracious Will for them as one's fellow-members of His Kingdom and His Church. Corresponding to this, Church-order will mean such forms of organizing corporate Christian piety as are from time to time regarded as best suited to its vital expression and furtherance, under the varied and changeful conditions of earthly life. . . .

Order, whether as a term or a definite conception, emerges

only gradually, being quite subordinate in the Apostolic Age proper, the first Christian generation which passed away about 70 A.D.

In the more pertinent of the two more-or-less relevant cases of the occurrence of the word in the New Testament, "Let all things be done seemlywise (εὐσχημόνως) and in order (κατὰ τάξιν)", "order" simply means the absence of disorder due to several persons exercising at the same moment the gifts of "prophecy" and ecstatic utterance (λαλεῖν γλώσσαις).[1] "For God is not a God of confusion (ἀκαταστασίας), but of peace" (and of "order" in that sense); "as in all the churches of the saints" (1 Cor. xiv. 33). Of order in the later sense of a fixed usage, defined by tradition or authority, there is no mention in connexion with Church-life in the New Testament, though there are allusions to a "tradition" or body of "traditions" (παραδόσεις) which missionaries of various grades were wont to "hand on" (παραδιδόναι) to fresh groups of converts, as expressing the common beliefs and usages of the Christian community. Thus, St. Paul writes to the church at Corinth, "Now I praise you that ye remember me in all things, and hold fast the traditions, even as I delivered (them) unto you" (1 Cor. xi. 2), before going on to discuss with it certain minor matters of order, in the sense already defined, viz., of seemliness, or the fitness of things. The "traditions" in question, embodying as they did what had grown up in "the churches of God" as customary, were of the nature of weighty precedents bearing on the application of the spiritual principles of the Gospel to the concrete conditions of corporate Church-life, and were to be passed on for the enlightenment and guidance of the local Christian conscience.

Thus, in dealing with one of the minor points in Church-practice, whether women might pray or prophesy bare-headed, the Apostle appeals not only to his own ruling in the other churches to which he stands in the relation of spiritual father and counsellor, but also to the usage (συνήθεια) of "the churches of God" (1 Cor. xi. 16), as opposed to the opinion of

---

[1] 1 Cor. xiv. 40. The other case of the use of τάξις with regard to the Church, "your ordered array (ὑμῶν τὴν τάξιν) and the solid front (στερέωμα) of your faith towards Christ" (Col. ii. 5), is apparently a military metaphor. The partially-cognate verb διατάσσομαι is used by St. Paul usually with the sense of "enjoin" (1 Cor. vii. 17, xi. 34, Titus i. 5: cf. 1 Cor. ix. 14, xvi. 1, Gal. iii. 19). The other verb used in Tit. i. 5 and rendered "set in order" (ἐπιδιορθώσῃ) means rather "amend the defects" (sc. of an inchoate Church-life).

certain persons at Corinth who were inclined to be "conten-
tious" (φιλόνεικος), to stand out stiffly for their own views on
the matter. But he does so only after he has discussed the
point on principle, and has appealed also to the local church's
own judgment (1 Cor. xi. 13) on what was a departure from
Jewish sentiment, as to whether the novel practice defended
by some was really seemly, when judged according to the mere
fitness of things.

· · · · ·

. . . For the action of this tendency in Church-order,[1] we
must be watchful, but not suspiciously so, just as we must for
the action of individualism and egoistic self-assertion, and the
love of change for its own sake—the opposite extreme,
representing full personal vitality in the units of human society.

As to the term "Church" as applied adjectivally both to
"life" and to "order", it will be used simply in the sense of
"corporate": and one result of our enquiry may be to bring out
the rather-changing stress and shades of meaning attaching to
the Church-idea in the development of ancient Christianity,
according to the senses in which that inclusive idea was understood. On this last point only one thing needs to be said at
this stage, to wit, that as prior to Christ moral personality
entered more and more as an important element into Biblical
religion, so (one may claim) it receives new emphasis and power
in Christianity, as conditioned by the personality of Christ
Himself and by the quality of His influence on others. If then
the value of moral personality does not become, in association
with the accession of religious vitality which emerged with the
Gospel, the most-distinctive characteristic of primitive Christianity, it must at least be very nearly that: and our eye must
accordingly be ready to mark the fortunes of this feature of
Christianity during our whole period.

[1] [I.e., the tendency towards a strict uniformity or fixity in corporate
procedure. C.J.C.].

CHAPTER I

THE APOSTOLIC AGE

CHRISTIANITY is pre-eminently the religion of moral personality. It appears in history as the fulfilment of the Hebrew national religion, raised as this was to a higher power and universalized in the personality of Jesus "the Christ", the Spirit-anointed Head of the Kingdom of God on earth.

According to the hope kindled and fed by a wonderful line of prophets, the final form of Hebrew theocracy, in which full knowledge of God and communion of life with Him should become the common possession of all His true People, was to come through a fresh mode of self-revealing activity on the part of God Himself. Direct inspiration of man's soul by the in-breathing of God's own Divine Spirit-life, communicating His very thoughts and will to human consciousness, was to be the distinctive mark and glory of "the Kingdom of God", the perfected reign of His Will in the Messianic Age. The People of that Kingdom and Age was to be essentially an inspired People, inspired for full communion with God and through Him with each other, in righteousness (or conformity to His Divine will), and so enjoying perfect life in peace and joy.

The human means through which this general salvation or wellbeing should be realized was to be a Person, the Messiah or Christ, supremely inspired or "anointed" with that "Spirit" whereby all this was to be realized in the experience of God's chosen and willing People. That is, the final form of Israel's religion was to be attained, not through the medium of God's sacred Law as such—sub formâ Legis—but rather through a sacred personality completely filled with the life which the Law aimed at producing. And in this he was to be the archetype of the life to be reproduced in His fellows in the Kingdom of God. For personality is the supreme, the only adequate, medium for the creation of personality. Thus Christianity is the one possible fulfilment of the prophetic ideal of Hebrew religion. It was to come in and through the Christ—sub formâ Christi. In Him God's "covenant" or revealed relation with

8

Israel, and through Israel with mankind, was to reach its new and final form.[1]

Now this is essentially what Peter and the other disciples dimly felt to have been fulfilled in their experience at Pentecost —an experience of new and inspired knowledge of God as revealed in the personality and life of Jesus of Nazareth. They now saw all the old as made new in the transfiguring light which flooded their souls with the triumphant assurance that all had been according to God's own counsel as regards His Christ, and that the Kingdom of God was verily on the eve of realization as the fruit of His devoted love. Forthwith their souls were aflame; they could neither contain the emotions evoked by this overwhelming intuition, nor fully utter them. Thus the powerful impulse to react immediately to the new revelation from above, and the inability to find expression for it in conventional or symbolic language (which is the creation rather of reflective or conceptual thought) issued in a new kind

---

[1] [Perhaps I might add here a few lines excerpted from Dr. Bartlet's book of rough notes for his first lecture.   C.J.C.]:—

This is not the occasion on which to examine the problem of the Person of Christ and of His unique influence on human life, collectively and individually. For our purpose it is enough, as it is also essential, to call attention to the historic fact—the most momentous in all history and probably the most significant—that it was by His personal influence that the manifestation of the Spirit at Pentecost was conditioned, and therewith the foundation of the Christian Church. What this may imply theologically it is not mine here to enquire. But the historic fact, a fact affording as much food for thought in the present connexion as in most, is that it was "sub specie Jesu Christi" that there broke forth a new religious and moral power, a "holy inspiration", adequate to carry the essential faith and ethic of the Hebrew prophets out into the heart of humanity at large (as that religion, under the form of the sacred Law of the Jewish nation, had been unable to go forth), so as to become the universal Church of God. Differ as men may in their further inferences, there can hardly be a doubt to-day that it was the specific spiritual quality of Jesus' personality, and of His teaching as illumined and vivified by that personality, that explained and still explains the unique dynamic energy of Christianity, first within Judaism, and then in ever-growing circles of humanity beyond its borders.

The special bearing on our present subject of this correlation of the historic personality of Jesus and the "holy inspiration" which accompanied faith in His name lies here. It was His personality and His supreme witness to the truth of His Gospel of God's Fatherliness (given in His own attitude to men and women as such, and in His self-devotion even unto the Cross), that gave content and direction to the enthusiasm of love to God and to men (whether actual or only potential members of His Kingdom on earth) which inspired the Church of the Apostolic Age for its wonderful enterprise and achievements. In that personality the ideal of the Divinely-inspired life was already presented as realized—under particular conditions, indeed, and in forms peculiar in part to Christ's own special vocation, but nonetheless writ large in the sphere of motive and principle. Thus in Christ's personality the Gospel was already implicitly revealed, in a form applicable, by the interpretative action of God's holy Spirit in the conscience, to all analogous circumstances in the life of each Christian, and still more in that of the Church.

of direct Spirit-speech later known as "speaking with tongues". It was in fact an immediate language of the emotions when overcharged with the impression of the profoundest religious ideas, those most moving to man as a spiritual being.

That was the psychological or purely-subjective aspect of such religious inspiration. But its rational or ideal content, implicit or in solution for the moment in the flood of emotion, was determined by the nature of the intuitive vision which occasioned it, and which conditioned its value as revelation to and for personality. The drawing-forth of this in explicit thought is what meets us in the New-Testament record of the growing faith of the primitive Church, regarding the meaning of Jesus as the New Head of the human race, and particularly as the Head of the Church which was the embodiment of His living Spirit. But this we may say by way of anticipation: that the vision at Pentecost was one of a new type of humanity embodied in the Messiah, one marked pre-eminently by what we in consequence of it have learned to call "moral personality"; that it lifted humanity on to a fresh level of moral maturity and holy liberty, as partaking in the Divine Spirit mediated by Christ its second Head; and that the principles proper to its corporate life of fellowship must be relative to the genius of *Christian* life as such. That is, they will be principles distinctive of Christ's Community or Church, just in so far as they express and foster moral personality like His own, and take effect by methods of corporate order which give adequate scope and liberty of exercise to the free and loving Spirit indwelling all its members.[1]

---

[1] [I insert here two detached notes found in different places among Dr. Bartlet's papers. C.J.C.]:—

It has been truly said that "The experience described as that of 'receiving the Holy Spirit' is beyond question the essential and distinctive thing in early Christianity".

This fact is one of abiding significance for our subject, both historically and theoretically. Historically, it serves to define the genius of Christianity in various ways. It does so by comparison, first, with its spiritual mother, Palestinian Judaism; and next, with its later and more abiding environment, the religion and culture of the Roman Empire, which even in their contrasts to Hebraism later contributed not a little to the Church's development. The specific differentia of the Christian Church was and must remain the *inspired* quality of its life. That life sprang originally from inward consciousness of God as directly active in it as Spirit, the source of religious insight and power. Such a consciousness of immediacy in the Divine presence, making God's people both corporately and individually the temple of indwelling Deity, and thereby "holy" or devoted to Divine ends and modes of living, has tended to recur all down the Christian ages, as often as revival has visited the Church. And, be it noted, such revivals are most characteristic of Christianity among historic religions.

Before going on, however, to trace the history of the Christian Church as an inspired community of men and women, we must make clearer what "the Spirit" and inspiration mean according to the New-Testament writers. Peter on the day of Pentecost declared that its phenomena meant simply the fulfilment of the anticipations of the Hebrew prophets that "in the latter days" God would "pour out of His Spirit on all flesh", so that Israel's sons and daughters would "prophesy" (Joel ii. 28 f.; Acts ii. 16–18), that is, speak under God's own direct initiative. In other words, the glory of the Messianic Age was that such inspiration as had been hitherto the experience of only this or that prophet should become the experience of God's People as a whole, if in varying degrees. Thus they should be in actual experience conscious of God's very life pulsing in them; and all their faculties and all their moral relations, especially to each other, should be raised to a higher power, one truly Divine in quality while human in form.

The agency whereby this came about was, after the mode of Hebrew thought, conceived as God's "Spirit" or energy, "poured forth"—or, as we should perhaps picture it to-day, "radiated"—from Himself into creaturely beings, according to their degree of receptivity. Such a metaphor was meant to express the most direct relationship possible between God's own essential nature, so far as communicable, and the human soul.[1] This, in principle, meant "inspiration", or in-breathing of God's own life, in the highest sense consistent with man's freedom or moral self-determination in the last resort, as involved in personal responsibility. In Jesus as *the* Anointed of God, His Messiah or "Christ", such inspiration or "anointing with holy" (i.e., Divine) "Spirit" had been absolute, or complete within the limits of human receptivity. Thereby had he become "the first-born among many brethren " (Rom. viii. 29), and the medium conditioning the fulfilment in others of the Divine idea of manhood as described in Gen. i—i.e., likeness to God. Proximately, then, it was from "the Christ", as God manifest in manhood, that the Divine Spirit or energy was understood by Peter, on the Day of Pentecost, to be "poured forth" in human experience (Acts ii. 33). The most characteristic form of the Spirit's action was revelation or intuitive insight,

[1] "To the Greek, man is more or less self-contained; to the Hebrew, his higher nature is directly dependent on God" (H. Wheeler Robinson, *The Christian Doctrine of Man*, p. 154).

immediate rather than taught by man to man, and producing full self-evidencing conviction (πληροφορία—1 Thess. i. 5, etc.). This was the Spirit's prophetic function in "the holy" (or Divinely-touched) "People" of God, the Church of His Christ, both generally in all, and specifically in some (the "prophets" and "teachers" par excellence—Acts xiii. 1; cf. 1 Cor. xii. 28). Reflective appropriation of Spirit-given intuitions marked the teacher rather than the prophet, the latter's special "gift" being the greater intensity of his intuition. But in the New Testament no contrast is drawn between these two functions or aspects of reason—the intuitive and the reflective. Here, therefore, in the relation between these two aspects of Divine revelation, the immediate and the mediate, the prophetic and the reflective, the exceptional and the normal, we have a point at which man's attitude was liable to change, and did in fact change as time went on.

According to this conception of the Spirit, its presence was a fact of experience, both for the subject of it himself and for on-lookers. It was no mere matter of inference from its fruits in character, though these were regarded as essential and were especially emphasized by St. Paul; it made itself, in some degree at least, directly perceived through the senses. This was particularly the case at the time of its first decisive manifesta-tion, which generally (after Pentecost), though not always (Acts x. 44–48, xi. 15), coincided with the rite of baptismal con-fession of faith in Jesus as "the Christ" or "the Lord". But St. Paul, at least, regarded the living faith that really brought a man to baptism as itself due to the Spirit, already implicitly active in the soul.

The above-described conceptions are relative to the dis-tinctively-Hebraic or Biblical notion of the Spirit and its rela-tions to persons, both as soul and body. "Spirit", however, was a term in religious use beyond Jewish circles and with different associations. As one of the gravest questions we must keep asking ourselves, all along, is whether and how far there is change from the one to the other type in the sense in which the work of the Spirit is understood in Church-life and Church-order. It is generally allowed that the ecstatic notion of "pro-phecy", which characterized (according to its critics) the Montanist prophets in the latter half of the second century, was un-Hebraic, inasmuch as reason, at least in any self-conscious sense, was quite in abeyance for the time being. But must not deviation from type be recognized also in any and every conception of the Spirit's action (through sacraments, for instance) which does not conform to the Hebraic type? This type was relative to the Hebraic conception of the Spirit, as acting directly only on persons (whether soul or body); so that while material things are used as media of suggestion, as symbols, they are not strictly-speaking used as instruments, or viewed as themselves receiving the Spirit and so conveying it literally to the human recipients. Finally, on the plane of the Spirit, all disability due to sex is transcended: women equally with men can "prophesy", whether to man or to God (as in prayer). On the purely-human plane, however, that of reflective reason, and so in "teaching" as distinct from "prophecy", the ordinary conventions of sex still applied in the Apostolic Age.

We have now to picture to ourselves the attitude of mind, to both the old and the new elements in their faith, with which the new community of Jesus' disciples started out on their mission to declare the Kingdom of God as made known in their own experience.

"The burden of the Baptist's message had been, The Kingdom of God is at hand. The discovery made by those who 'believed on' Jesus, was that He was the King, inasmuch as where He was, there was the Kingdom of God. The witness of the Apostles included both, and was, in effect, The Kingdom is coming, for the King has come. . . . It was the expression of a religious conviction founded on a religious experience, an expression which, though the best which was then available, nevertheless failed to convey adequately all that Jesus had come to mean for them. If He was the Messiah, He was the representative of God".[1] And He was not only the representative of God. He was also the manifestation of God's attitude to man, and that in a new and more vital way than ever before—the way of personality. He had lived among them as a Son reflecting the character of a Father, not Himself visible. Thus "He made God real to them. He brought God near to them. And it was in that aspect of His character and relation to men which is expressed by the Fatherhood of God. It is true that it was not to them a new doctrine. But in the place that Jesus gave to it, the emphasis He laid upon it, the use He made of it, it was utterly new. And whatever He may have taught upon the subject, the truth of it

[1] C. Anderson Scott, *The Fellowship of the Spirit* (1921), p. 23.

was borne home by His own life, by His whole bearing, by every action, tone and gesture. He revealed the Father by revealing the perfect Son.

" And there was yet more than this. It was not only that knowing Jesus they had come to know God as Father, but that somehow, being in touch with Jesus, they were in touch with God, with God acting like the father in the parable of the Prodigal Son. In fellowship with Him they found 'rest unto their souls'. In loyalty to Him they somehow found 'peace with God' ".[1]

So had it been during the period of His bodily presence: so, too, was it now, since Pentecost; herein lay its wonder and its creative power. He had come to them anew, in the Spirit, His Spirit as well as the Father's; and He was now spiritually, that is, in inward reality, more with them, and they in deeper fellowship with Him, than when their intercourse on both sides was under the conditions of the body. Then, "the veil of flesh hung dark between" their soul and His: now they saw into His heart and mind in quite a new way; and so they experienced His spiritual power energizing within them as the Life of their life. And it was the very life of God, "holy Spirit", given forth through Messiah from the Holy Father acting as Spirit. This was the essence of the matter. It was also largely its sum and substance in those first days. For, as has been well said, "The belief of these disciples in Jesus as Messiah was restored, but the contents of their faith", while already "enriched by the presence of important new elements", was yet "waiting to be clarified through further experience and intuition".[2] "If the King had returned" to themselves, invisible, but with more inward reality, "the Kingdom could not be far off".[3] In a sense, one far deeper than they could at first grasp, it had already come, as St. Paul, who had never known his Lord in the flesh, realized and taught with characteristic emphasis (Rom. xiv. 17). In any case they were left behind to be their Master's witnesses. "The task of witnessing and propagating 'truth as it is in Jesus' was at once accepted by the 'disciples' . . . The task of interpreting and applying it to life is one which occupies us still".[4]

During the whole of the Apostolic Age, however, not only did their conception of "the Kingdom of God" and of His Christ, as regards many of its time- and space-relations, remain

[1] C. Anderson Scott, *op. cit.*, pp. 24 f.   [3] *Op. cit.*, p. 27.
[2] *Op. cit.*, p. 28.   [4] *Op. cit.*, p. 29.

confused, owing to the persistence of old forms of thought framed on a lower stage of spiritual training, but their conception of "the Church" also, as constituted by the coming of the Messianic Spirit at Pentecost, was also for a long time in a tentative state.

"They are not at the first conscious of any such distinction between the Jews and themselves as would necessitate their separation from the Church of Israel. They are 'continually in the temple praising and blessing God'. They remain, as most of the believing Jews in Jerusalem remained for thirty years, 'all of them ardent upholders of the Law'. Unconscious as yet of the profound difference Christ had made, they recognised as the one formal distinction between themselves and the Jews of the old faith their conviction that 'God had made this very Jesus whom they had crucified' to be Messiah, and also Lord. But step by step we see them led to the discovery that what they had first called a new Way was really a new Religion. It rested on a new form of relation to God, and involved a fundamental conception of God which was other than that of Judaism".[1]

This new, creative experience, which opened a fresh era in religion, involved two things. Firstly, it meant that Christ, as the realized ideal or type (under given conditions) of Christian life, was the objective content of Christian faith, i.e., of personal trust in God, as quickened subjectively or interpretatively by His Spirit in the form of "holy" or Divine "inspiration":[2] and secondly, it meant that the vital bond of the Apostolic Church was the common privilege of being possessed by and of possessing this experience. These two correlative aspects of Christian life radically determined Church-order in the Apostolic Age. Every type of order is relative to the nature of the life it expresses. In the corporate life of the primitive Christian com-

[1] C. Anderson Scott, op. cit., pp. 11 f.

[2] Such is the best rendering of "holy Spirit" ($\pi\nu\epsilon\hat{\upsilon}\mu\alpha$ $\overset{\text{\'{}}}{\alpha}\gamma\iota o\nu$) in the large number of cases in which the phrase appears in the Greek New Testament with no definite article. But this is far from exhausting the cases where such a rendering holds good, inasmuch as the psychological and experimental aspect of the spiritual fact of heightened human consciousness is intended, rather than the objective, transcendent Divine activity or energy to which, on occasion, such a fact is referred—"the Holy Spirit", par excellence. There are passages too in which "Spirit" or "holy Spirit" describes the element as such, in contrast to terms like "flesh" (Gal. iii. 3, v. 16 ff., 25) or "water" (Acts i. 5, cf. 2), wherein the new personality or "man" lives, moves, and has its being as "spiritual". This applies in some cases even where the definite article occurs (in the Greek as well as in the English version), particularly where the word "Spirit" has just been used without the article (e.g., Gal. v. 16–18, "by Spirit", "against the Spirit", and again "by Spirit": cf. Gal. iii. 3–5 with Acts viii. 15–19 in the Greek). Thus in the last resort the context fixes the sense.

munity, the more-subjective aspects manifestly represented its common sense of Divine inspiration as at work in them; whereas the objective aspect, its circle of moral ideals, and the customs in which these found expression, rested on its impression of the historic personality of Jesus. He was the absolutely Spirit-filled Head of His Body, the Christian Community, as one in life with Him. But in this instance the unity between the objective and subjective aspects of the Christ-life was so complete in the experience of God's Messianic People, that their distinction was hardly felt in the first stage of the Gospel and of the Church. "The Word" and "the Spirit" of the Gospel, or truth about God and His gracious Will, were but two aspects of one and the same revelation of Divine Life, originally embodied in Christ as the truly "living One", and now being reproduced in Christians.

The blending into unity of these two elements, Christ as the historic revelation or "Word", and the interpretative Spirit of God, as realized in Christian experience—and in its complete form found only in the Church as a whole—is described most strikingly in the magnificent outburst in Ephes. iii. 14–19, where the greatest of New-Testament prophets sets forth in impassioned language the central idea of experimental Christianity. There he prays that "the Father", the proto-type of all fatherhood, "would grant . . . that ye may be strengthened with power through His Spirit in the inward man, that Christ may dwell in your hearts through faith; to the end that ye, being rooted and grounded in love, may be strong to grasp with all the saints what is the breadth and length and height and depth, and to know the love of Christ which passeth knowledge, that ye may be filled unto all the fullness of God". "With all the saints": the Church, then, is the sphere of the full revelation of Christ as the love of God made manifest. Apart from it, the Body of Christ, a complete vision cannot be gained of Christ its Head, the Jesus of the Gospels, now become the Christ of all human history. For the Church is called, in and through her corporate Christ-inspired life, to body forth the full reality potential in Him as its Head, Who is in process of total realization in His members one and all (Ephes. i. 23).

But to be called and to be able to represent means also the ability and danger of misrepresenting. The Church-order or organization relative to such a religion must needs be special and distinctive, when compared with those relative to religions of a less-vital and less-personal type. To overlook or forget this inspired quality of the primitive Christian consciousness, and not reckon with it everywhere in one's interpretation of the Church's life and order in the Apostolic Age and in later times too, would be to fall into anachronism and historical unreality. Spirit and form; idea (or "word" of God in the soul) and its outward expression to the senses; the personal and the corporate; these were at first in full accord and organic unity. Inner and outer were at one, the former being and remaining primary, determinative, and ever newly-creative; and the latter secondary, conservative of the best experience and so educative—the basis for fresh advances of the personal towards the ideal through the freedom of the Spirit.[1] Such was the spirituality, the Spirit-prompted nature of the Apostolic Church, incarnating afresh in its derivative life the Spirit of its Messianic Head, a Spirit of love and therefore of true liberty in fellowship.

The[2] first description (in Acts ii. 42) of the corporate Christian life as an inspired fellowship or brotherhood reveals the essential genius and lines of such "order" as it had at the first. "They were diligently attending on the teaching of the Apostles and the fellowship, the breaking of the loaf and the prayers". These and these only marked off the new People, within the Old, as "the holy remnant" (according to ancient prophetic language and idea), in which the full Divine purpose was being realized. Alongside of these distinctive outer forms of the inward Spirit-bond of love, the Christian community shared in the old Jewish religious order of Temple- and Synagogue-piety, as long as it was suffered by the national authorities so to do. Let us look, then, at these new Christian "wineskins" of corporate order for the expression of the new Spirit-life.

The central things were the specific Christian type of fellow-

---

[1] This is the real meaning of St. Paul's contrast of "letter" and "spirit" (2 Cor. iii. 6), as typical of the Old Covenant of Law and the New Covenant of Grace. In both the Divine Will was embodied, but on different levels of spiritual reality, as the Epistle to Hebrews puts it. In the former that Will was embodied in rigid, inflexible, unprogressive forms: in the latter, in flexible, plastic, progressive ways, more and more adequate to express the inward impress of the Spirit of Life in Christ Jesus, in all its sovereign freedom of application to concrete cases. In that sense "the Lord", the Christ, is Himself "Spirit", not "letter", because a person, not a code (2 Cor. iii. 17).

[2] [This portion of Dr. Bartlet's work, pp. 17–19, was found apart from the rest of the typescript, and does not appear to have been ever finally incorporated in it. Hence it may read a little disjointedly as related to what precedes and follows. Yet it is clearly germane to the subject; and I have accordingly inserted it at what seems the most suitable place for it. C.J.C.].

ship itself among those devoted to the Kingdom of God, as revealed by Jesus the Messiah, and the Apostolic witness to His life and words. This perspective, namely, the centrality of the Messianic Kingdom as the supreme object of hope and as already represented on earth by the holy People of God, consecrated and so heirs of that Kingdom in full fruition, is characteristic of Jewish Christianity throughout the Apostolic Age.

The Apostolic teaching (διδαχή) was twofold. It related (1) to the Christian facts, the historic ministry of Jesus as the Christ, and (2) to the Christian ideal of life. This latter came, as time went on, and as the basal facts had all become familiar, to constitute the staple of "the teaching" or instruction in morals and in fellowship-relations generally. Such teaching was essentially practical in scope and spirit, as we see from the references to it in the New Testament and in other earliest Christian writings, notably that styled 'The Didache of the Lord'. The last-named purports, probably with full warrant (in its original form), to set forth the substance of the central Apostolic tradition as to the instruction given, prior to baptism and as its condition, to converts from outside Judaism in particular. The ground-work of such baptismal instruction was taken over from that for proselytes to Judaism. That some more-or-less regular type of instruction in the Christian moral ideal was early taught for committal to memory, as part of the Christian "traditions" handed on from the missionary to his converts, is most likely from what we read in the Epistle to the Romans (vi. 17, xvi. 17) and elsewhere (e.g., Heb. v. 12). From the contexts in which the term διδαχή and the largely-synonymous term διδασκαλία occur, one would naturally infer that the teaching in question was of the connected kind, such as we usually mean by "instruction", as distinct from "preaching" or proclaiming central aspects of the Gospel as a whole. With this agrees the distinction between "prophet" and "teacher" (διδάσκαλος: see Eph. iv. 11, Acts xiii. 1). Further, as addressed to Christians or catechumens, teaching was usually moral or practical in scope (cf., e.g., Mark vii. 7). It dealt with precepts or rules for conduct, otherwise called "traditions", as meant to be passed on from teacher to taught (2 Thess. ii. 15, iii. 6; 1 Cor. xi. 2). An illuminating case of the use of the word διδαχή and its connexion with Church-usages, both being aspects of Church-order—as in the two parts of our 'Didache'—occurs in Heb. vi. 1 f.

But such Christian ethical instruction, though it gradually

settled into the cooler, connected form of an "order" for catechetical instruction, often came originally to the Church in the form of prophetic intuition. There was in fact no sharp dualism between "the word of God" as inspired "prophecy" and the ordinary practical "wisdom", taught in more reflective forms, with more-or-less spiritual insight of explanation, by the "teacher"; but in the one case it came direct from the inspired soul, in the other it was more a matter of memory. Hence the inspired or "charismatic" element in teachers varied almost from the prophetic burning-point to charismatic zero.[1] This explains its very different uses both in the New Testament and in the 'Didache'.

The disciples expected at first that their nation would soon repent of its rejection of Jesus as the Messiah; and so they viewed themselves simply as that part of Israel which was already prepared for His return in power to set up the Kingdom of God in manifest form, and as "sealed" by the Spirit of grace and adoption as heirs of that Kingdom. But by the sheer course of events, both persecution from the leaders of the nation and the extension of their community itself (the true "Israel within Israel")—Divine "faits accomplis" of the Spirit in advance of their preconceived ideas—they came to find themselves in large part organized independently of the national order in religion. Their independent Church-order grew up around the two distinctive elements in their faith and life of fellowship, viz., baptism into the Name and Spirit of the Christ, and their sacred meal of fellowship, "the breaking of bread" or the "eucharist", so called from the initial act of thanksgiving by which the whole was hallowed. To the significance of Christian baptism, as baptism with the Spirit, we have already alluded incidentally; and to the other of the two sacramental acts which determined their distinctive Church-order we shall return presently.

The idea of Christians as "holy" or devoted to God's ends as

---

[1] [Dr. Bartlet is here using the (late-coined) adjective "charismatic" in its rather narrowly-technical sense of "spontaneous", i.e., inspired by Divine grace at the very moment. It must, however, be borne in mind, as was pointed out by A. J. Mason in *Essays on the Early History of the Church and the Ministry* (ed. Swete [1921], pp. 30–33), that, especially under the guidance of St. Paul, *all* ministries in the early Church, being believed to be exercised by virtue of the minister in question being Divinely capacitated therefor, were strictly speaking "charismatic", not the spectacular or inspirational only. See below, pp. 22–25, p. 25, n. 1. C.J.C.].

summed up in His Kingdom, for the perfected form of which their whole life was but one long-sustained expectancy, was absolutely determinative for primitive Church-order, as expressive of Church-life. Such holiness was far wider than our notion of religious devotion. It was synonymous with living unto God, with Him and His ends as the centre of thought, feeling, and will. But God's prime practical interest on earth was His holy People or Church, as actual heirs of the Kingdom and as its primary embodiment.

Preoccupation with this thought comes out most strikingly in the eucharistic prayers in the 'Didache', which contains our oldest specimen of a connected Church-Order. These prayers may well preserve the use of the Apostolic Church in Palestine and Syria, so much are they on the lines of the Petrine speeches in Acts and all our other non-Pauline evidence. The first of them, that over the cup as associated with the breaking of bread (of which we read in Acts ii and elsewhere),[1] runs as follows (ix. 2):

"We give thanks to Thee, our Father, for the holy Vine of David Thy Servant, which Thou didst make known to us through Jesus Thy Servant. To Thee be the glory for ever." Here the "holy Vine", described in terms of God's chosen King of old, David, His true servant (παῖς), is plainly God's Messianic People, the Church. This is also alluded to explicitly in two of the petitions which follow (ix. 4, x. 5), and is indeed central to the general outlook of these eucharistic prayers as a whole.

To the original Apostolic circle in Jerusalem Jesus was primarily and essentially the Prophet of the Messianic Kingdom: all else followed in the main from this. So in the early days Peter claims that Jesus is he of whom Moses said, "A prophet will the Lord God raise up unto you from among your brethren as He raised up me" (Acts iii. 22), but with even greater right to absolute obedience. Even in his latest days, Peter still thinks of His Lord mainly in the character of the utterly-devoted Servant of the Lord, through Whose meek, sacrificial love unto the passion on the Cross the sins of God's People were atoned for and they themselves saved. He was, then, the indispensable element in the new building of the true Spiritual Zion, occupying the key-position in its structure, as the "chief corner-stone". For it was by union with Christ in this character

[1] See also below, pp. 29 f. on Jewish Table-Communion.

—according to Peter's own strangely-mixed metaphor—that Christians, "coming as to a living stone", were vivified with a life Divine, and so qualified to be "built up into a spiritual house" or temple, "to be a holy priesthood, to offer up spiritual sacrifices, acceptable to God through" Him (1 Peter ii. 4–6).

We have essentially the same conception of Jesus and His relation to the new Ecclesia as the Messianic People of God, objectively made holy to God by the self-oblation of their personal Head, the Servant of the Lord, underlying the more speculatively-developed Christology of the writer to Hebrews. For he says (ii. 10) of Jesus as "the Son of Man", i.e., the representative of humanity as God meant it to be when He created man, that it suited God's character and ways, "in bringing many sons unto glory, to make the pioneer-leader (τὸν ἀρχηγόν) of their salvation" (later on [xii. 2] called also "faith's pioneer-leader and perfecter") "perfect through sufferings". Now this is exactly the perspective in which Jesus and the Kingdom of God are viewed in the thanksgiving or eucharistic prayers in the 'Didache', which have often been treated as of hole-and-corner origin, possibly also of rather-late date, simply because they are not on Pauline or Johannine lines of thought. On the other hand, when they are approached purely along the lines of the Apostolic Jewish Christianity of the New Testament as a whole, there is no reason to regard them as other than the direct lineal representatives of those referred to in Acts ii. 42 in connexion with the breaking of the holy loaf. That sacred rite of the Koinonia or brotherhood of the Church, the original symbolism of the one loaf shared among the many, was what the 'Didache' (xi. 11) itself calls "a mystery" or symbol "of the Church" in terms of the senses (κοσμικόν). This was a different form of prophetic symbolism from that which Jesus Himself gave to the breaking of the loaf on one special occasion only, that of the last or Paschal meal.[1]

Nay more, who can venture to deny that alike in form and in idea the eucharist of our 'Didache' may be continuous with the yet-earlier and habitual symbolism given to the regular Jewish rite of hallowing a solemn meal, where a group of male Jews

---

[1] The associations of this special occasion I believe were first fixed upon and grafted on to the original Jewish-Christian Apostolic type of the breaking of bread by St. Paul. This was in keeping with his special sense of the centrality of the Cross to *all* Christian life and thought, and not only as consecrating believers in Christ once for all as "saints", devoted through Messiah's vicarious sacrifice to membership in the Messianic Kingdom.

partook of God's blessings of food and blessed His name for them? In this connexion should we not recall how it was "in the breaking of the loaf"—i.e., an act reminding them of something distinctive in Jesus' own manner of performing the priestly function of the house-father in these domestic "eucharists" or "benedictions", whether by gesture or words or both— that He was recognized at Emmaus by the two disciples, whom He had met on the way thither after His passion (Lk. xxiv. 30 f., 35)? But if so, we may here be in presence of the most venerable of all devotional and liturgical formulae due to the prophetic spirit, the inspired consciousness of the Apostolic Church, in the earliest days of its Jerusalem-fellowship. For these prayers may be in substance, if not in ipsissima verba, part of "the prayers" associated in Acts ii. 42 with "the breaking of the loaf" in fellowship. They may, that is, be eucharistic prayers which, under full Apostolic lead, were shaped by a usage that would in time crystallize; and they may contain certain turns of thought and phrasing felt to be inspired by the common mind of the Spirit-filled Society. And such eucharistic prayers would tend to spread beyond Jerusalem, e.g., when Barnabas went to Antioch (Acts xi. 22–24).

I have dwelt thus fully on certain preliminary matters of principle, because I am sure it is only in the light of these, kept constantly before us, that anything like a real reconstruction of the primitive Church's life and order is possible. In particular, apart from sustained and serious reckoning with the pervasive consciousness of the energy of "holy spirit" at work in each and all of the Church's members, nothing will be seen by us as it was seen by the actors themselves; for the atmosphere and spirit of the whole will be lacking.

Having, then, done our best to escape this danger, so far as a sound method of approach can carry us, let us consider some salient features of Church-order in the Apostolic Age, including for that purpose such parts of the written traditional Apostolic instruction or 'Didache', as seem to belong to the period before 64 A.D. rather than to that which follows it.

As we have already seen, all Church-order, in the positive and not merely the restrictive sense, sprang out of the inspired quality of Christian life within the unity-amid-diversity of the membership of the Church, viewed as the body or organism animated by the Christ present in all by the Spirit.   Here

Romans xii is of quite fundamental significance. The Church being in principle the fellowship of the Spirit of Christ, the law of its corporate life of common inspiration is that of loving and dutiful membership of the one Body, in an active rather than a passive sense. "And having gifts of grace (χαρίσματα) differing according to the grace given unto us, whether prophecy, (let us prophesy) according to the proportion of our faith; or practical service (διακονία), (let us engage) in our service; or he that teacheth, in his teaching; or he that exhorteth, in his exhorting. He that shares his goods, (let it be) without reserve (of heart); he that superintends, with zeal; he that does deeds of mercy, with cheerfulness" (Rom. xii. 6–8). Here there is no line drawn between services to the brotherhood rendered in Church, or corporately, and those in a more private capacity, or again between what would later be reckoned sacred and what would be reckoned secular forms of ministry. Even the ministry of the Word or the living message received in the soul by direct illumination of the Spirit—the genus to which belong the higher kinds of χάρισμα on the Apostle's lists of Spirit-prompted graces and functions—is not marked off in idea from the more-material services to human need which elsewhere come lower on the list, particularly in 1 Cor. xii. 28. There the gifts qualifying for "assistance" and "guidance"—as of the steersman who shapes the ship's course—come nearly last, probably as less super-normal in form; while "deeds of power" and "healings" of the body come in-between in an intermediate position. The whole series is one of graded manifestations of holy inspiration, as quickening to higher potency all natural faculties whether spiritual, psychic, or physical. Finally there is appended, as it were by an afterthought, to the "acts of guidance" the gift of rapt or ecstatic utterance—the natural language of the emotions when stirred by "holy Spirit", as at Pentecost and on other occasions referred to in Acts. The gift of interpreting such "tongues" is mentioned alongside of it in a final enumeration (1 Cor. xii. 29 f.). The relative valuation here implicit was probably peculiar in part to St. Paul,[1] especially as regards the subordination of the more spectacular type to the more spirit-ually-significant and revealing variety of gifts, which minis-

---

[1] Such varieties of valuation as may have existed in the Apostolic Church would tend to influence the order or method of exercising ministries in Church-assemblies and otherwise, as was certainly the case in the later treatment of them at different times and in different parts of the Church. On this we shall have something to say in later chapters.

tered most to the education or building-up of Christian character through fresh insight into the mind and ways of God.

The striking things to observe, thus far, are the universal distribution of Spirit-gifts of one kind or another, and the universal use made of them in Church-life, including its corporate meetings for worship and for mutual edification. This life of mutual love, and of concern for the welfare and up-building of all in the fellowship, led naturally and instinctively, in churches where the Spirit was felt by all to be the prompter of loving impulses, to a general mutual ministry of gifts of grace. Paul's first letter to the Corinthians, particularly ch. xiv, shows us this clearly. The Corinthians, zealous for spiritual gifts, are bidden, "with a view to the edifying of the Church", not to be satisfied with an ecstatic type of gift like a "tongue", but to seek by prayer for the further and supplemental gift of interpretation. For unless this be added, either by the speaker in a "tongue" himself or by some fellow-member, the Church gets no real benefit; and similarly with spirit-songs, and rapt benedictions or thanksgivings addressed to God in the church-meeting by one or another (xiv. 12–17). Nor is there any reason to doubt that a like general "charismatic" ministry obtained also in less-Pauline circles (see 1 Peter iv. 8–11).

Here the leading principles plainly are: "where the Spirit of the Lord is, there is liberty" (2 Cor. iii. 17), and "Quench not the Spirit" (1 Thess. v. 19) by despising "prophesyings" (1 Thess. v. 20), even when the form or degree of the Spirit-gift may not be of the most edifying order. These are the two contrasted aspects of the matter, viewed from the side of the duty of the Spirit-prompted member and from that of the Church respectively. The latter's true part, as itself Spirit-illumined, is to "prove all" messages by spiritual discernment, and then to "hold fast that which is" found "good" in them (1 Thess. v. 21).

Such a state of Church-life would seem, if judged by later standards, to lack something of "decency and order" (1 Cor. xiv. 40). Yet there is nothing in it that would seem other than natural to a meeting of the Society of Friends. Nor did the care for the common good, and for "the things of others" as individuals, stop at the positive aspect of mutual building-up: it included also the more-negative aspect, the discipline of wrong-doing, and the restoration of the offender to a right mind and to living unity with the fellowship. Not only does Paul bid those

who are "men of the Spirit" more than others to devote themselves voluntarily to such a task (Gal. vi. 1); he also lays on the
whole brotherhood the duty of discipline. They are to "withdraw" their fellowship (individually) "from every brother that
walketh disorderly," i.e., "not after the tradition" governing
general Church-usage, handed on by their Apostle (2 Thess.
iii. 6). All, too, shared in the exercise of corporate discipline on
cases of serious disloyalty to the Christian ideal, necessitating
temporary or abiding suspension from the corporate fellowship
of the Church (1 Cor. v. 1–8). And this practice was a corollary
drawn very directly from the general idea of the inspired nature
of Christians as such, and particularly from their corporate
consciousness in Church-meeting. Indeed, it was largely out of
such voluntary efforts at fraternal service by remonstrance,
advice, encouragement, and what-not, that there gradually
emerged a more-regular, because generally-recognized, ministry
on the part of those possessing a special degree of Spirit-
bestowed gift or heightened aptitude; and this in the end
received formal sanction for representative exercise (see 1 Cor.
xvi. 15 f., 18; cf. 1 Thess. v. 12 f.).[1] In such cases, however,
there often blended from the first another factor than the
purely-spiritual, viz., the advantage enjoyed in respect of
superior social position, education, and wealth. Such advantages
put certain brethren in a position to exercise a ministry not unlike that of a patron towards his clients. This is seen even in the
case of women like Lydia at Philippi and Phoebe at Cenchreae,
the latter of whom performed there a ministry of helpful
beneficence as patroness (Rom. xvi. 1 f.).

A particular case of such pre-eminence, due primarily to
advantages not strictly spiritual, was that in which a relatively-
wealthy believer made his house the meeting-place of the local
brotherhood. The original churches must all have been in some
sense house-churches. This would give the host a certain natural
right to the function of presiding and controlling the conduct of

---

[1] [I append here a detached note found among Dr. Bartlet's papers and
relevant to the topic handled in the text above. C.J.C.]:—
Liberty for mutual edification and common responsibility for corporate
decisions are integral to true Church-life and -order. Very characteristic is the
relation of each church to its ministers. All ministry, in the widest sense, rests
on Divine "gifts" (1 Cor. xii–xiv; Rom. xii. 3 ff.; Ephes. iv. 7, 11–13): the
regular ministry is but a special form of what is incumbent on all (1 Thess. v.
12–15); and the exercise of its special gifts depends on the recognition of these
by the Spirit-guided Church (1 Cor. xvi. 15–18). Full authority remains, however, resident in the church itself as a representative form of the Church
Universal.

the community in the exercise of the ministry of "gifts" open to all the brethren. This might happen even prior to and apart from regular election (let alone ordination or solemn setting-apart with prayer) for the representative exercise of gifts. Such a state of things, in which a plurality of house-churches arose with the increase of members, would raise serious problems of order in relation to local unity, such as we seem to meet in the Ignatian Epistles.

No further working out of these principles, as lying at the base of the Christian Church, God's new Ecclesia, is here called for,[1] especially since a convincing picture in these terms has been presented by Dr. C. Anderson Scott in the work already cited, as well as in his fine study entitled 'What happened at Pentecost?'[2] What really resulted from the Pentecostal experi-ence of Divine inspiration, as the source and essence of religion of the Christian type, was a new kind of "fellowship" ($\kappa o\iota\nu\omega\nu\iota\alpha$), intenser, and more suffused with the Spirit of Divine love, than any heretofore. It was not immediately or primarily "the Church" as an institution, or even as a definitely-constituted order of corporate life, set up (in keeping with any supposed Apostolic commission) in order thus, and thus only, to organize a community on the foundation of faith in Christ's Messiahship, or to mould its development in certain ways, still less to do so with authority intentionally bestowed ad hoc for this purpose.

All such notions, alike of the primitive Christian Ecclesia and of the Apostolic function, which Dr. Hort has shown to have been simply one of authoritative witness, not of governmental and administrative commission, are pure anachronisms. They are shown to be so chiefly by two simple considerations of the broadest but most conclusive nature. First, the fact that the Twelve and their fellow-disciples are recorded early in Acts to have asked their Risen Master whether He was about, then and there, "to restore the Kingdom to Israel" (Acts i. 6). Such a question, both by its time-perspective and by its national conception of the Kingdom to be restored, implies a purely-Jewish view of the form of the Kingdom, and so of any Church

[1] The true conception of *The Christian Ecclesia*, as continuous with and fulfilling the Jewish idea of *The People of God*, is clearly set forth in Dr. F. J. A. Hort's work under the former title (1897); and his position has been further developed, under the latter title, by the late Dr. H. F. Hamilton, of Bishop's College, Lennoxville, Canada (Oxford, 1912: two vols.).

[2] In *The Spirit*, a volume of essays edited by the late Canon B. H. Streeter in 1919 (pp. 117–157).

which they could then conceive to be in their Lord's mind. It was still one resting on a national and not on a universal basis; that is to say, it was not a Catholic Church at all.[1] Secondly, the facts which the Book of Acts goes on to record touching the behaviour of the Apostles, as witnesses to the Messiahship of Jesus, imply (a) that what Peter and his colleagues were at first expecting, and what they continued for an indefinite time to expect, was simply the conversion of Israel from its perversity in rejecting its true Messiah (Acts iii. 19 ff.); and (b) that the piece-meal and tentative expansion of the Christian Ecclesia, so as to include fresh classes of those outside the Law, was accepted only out of sheer loyalty to the unlooked-for manifestation of the Spirit's gifts beyond Israel itself and in ever-widening circles of unlikely converts, notably the Samaritans and (later on) uncircumcised Gentiles like Cornelius.

From what has just been said it is also manifest that there was not in the Apostolic Age anything really like the later ecclesiastical rite or sacrament known as "confirmation". The coming of "holy Spirit" was normally not manifested later in time than the rite of baptism; alike in idea and in fact it was part of this rite, or rather it was its very essence, the special prerogative of Messiah's baptism as contrasted with John's, which was with water (Matt. iii. 11, Lk. iii. 16, Acts i. 5, xi. 16; cf. xix. 4–6, Heb. vi. 1 f.). This principle seems in evidence in the case of the Apostolic circle at Pentecost, which does not appear to have been baptized with water in the name of Jesus at all, having already in all probability received John's water-baptism unto repentance—as penitents prepared to receive the Messianic Kingdom and its *Spirit*-baptism when it should be manifested. Of them we simply read in Acts i. 4 f., that they were "to await the promise of the Father", heard from Jesus; for whereas John had baptized with water, they were to be baptized ere long with holy Spirit—the specific Christian gift promised by the Father to the Messiah's People (Luke xxiv. 49). As regards the pair of other exceptional cases in Acts—in that of the Samaritans, the gift of "holy Spirit" follows after an interval their baptism with water in the Name of Jesus Christ (Acts viii. 14–17); in that of Cornelius and his

---

[1] Viewed in relation to this limited outlook, the idea of Apostolic *succession* is obviously out of keeping with the thought of the Apostolic age, and can have formed no part of the Apostles' commission from Christ. It could have originated only after the real historical situation of the Apostles was no longer conceivable.

friends it precedes, being coincident with their inward faith in the Gospel-message (Acts x. 44–48). But both are to be understood in the same way. They are special cases, mentioned by the author of Acts as Divine evidence, afforded by the "falling" of the holy Spirit on new classes of believers, touching God's will as to their eligibility for membership in His chosen Ecclesia, for the inheritance of the Messianic Kingdom. In both cases, Peter, as representative of the leaders of the Mother-Church in Jerusalem, is recorded to have been participant in the matter, and so to have witnessed to the fresh departure in principle as actually an act of God and therefore to be accepted as valid. The laying-on of hands was not of the essence of the matter. It was the usual accompaniment of Christian baptism, even though the member of the Church who thus identified himself with the new candidate for incorporation was, like Ananias who laid hands on Saul, simply an ordinary Christian brother.

Any member of the Spirit-filled Ecclesia was competent to be the human medium through whose symbolic act of self-identification, in faith, the welcome of the Body of Christ was given to a fresh candidate for incorporation, and thereby his reception of the Spirit facilitated and brought to fruition. The more-fully representative such a member was, say, an apostle or a prophet, the more fitting and psychologically helpful the laying-on of his hands would be. But that was all.

Fixing our attention, then, for the moment on the decade just before the ruin of the Jewish State and its holy City, which we may regard as the transitional epoch par excellence, we may say that the following features, characteristic of primitive Christianity generally, co-existed side by side, if in varying degrees in different localities.

First and foremost, it was still an age of the Spirit, of conscious inspiration, both corporate and individual, of spontaneity and large liberty in the expression of a life felt to be Divinely prompted, yet for that very reason directed not to self-centred ends but to the Will of God; for to Him all must give account of the use made of His gifts, both spiritual and material, received and held on trust.

Secondly, the all-inclusive idea, regulative of thought and feeling, was the Messianic "Kingdom of God". Of the presence of this Kingdom in some degree the holy inspiration of the new

Christian life was the token, as it was also the earnest of its future consummation and full power at a date still thought to be very near.

Thirdly, and as related to this pre-occupying idea of the inspired and Messianic Kingdom, the person of Jesus, the Spirit-filled "Servant of the Lord" or Messianic Son of God, its appointed human head, occupied a place of sovereign pre-eminence. As Peter puts it in his sermon in Solomon's Porch (Acts iii. 12 ff.), Jesus was "the Holy and Righteous One" of Messianic prophecy, "the pioneer-leader of life". Him, in his character as "Servant of the Lord" described in Isaiah liii, "the God of our fathers has glorified", by raising Him out of the seeming defeat of death into new life. To witness to all this from their own experience, Peter and his fellow-witnesses were chosen: and the gift of the Holy Spirit was God's seal set to Jesus' Messiahship. "Him did God exalt by His right hand as pioneer-leader and Saviour, to give repentance to Israel and remission of sins" (Acts v. 31).

APPENDED NOTE ON

JEWISH TABLE-COMMUNION[1]

The house-father takes a loaf and blesses, saying,"Blessed be Thou, O Lord our God, King of the world, Who bringest forth bread from the earth".

He breaks the bread and shares it with his table-fellows.

If wine be used, he now takes a cup of wine and utters the Bene-diction, "Blessed be Thou, O Lord our God, King of the world, Who hast created the fruit of the vine". The cup is passed round.

Then follows the meal, with every sign of gladness, and with thought for the poor.

The solemn thanksgiving is pronounced after food. (Aliens,[2] women, slaves, and minors are excluded—so sacred is it, as a sacri-fice; cf. 'Didache' xiv. 1 f.). It included

(a) a preface; the house-father and his fellows reminding one

---

[1] [For this "appended note" Dr. Bartlet utilizes the material he had prepared for and embodied in his contribution to *Mansfield College Essays* (1909), pp. 53–59,from which it is clear that he was mainly dependent on E. von der Goltz's *Tischgebete und Abendmahlgebete* (in *Texte und Untersuchungen*, N.F., vol. XIV, iib [1905], pp. 5–13). It may be observed that, while the usages here described are probably in substance quite ancient, the actual written documents from which they are drawn are comparatively late. There is a fuller study of Jewish table-prayers by L. Finkelstein in *The Jewish Quarterly Review*, vol. xix, pp. 211–262 (Jan. 1929). C.J.C.].

[2] Hence the gravity of the issue in Gal. ii. 12 ff., Acts xv. 19 f., 28 f.

another that blessing and praise are due to God for His gifts and goodness, by which men live:

(*b*) a fourfold prayer of thanksgiving (cf. "the prayers", Acts ii. 42) with responses:

    (i) for God's favour to all flesh, and to Israel for His Name's sake, in giving food;

    (ii) for life in the goodly land of Israel after bondage in Egypt, for God's covenant-pledge of circumcision in their flesh, for His Law and its teachings, for the life bestowed by His grace and mercy, and for His daily nourishment;

    (iii) for God's grace to His Jerusalem (which He will yet build again, and into which He will gather Israel);

    (iv) that the Good and Merciful One may in the future yet more fully show grace and mercy as King of the world and Israel's fatherly King (the ejaculatory nature of this section is marked).

(*c*) the Amen.

APPENDED NOTE ON

TABLE-COMMUNION IN 'THE DIDACHE'

ix. 1. "Now as touching the Giving of Thanks, thus give thanks:

2. "First, as touching the Cup: 'We thank Thee, our Father, for the holy Vine of David Thy Servant, which Thou hast made known to us through Jesus Thy Servant . . .'

3. "But as touching the broken bread: 'We thank Thee, our Father, for the life and knowledge which Thou hast made known to us through Jesus Thy Servant . . .

4. " 'Just as this broken bread was once lying scattered upon the mountains, and being gathered together became one, so let Thy Church be gathered together from the ends of the earth into Thy Kingdom; for Thine is the glory and the power through Jesus Christ for ever' ".

5. Only the baptized Christian is to partake of "the Eucharist" as being a holy thing.[1]

x. 1. "But after being filled, thus give thanks:

2. " 'We thank Thee, holy Father, for Thy holy Name, which Thou hast enshrined in our hearts,[2] and for the knowledge and faith and immortality which Thou hast made known to us through Jesus Thy Servant. . . .

3. " 'Thou, Sovereign Almighty, didst create all things for Thy Name's sake. Both food and drink didst Thou give to men to enjoy,

---

[1] Compare the practice of the Essenes regarding their common food, as described by Schürer (*Gesch. des jüd. Volkes*, vol. ii, pp. 663 f. [Eng. tr. II, ii, p. 200]).

[2] Perhaps replacing "Thy covenant which Thou hast sealed on our flesh" (see above).

that they might give thanks to Thee; but to us didst Thou graciously give spiritual food and drink and eternal life through Thy Servant.

4. " 'Above all, we thank Thee that Thou art powerful . . .

5. " 'Remember, Lord, Thy Church, to rescue it from all evil. . . .

6. " 'Let grace come, and let this world pass away. Hosanna to the God of David. If anyone is a saint, let him come (to meet the Lord): if anyone is not, let him repent. Maranatha. Amen' ".

CHAPTER II

THE SUB-APOSTOLIC AGE

As one looks back upon the Apostolic Age, the prevalent impression is that of the spiritual atmosphere of a religious revival; and such in fact was the atmosphere of the Apostolic Church. Forms of true religion, of the Hebraic type, were already existing in Israel; what was needed, when the Christ came, was that they should be revitalized by a new spirit of life. It was natural then that the emphasis should fall upon this new or distinctive element, which was of the kind known generally as religious enthusiasm. But the new consciousness of God's inspiring energy, at work in the Christian experience, did not mean that the old forms were thrown aside, but only that they ceased to be regarded in a fixed or rigid way, as if established by a Divine Law, and therefore to be obeyed with the literal obedience of a bondservant. Henceforth they were to be fulfilled in their spirit, or inner meaning, as Christ had fulfilled them, that is, in the spirit of a loyal and loving son. The old forms were all seen in a new light, that of the Divine Fatherhood, simply as ways in which His loving Will could best take effect in and through His children. In a word, Law had become Gospel. In modern language, the method of "repression", which had prevailed in current Judaism, was replaced by that of the "expression" of the essential Divine ideal, namely, the kinship of the human with the Divine as regards man's higher or essential nature. But such expression rested upon God's own living action within the soul, impressing on it the vision of the ideal to be realized: and this Divine initiative was what was meant by the characteristic Apostolic words, "holy Spirit" and "Grace".

One passage is worth quoting from the so-called 'Epistle of Barnabas' (about 75 A.D.), as showing how strong the sense of Divine inspiration still was at the heart of Christian experience. In contrasting the outward temple of Judaism (which had just been destroyed) with the Temple of the Lord which was rising before his eyes as the Christian Church, the author exclaims, "Wherefore in our habitation truly God dwells in us. How? His word of faith, His calling of promise, the wisdom of His ordinances, the precepts of the teaching (διδαχῆς)—*He* Himself, prophesying in us, He Himself dwelling in us, opening for us, who had been enslaved to death, the door of the Temple, to wit the mouth (in confession), giving us repentance, leads us into the incorruptible Temple. For he who longs to be saved (and so seeks Christian instruction) looks not to the man (i.e., who speaks God's word), but to Him Who dwells and speaks in him—being amazed at this, that he has never either heard the Speaker's words (as they sound in his inward ear) from His mouth, nor himself ever desired to hear them. This is a spiritual Temple in process of being built for the Lord" (xvi. 8–10). Here we have a deeply-experimental utterance on the lines of John v. 34–38, touching the Father's inner "witness" heard in the soul.

At the same time there operated as a controlling, if at first latent, element in the primitive Christian consciousness, the acceptance of an objective type of human life, relative to which alone the intense, vital, free subjectivity of its own life had its real meaning and value. It was freedom to seek righteousness as the loving Will of God that was the very essence of the matter, what was called "salvation" or "eternal life". That life was from the first and throughout conceived as one realized in personal relations within a social order, known as the "fellowship" or "brotherhood", derived from God, and made sacred in all eyes by its relation to Him.

The Apostolic Age then, with all its enthusiasm and sense of direct inspiration throughout the Brotherhood, saw in the Spirit the power by which God's Will was to be done on earth as it is in Heaven—that is, completely. The sum of that Will was an attitude of the whole personality to other personalities one and the same with God's very own attitude, namely love. But Christian love, while an emotion, was inspired by the profoundest and most constructive of ideas, that of the absolute value of human personality, because of its Divine origin, nature, and destiny. The most adequate, as also the most moving, expression of this fact is St. Paul's psalm of love (1 Cor. xiii). Accordingly the enthusiasm of the Apostolic Church was an "enthusiasm of humanity", to use the classic phrase of the author of 'Ecce Homo'. This is what we meant by saying in the opening sentence of our last chapter that Christianity is the religion of moral personality.

We were justified, therefore, in ascribing to the Apostolic Age an atmosphere and a temper of inspired spontaneity. No other representation of it would be historical. But this does not mean anarchy or lawlessness of spirit. All the background of the religion of the Hebrew prophets is presupposed; and this makes itself more and more evident in the latter part of the Apostolic Age, and particularly in the later Pauline Epistles, where the outlines of the new Church-order are discernible with ever-growing distinctness. In the vivid reflection of Christian life and order there is a growing emphasis on the *ethical and social* application of the inspired life. That life had never been individualistic or purely subjective in temper; for it had always been inspired and controlled by mutual love. St. Paul well knew that we know in part, and prophesy, or utter our deepest and most inspired intuitions, with only partial truth or adequacy. Here the common, or corporate, consciousness supplements, corrects, and completes, what the individual apprehends in a more partial and one-sided fashion. "We were all baptized by one Spirit into one body, . . . and all made to drink one Spirit", says the Apostle (1 Cor. xii. 13); but there are varieties of spiritual gifts due to the same Spirit. The insight, therefore, of an Apostle or a prophet has greater validity and, therefore, authority, than that of a less-gifted member of the Church; while the common, corporate mind of the whole Body or spiritual organism, of which Christ is the Head, has the completest human authority of all. While then "conscience", in the sense of reverence for moral principle as directly revealed by God to the soul, is as characteristic of Christian and particularly Pauline thought as is the idea of love, yet the action of the former is in practice always to be subject to the wider interests of the latter, rightly interpreted. In other words, reverence for "holy spirit" as revealed within oneself is always bound to seek harmony with the same Spirit revealed within the common consciousness of the Church. It was on these lines

that the great Apostle of the Gentiles restrained the individualism and intellectualism of his non-Hebraic converts at Corinth
and elsewhere. In so doing, he laid down for all time the principle of harmony between Christian liberty in the Spirit, including the duty and right of Christian prophecy or utterance
of God's truth for the conscience, and that order in common
Church-life which is the practical corollary of considerate love.

Such are the principles of Church-order which grow out of
Christian life in the Spirit itself, and of Church-authority as
connected therewith. But there is another and even more
vital element in the illumination of the Christian mind and
conscience to which reference must be made, as the greatest
safeguard against mere subjectivism or one-sided religious
enthusiasm. For Christianity has the unique privilege of having
its ideal already realized in the person of its Founder, the Head
of the Church. In His personality as reflected in the Gospels,
and in His words there recorded, when read in the light of His
own character and spirit, Christians have an abiding ultimate
standard of Divine truth, in the sphere of moral personality in
particular, which affords a permanent corrective to all subjective aberrations, whether of the individual or of the Christian
consciousness at large. Finally, reference to the Gospels has
brought into view the last in order of thought, but the first in
practice, of the Christian standards of Church-life and -order—
I mean the written Word as a revelation of the Divine Will.

The sum-total of these objective sources of Church-order
expressed itself in the Christian tradition or traditions on
specific points which gradually took shape during the Apostolic
Age. A selection of what was felt at the time to be practically
the most important of such traditions came to be current under
the title "the Teaching" ($\dot{\eta}$ $\Delta\iota\delta\alpha\chi\dot{\eta}$). This was regarded as having
behind it full Apostolic authority, which was tantamount also
to full Church-authority; and there are references to its use in
several of the Pauline Epistles, and that in increasing measure,
as the dangers attending the free exercise of crude or uneducated
consciences came in actual experience to be realized. St. Paul
was a great missionary before he was a great theologian; and a
missionary is quick to adjust his methods of presentation to the
psychological needs of his converts. There seems, therefore, no
valid reason, in the light of the analogy of the mission-field to-day
as in other ages, to doubt that the emphasis upon the need
and value of "the healthful teaching" ($\dot{\eta}$ $\dot{\upsilon}\gamma\iota\alpha\dot{\iota}\nu o\upsilon\sigma\alpha$ $\delta\iota\delta\alpha\sigma\kappa\alpha\lambda\dot{\iota}\alpha$

—1 Tim. i. 10; 2 Tim. iv. 3; Tit. i. 9, ii. 1: cf. 1 Tim. vi. 3, 2 Tim. i. 13, Tit. ii. 8), prominent in the Pastoral Epistles, is true to St. Paul's own method of teaching.[1] We may, therefore, well imagine that the substance of 'the Two Ways', which forms the first part of our 'Didache', was used by St. Paul, as by other teachers, in the Apostolic Age.

The Apostolic and Sub-Apostolic Ages blend insensibly into each other. Take what date one may, short of the death of the last of the Apostles proper, there will be large overlapping of features characteristic of each. This is eminently true as regards our special subject, that of Church-life and -order, and their mutual relations. For while, as we have already seen, the Apostolic Age was by the very nature of its opening unique in its general character, yet the inspired and intensely-fraternal quality of the Messianic People or Church of God persisted down to the end of the first century, and indeed well into the next. On the other hand, the informal beginnings of the reflective and connected "order", alike in instruction and in Church-usages, such as marks the Sub-Apostolic Age, can be traced back far into the preceding period.

As the Apostles themselves began to be withdrawn from the Church by death, and their spoken instruction ceased to be heard, the value of what was believed to be Apostolic tradition would be immensely enhanced. It would be but natural, then, if the first edition of our 'Didache' was written down as representing current Apostolic tradition in northern Syria, soon after the death of Peter in A.D. 65. In it there stood not only the moral order of 'the Two Ways', but also appended to this a simple order of Church-usages on baptism and the eucharist or breaking of bread—including a brief allusion to the prophetic ministry in connexion with the latter—the whole being rounded off with an exhortation to fidelity in view of the approaching fiery trial of Antichrist's epiphany and the return of the Church's Lord.[2]

Here we have, side by side, in harmonious co-operation,

---

[1] This view of the matter is well set forth in the Commentaries on the Pastoral Epistles by Dr. R. St. J. Parry and Dr. W. Lock.

[2] See below, pp. 53–56. The clearest proof that the *Didache* or Instruction proper, apart from a hortatory peroration, once ended at this point [x. 6? C.J.C.], is afforded by xi. 1, with its reference to πάντα τὰ προειρημένα as the test of a true teacher. [But see below, p. 53, n. 2. C.J.C.].

[A pencil-note indicates that Dr. Bartlet regarded the missionary-instructions given to the Apostles in the Gospels of Matthew (x, xxviii, etc.) and John (xx f.), and the appointment of the Seven in Acts vi, as also illustrating the process by which the missionary-functions of the early Church came to be separated from her local administrative functions. C.J.C.].

(a) the traditional or fixed element of Church-order, and (b) the fresh, flexible, and progressive element of prophetic inspiration operating in the ministry of special gifts of grace (χαρίσματα),[1] as distinct from the regularly-appointed and administrative leaders of each local church.

Some quarter of a century later than the first draft of the 'Didache', we have in 'the Ascension of Isaiah' a companion-picture of this twofold order of ministry, the prophetic and the official; only the latter is now the more prominent, and the former seems to be for the most part dying out.

This relative fading of the prophetic or manifestly-inspired type of ministry was probably due in part to certain abuses to which it was easily liable. The class of travelling missionaries —"apostles" in the wider sense, to which we have reference also in our present 'Didache'—was in special danger from inter-ested personal motives, quite apart from the discredit into which those fell whose doctrine was out of keeping with the tradition represented by the Twelve Apostles and St. Paul (cf. Apoc. ii. 2; Ep. of Jude). It was then probably about this period, say 80–90 A.D., that our 'Didache' first underwent revision and expansion, in order to bring it into closer touch with the existing needs of the Church.[2] The attitude now taken up to this itinerant charismatic ministry is one of reserve and discrimination. At the same time, true representatives of this type are still assumed to be active, and are highly honoured. There is no suggestion that "prophets" are a merely-temporary type of ministry and not an integral part of the permanent Church-order.

The beginnings of yet another stage in the Church's life are indeed visible in our present 'Didache'. I mean the stage at which the functions previously performed for the most part by men with distinctively-prophetic inspiration—particularly the offering of the church's sacrifice of thanksgiving in its corporate eucharistic gathering—were more and more devolving on the regularly-appointed or ordained administrative officials. But internal evidence points strongly to the section in question being part of a third stage of growth, say about 100 A.D.[3]

---

[1] [In the *Didache* itself the word occurs only in i. 5, and there refers to material possessions. C.J.C.].

[2] For details, see below, pp. 53 ff.

[3] [Yet one would have thought that the stage here described by Dr. Bartlet must have been *contemporaneous with*, not subsequent to, the stage at which the more palpably-charismatic ministry of "the prophets" was in a state of noticeable decline. C.J.C.].

It is in the light of this development of the 'Didache' that we can best study the other evidence for the Sub-Apostolic Age.

Clement of Rome, writing about 96 A.D. in the name of the church of which he was secretary, describes the established Divine order to which it was his aim to persuade the Corinthian church to return, after having set it aside as regards the local bishops entrusted with the church's eucharistic prayer. The idea of the traditional Church-order as sacrosanct (vii. 2), so that modification of it or departure from it is disorder (xliii. 6) and sin (xl. 4) against the sovereign Master's institutions, is so unlike what we have met with thus far under the New Covenant of the Spirit, rather than the Old one of "the letter" of the Law, that we do well to pause and ask what it means.

It is surely significant that the new sentiment appears in a new psychological climate, the Roman as distinct from the Jewish or Greek: and it is natural to ask whether it does not denote a certain reaction of this new temper of mind upon the genius of the Gospel of Christ and upon the liberty of the Spirit, as seen in the New-Testament writings and those nearest to them in time and spiritual tradition. We have here, at any rate, a new note, and also a new factor at work, of which we shall find yet other examples as we go on. It will be well, then, to take account of it when it first appears, that we may be the better able to identify it and its cause or causes on later occasions. For in this case we have ample means of judging its real significance in the sustained argument which supports this protest against change in the established order. That the change has disturbed the concord and brotherly love proper to Church-life settles nothing. In order to grasp the exact situation, we must summarize the whole letter.

The writer traces the trouble back to spiritual degeneracy, due to prosperity issuing in "jealousy and envy", particularly on the part of "those without honour against those in honour" (especially the honour due to seniors, cf. xxi. 6), "the young against their elders"—phrases borrowed from Isa. iii. 5, but presumably corresponding in some degree to the facts, as when he adds on his own, "the foolish against the wise". The spirit now prevailing Clement regards as evil and self-willed, springing from "unjust and impious jealousy" (iii) like that of Cain, when Abel's gifts in sacrifice to God were preferred to his own. He then goes through several Old-Testament and Christian

examples of such a spirit (iv–xix). That spirit, says he, is one
unlike God and His ways, as visible in the providential order
of the Universe, marked as it is by peaceful and harmonious
order (xx). Let us, then, order our lives in like reverential regard
to His will, "not breaking ranks" in His army nor heeding
"foolish" men, who are puffed up "in vain-glory of speech",
but "revere our leaders, honour seniors, discipline young men
in the fear of God. . . " (xxi. 4–6). God bestows his favours on
"those who draw nigh to Him with a single mind. Wherefore
let us not be of two minds, nor let our soul indulge idle notions
as to His exceeding and glorious bounties" (xxiii. 1 f.), promised
to those who fear and wait for Him, Who shall yet come speed-
ily, having His reward with Him. Some, indeed, are of two minds
as to this, owing to such delay as has occurred (xxiii. 3–5,
xxxiv. 3). But doubt not as to resurrection and judgment (cf.
2 Peter iii. 4 and the [so-called] 'Second Epistle of Clement',
xi. 2), and so wax indifferent to His will and ways (xxiv–xxxiii).
Wherefore be diligent in every good deed, and "be subject to
His will", and ever do Him sacred service as the angels do
(λειτουργοῦσιν), "gathering together in concord" for united
worship such as He approves, because He has appointed that it
should be done thus and not otherwise (xxxivf.). So shall Jesus
Christ act as "the High-Priest of our offerings" (xxxvi). The
Roman army, in its disciplined order, as also the human body,
with the organic subordination of its parts to the common welfare,
are models of the good order God approves (xxxvii). So in our
corporate Church-life, let each play the part assigned to him
"in the lot appointed him by grace " (καθὼς ἐτέθη ἐν τῷ
χαρίσματι αὐτοῦ), whether by nature or direct spiritual gift.
Humility must not blow its own trumpet, nor the pure in
flesh (the voluntary celibate) boast therein, knowing that it is
Another Who furnishes him with the ability of self-control.
Mindful of our dependence on our Creator for all, "we ought
in everything to give thanks (εὐχαριστεῖν) to Him " (xxxviii).

All this being so, our duty is to observe due order in so doing.
"Both offerings and (Divine) services (λειτουργίας) He has commanded to take place, not at random or disorderly, but at fixed
seasons and hours. Both where and by whom He would have
them performed He has himself fixed by His own supreme wish,
that all things, being done dutifully according to His good
pleasure, might be acceptable to His will. They, then, who make
their offerings at the appointed seasons are accepted", as

"following the supreme Master's institutions. . . . For unto the High-Priest his proper services (λειτουργίαι) have been assigned, and to the priests their proper station appointed, and on the Levites their proper ministrations devolve. The layman is bound by the ordinances for the laity "(xl. 2–5).

Here we have the terminology of the Mosaic hierarchy of Divine service applied by strict analogy to the Christian Church and its order, in spite of what the whole New Testament implies as to the *difference* between the dispensations of the Law and of the Gospel in the sphere of corporate life and order. Christ is the High-Priest; the presbyter-bishops are the priests (no longer conceived mainly as exercising a Divinely-inspired charisma, but as filling an appointed post, with corresponding rights and claims on others); the Levites are the deacons, assisting the former; and finally the People of God as such, the laity, are bound on pain of sacrilege to refrain from any possible initiative in leading the Church's acts of Divine service, such as Paul's first letter to Corinth (xiv), to which he elsewhere appeals, clearly implies, or in corporately empowering its specially-gifted members to do this representatively on their behalf and in their name. In contrast to any such Church-order, each, Clement insists, is to please God in his own rank—not transgressing the appointed rule (κανών) of his service. Just as it was under the Law of Moses, so is it to be in Christ: only under the latter the penalty of breach of the Divine order is heavier, because it is in the face of fuller knowledge of the Divine will (xli: cf. vii. 2). How different is this analogy from the parallel and contrast between the Old and the New Covenant in the 'Epistle to the Hebrews'. There all the "shadow"-ritual of priesthood and sacrifice is viewed as summed up in the spiritual reality of Christ, without mention of any other Divinely-ordained priest as necessary to the normal worship of Christians. Rather do these worship in virtue of their status as "perfected for ever" for the act by their High-Priest's "one offering" (x. 14), as those thereby having "their hearts sprinkled from an evil conscience" (x. 21 f.). It is their prerogative, then, as "a holy priesthood," to offer up spiritual sacrifices acceptable to God through Jesus Christ" (1 Pet. ii. 5), and with no other conditions of acceptability, such as a particular type of ministerial order appointed by God rather than by themselves, to voice representatively their corporate worship. The latter kind of "ministerial priesthood" (to use Dr. Moberly's phrase), in the name of God's People as such, would, on the principles of the Apostolic Age, not be regarded as commissioned "from below", but as created on the level of the Church's own life in the Spirit, than which no higher level of spiritual authority among men was at that time thinkable.

Here, then, we are at the watershed of two radically-different conceptions of Church-order and ministerial authority. Clement's type, which gradually—more so than is often realized —came to prevail in ancient Catholicism, made validity depend upon an authority given, not through the Spirit-indwelt fellowship of saints acting corporately, but through certain ministerial organs constituted by Divine action, over its head as it were, in virtue of an Apostolic commission. The first trace of this theory of Divine constitution imposed from above upon the People of God is now before us in a letter from Rome; and the presumption, against which there is nothing to be set, is that it was due to Roman mentality which saw in the Mosaic Law precedents regulative also for the New Covenant.

Here is the way in which Clement describes the matter, as though it were a thing of common knowledge—simply because it came naturally to him and to the Roman Church so to see things. "Jesus the Christ was sent forth from God" with the Gospel (xlii. 1); He gave it to the Apostles. Both these things happened in due order by God's will (xlii. 2). "Having, then, received charges"—note how the Roman thinks of the Gospel as itself a body of commands "received as from a superior officer"[1]—they went forth, once they were convinced by the Resurrection and the coming of the Holy Spirit, "preaching as Gospel that the Kingdom of God was about to come" (xlii. 3). Then "they appointed their first converts, after testing them by the Spirit, to be bishops and deacons of those yet to believe" (xlii. 4). "And that was no fresh departure; for so it had long ago been written in Scripture as to bishops and deacons", viz., in Isa. lx. 17, quoted loosely or rather twisted by several changes to fit the strained use thus made of the original Greek version, which ran, "I will set thy rulers in peace and thine overseers (ἐπισκόπους) in righteousness". In keeping, then, with this intimation of the Divine will, those entrusted by God with such a function, established in office the aforesaid persons, just as Moses knew God's mind beforehand when he took steps to make

[1] Lightfoot, note ad loc.

clear the exclusive choice of one tribe (Aaron's) for the priesthood (xliii).

Similarly, the Roman church proceeds to say to its sister at
Corinth, the Apostles had through Christ foreknowledge of
future strife for the title of "episcopate" when they appointed
the aforesaid persons; and subsequently for the same reason
they added a supplemental rule, namely, that, should these die
(before Christ's return), other approved men should succeed to
their ministry (xliv. 1 f.). Those, then, who have been appointed
in due order, under one or other of these conditions, the church
as a whole consenting, and who have ministered blamelessly to
the flock of Christ, cannot in our opinion be rightfully set aside
from their ministry (xliv. 3). Nay, it will be no light sin to cast
out of the episcopate those presbyters who have blamelessly
and dutifully offered the gifts in the eucharist, as the Corinthian
church has displaced certain from the ministry which they have
honoured by dutiful conduct (xliv. 4–6).

Inspired Scripture, the letter continues, yields no precedent
for righteous men being cast out by dutiful men (xlv). Why this
strife and division, when we have one God, one Christ, one
Spirit of Grace, and one calling in Christ? Why tear apart the
oneness of the Christ? Remember the Lord Jesus' words as to
causing even one of the elect to stumble. Yet your σχίσμα has
turned many aside, and brought doubt to many (outside
Corinth) and grief to us all (xlvi). The Apostle Paul himself in
your early days reproved your partisanship even as between
Apostles. What of faction against your presbyters for the sake of
one or two persons? (xlvii). Granted that so-and-so is faithful,
granted he is able to utter knowledge, wise in discrimination of
ideas (λόγων), energetic in deeds, pure. The greater he seems to
be, the more humble should he be, and the more should he
seek the common good of all, and not his own (xlviii. 5 f.).
Love is the sovereign grace; "love unites us to God" (xlix. 1–5).
Pray for it (l. 2), and for forgiveness for yielding to the adver-
sary's assaults, especially the leaders of faction and division
(li. 1 f.).

Who among you is noble and loving? Let him be ready,
on the occasion of strife, to withdraw in obedience to "the
behests of the whole people" (ὑπὸ τοῦ πλήθους), that the flock of
Christ may be at peace with the appointed presbyters (liv. 1 f.).
History knows cases of such loving self-sacrifice (lv). "Ye, then,
who laid the foundation of the sedition, submit to the presbyters

and be disciplined into repentance" (lvii. 1). For, be sure, he who humbly accepts the ordinances and commands of God shall be enrolled in the number of those being saved through Jesus Christ (lviii. 2). If any disobey the things said by Him through us, they shall incur great danger; but we shall be guiltless of this sin, praying with urgent entreaty that the Creator of all "may preserve the number of His elect in all the world undamaged through His beloved Servant (παιδός) Jesus Christ" (lix. 1. f).

And so the epistle passes insensibly into a prayer of intercession (lix. 3–lxi), which was probably that preceding the prayer of oblation in the eucharistic service of the Roman church of Clement's day. It illustrates the important fact that Christian corporate prayer was at first and for long moulded on the lines of Jewish models. In its final sisterly appeal for concord, and for the requisite bowing of the neck in obedience to God's truth on the part of some, the Roman church refers to "the joy and exultation" which this will afford to those who have written thus "through the Holy Spirit" (lxiii. 2). Here we have a touch of the primitive sense of inspiration as proper to Christ's Church, and not of any special claim for this in the case of the church at Rome, as is clear from its calling the letter its "entreaty" (ἔντευξιν, lxiii. 2), made as to "men faithful and most distinguished and deeply versed in the oracles of God's instruction" (lxii. 3).

The situation which occasioned this letter, so typical of the spiritual solidarity of love among the whole People of God, was apparently somewhat as follows. The eucharistic service at Corinth, including the reception and presentation of the church's gifts to God's uses, as well as the consecration-prayer over the bread and wine to be used for the communion proper, had for some time been assuming a more-or-less traditional form, doubtless on the basis of earlier local prophetic or freely-inspired ministry on such occasions. Thus even the eucharistic prayer itself was offered, perhaps in rotation, by one or other of the official presbyters, who were called also "bishops", largely (if we may judge from Clement's close correlation of the terms ἐπισκοπή and ἱερωσύνη) because of this central and most-honourable function of "oversight" over the eucharistic service. Recently, however, one or two men of more-striking spiritual capacity, as it seemed to many, had had their superior fitness for this most sacred ministry of prayer put forward by a section of the church; and the church as a whole had sanctioned the substitution of these for some (xliv. 6) of those who had been acting as "overseers" (presumably, of the eucharistic oblation). It appears also as if, at the same time, there was some reversion to older usage as regards eucharists at other times and places than in the recognized corporate gatherings of the church for worship, especially on Sunday, on the part of these more-charismatic ministers of the earlier prophetic, rather than of the formally-ordained, type. It is quite possible that the usage reflected in our 'Didache', known in one of its earlier forms, was cited in support of both these practices as but a return to the usage of an earlier and a better day. But the general attitude of the senior and official element of the church—the "elders" in both senses—was one of opposition to the change of existing practice: and so a serious schism had arisen, with resulting breaches of peace and love and a general state of disorder.

Clement suggests that the supporters of the fresh ministry were mostly drawn from the younger, less-responsible, and less morally-sound part of the church; and that some of them at least were the less responsible in attitude because the delay of the Return of Christ made them take no practical account of "the fear of God" as a restraint on ambitious, self-willed, and unloving action (cf. iii. 4, xxii. 1, xxiii. 3–5, lvii. 5, lxiv). That the Roman view of the two sides in the issue was strictly objective and equally fair to all, we cannot safely assume. The letter displays too strong a bias in favour of an historically-dubious view of the ministry of the Apostolic Age and its sequel (a view based on a-priori Scriptural arguments) to be entitled to rank as a complete diagnosis of the case. In fact, Clement's letter and the 'Didache' look at the normal eucharistic ministry from opposite sides. To the latter, purely charismatic or pro-phetic ministers are the ideal: the less-charismatic, dependent upon the local church's election and appointment, are the second best; for a section of the 'Didache' (xv. 1 f.), possibly added about the date of 1 Clement, says of "bishops and deacons", "they *too* minister (. . . λειτουργοῦσι καὶ αὐτοί) to you the ministry of the prophets and teachers: therefore despise them not. . . ." To Clement, on the other hand, the latter alone were legitimate, as being commissioned by Christ through the Apostles. In other words, the traditions of northern Syria and of Rome differed on the point; and that of Corinth came some-where between the two.

This brings us to the situation in Antioch and in the churches of the Roman province on the western coast of Asia Minor, as reflected some ten or fifteen years later in the letters of Ignatius, the single bishop or president of the church of Antioch. His second name "Theophoros" ("God-bearer"), which Lightfoot thinks he assumed at his conversion or baptism, seems significant of his enthusiastic temperament, and his strong sense of being directly inspired by God (e.g., with "revelations" touching matters of spiritual insight).[1] Lightfoot thinks he came to his Christian faith by a striking personal experience; and this conjecture suits the fundamentally-Pauline type of his language and his conception of Christ as "our life".[2] But besides this strong feeling for the mystical side of religion, and that of a deeply-ethical type, he had in him another element not often accompanying the mystical bent—a strong and indeed overpowering sense of the importance of an outward order expressive of the inward unity of love, love being the essence of the Divine life in man. Such a man, writing as he was in a white heat of excitement and emotion, while on his way to approaching martyrdom, and amid conditions of pressing spiritual danger for the churches he had seen only hurriedly on his way towards Rome, was perhaps hardly likely to express himself in a way easy to interpret objectively and precisely. All the more needful, then, is it for us to try here also to understand how he correlated Church-order and the kind of life it was meant to express.

The following passages, taken in their order in Ignatius's letters, tell their own tale.

"It is profitable for you to be in blameless unity, that ye may also be partakers of God always".[3] "Let no man be deceived: if any one be not within the altar-precinct" (i.e., the congregation met for prayer), "he lacks the bread of God.[4] For if the prayer of one and another has so great force,[5] how much more that of the bishop and the whole church.[6] Whosoever, then, comes not to the congregation (ἐπὶ τὸ αὐτό), thereby

---

[1] Cf. Ignat. *Eph*. xx. 1 fin.: . . . μάλιστα ἐὰν ὁ Κύριός μοι ἀποκαλύψῃ. We may note in passing the high religious inspiration of the *Odes of Solomon*, which Rendel Harris is now inclined to bring into close relation with the type of devotional enthusiasm which breathes in the *Letters* of Ignatius.

[2] Ignat. *Eph*. iii. 2.

[3] Ignat. *Eph*. iv. 2.

[4] I.e., Christ: cf. Ignat. *Rom*. vii. 3.

[5] I.e., for securing Christ's presence: cf. Matt. xviii. 20.

[6] I.e., the eucharistic prayer.

shows himself overweening, and has separated himself".[1]
"Be diligent, then, to meet together more frequently for
thanksgiving to God and for His glory".[2] A little later he speaks
of the Ephesian Church as united in "breaking one loaf, which is
medicine of immortality, an antidote that one should not die,
but live for ever by (ἐν) Jesus Christ" (as the bread of God).[3]

Certain persons, while acknowledging the bishop with their
lips, "do not assemble together validly according to precept".[4]
"Attempt not to think anything right for yourselves apart
(from others);[5] but let there be one (eucharistic) prayer in
common, one supplication,[6] one mind, one hope, in love and
in joy unblameable, which is Jesus Christ. . . . Hasten all of
you to come together, as into one temple of God, as to one
altar-precinct, to one Jesus Christ . . ."[7] "Be ye careful to
observe one eucharist[8]—for there is one flesh of our Lord Jesus
Christ, and one cup unto union in (lit. of) His blood; there is
one altar-precinct, as there is one bishop, together with the
presbyters and the deacons . . .—that whatsoever ye do, ye
may do it after God".[9] "Let not position" (e.g., as a prophet)
"puff up any man. For the whole (business) is faith and love. . .
But mark ye those who hold strange doctrine touching the
grace of Jesus Christ which came to us, how contrary they are
to the mind of God. They have no care for love (shown in acts),
none for the widow, none for the orphan, none for the afflicted,
none for the prisoner, . . none for the hungry or thirsty.[10] They
abstain from eucharist and prayer, because they allow not that
the eucharist is the flesh of our Saviour Jesus Christ, which
flesh suffered for our sins, and which the Father of His goodness
raised up."[11] "They therefore that gainsay the free gift[12] of God
are dying by their questionings. But it were expedient for them

---

[1] Ignat. *Eph.* v. 2 f.
[2] Ignat. *Eph.* xiii. 1.
[3] Ignat. *Eph.* xx. 2. Note that the broken loaf is in memory of Christ's Passion, but that there is no hint of its needing to be consecrated.
[4] Ignat. *Magn.* iv: cf. *Did.* xiv. 1, and Ignat. *Trall.* vii.
[5] Cf. *Did.* xvi. 2.
[6] Δέησις (as distinct from προσευχή), perhaps with the sense of intercession.
[7] Ignat. *Magn.* vii. 1 f.
[8] The heretics apparently had their own rival or sectional eucharists: cf. Ignat. *Smyrn.* vi. 2, viii.
[9] Ignat. *Philad.* iv.
[10] For this non-ethical Docetism, cf. 1 John ii. 3–6, 9f., iii. 18–22, iv. 1–3.
[11] Ignat. *Smyrn.* vi. 1 f. Ignatius's point here, as above, is the principle of "Life through Death", whereof Christ was the symbol and archetype. As Head, so members: but only on condition of their remaining in loving unity with his other members, especially in the eucharist as the Church's central rite.
[12] τῇ δωρεᾷ: see Rom. v. 15, 17, and cf. vi. 23.

to love, that they may also rise again".[1] "But shun divisions, as the beginning of evils".[2]

Only a few words are needed to draw out the situation, as concerns the Church-order here implied. The historical background, which determines the points of emphasis and their meaning, was somewhat as follows. There was developing in the churches of the Roman province of Asia, with Ephesus and Smyrna as typical centres, a religious crisis (reflected in the Johannine Epistles) such as had already reached its head in Antioch, where Ignatius had himself been the protagonist and framer of a definite policy to meet it. Hence the sharply-defined and uncompromising confidence of his counsel to those still hesitating as to the new phenomena. There had emerged a Docetism which denied, on a-priori grounds of dualistic prejudice against matter as inherently evil and unworthy of positive relation to God, the reality of Christ's body or fleshly nature, and so the reality of his true humanity. In its denial it was confronted with the Church's unbroken tradition as to the full humanity of Jesus the Christ. Hence its tendency to keep aloof from normal church-meetings and to promote hole-and-corner group-meetings of Christians, where the new views could be argued for with little or no check, especially with an arbitrary or allegorical exegesis of such Scriptures as were then read in public worship, viz., the Law and Prophets of the Old Testament, along with the Gospels and certain of the Epistles. It was argued that the Old Testament knew no Passion or Cross for its Messiah; and that therefore this could not be an essential element in Christian faith. As we have seen, reference to the Passion in eucharistic symbolism, as reflected in the eucharistic prayers of the 'Didache' (probably now in wide use, especially at Antioch), was not part of the older Jewish Christian traditions, the broken loaf being applied rather to Church-unity as made up of many members. The eucharist, then, as understood by St. Paul, became the touchstone of the issues between them and Ignatius. Ignatius accepted the Pauline symbolism of the Church's central sacred rite, as well as that which saw in it the symbol and inspiration of Church-unity. That unity, moreover, Ignatius construed in a different and more-complete sense than did the Docetists, who understood it rather in an ideal sense. Over against this, he set the doctrine of the one corporate eucharist of the whole local church; and, with a view to this, he

[1] Ignat. *Smyrn.* vii. 1.   [2] Ignat. *Smyrn.* viii. 1.

pressed the necessity of the presence (or at least the sanction) of the one bishop or presiding officer of that church, as the living symbol and guarantee of such unity. The hole-and-corner eucharists, then, of the Docetic schismatics, though in a formal sense they had long precedent in their support, as those held in house-churches or group-gatherings for convenience, were henceforth to be sternly set aside, in order to avoid their being abused in the service of doctrinal error. We can well understand that the Ignatian letters, so full of passionate Christian feeling and devotion, would make a profound impression upon the Church generally, at any rate in the East, and would both indirectly and directly create a strong feeling against church-usages which lent themselves most easily to such abuses as Ignatius stigmatizes. Further, Ignatius himself would become the type or beau idéal of a true bishop or local pastor-in-chief. This view of him would be accepted the more easily in that he combined in himself both the pastor and the prophet, the two forms of the ministry which tended most readily to fall apart and to enter into rivalry, so destroying that corporate unity which is the proper, visible, or sacramental expression of the church as the home of love. This loss of unity we saw to have happened at Corinth, where men of prophetic gifts seemed to have been put forward as rivals to the existing eucharistic ministers appointed by the community for that and other functions. For such segregation there was theoretical justification in earlier usage, as we see from the 'Didache', where prophets are the primary ministers of the church's eucharistic prayers. In the nature of the case, it seems as though they ought to have retained this privilege, even though not to the exclusion of ministers endowed with less personal fitness for the function, and accustomed to use more-traditional types of prayer. Both types of eucharistic ministry, that is to say, might have existed side by side, without loss and even with gain to the Church's worship. But it seems that concern for the formal unity of leadership in the Church, as a safeguard against such divisive tendencies as the Ignatian letters combat, proved the decisive factor in the general Church-policy in the matter. Accordingly the prophet, having been subordinated to the official ministry at the point where his claims were strongest, was at a disadvantage for maintaining his earlier right, which rested upon his possession of a Divine gift, to play a leading part in Church-life and -order. It cannot be said, in any case, that the Church had here found a final solution of the difficulty of harmonizing, to the greater benefit of itself and the Gospel with which it was entrusted for mankind, the rich variety of the Spirit's gifts which had been bestowed upon it—for permanent use, on the lines of the Apostolic precedents. Something was lost by this failure, the true seriousness of which it is hard for us rightly to appraise.

As regards the outward order of the eucharistic fellowship of the Church, it is not quite clear whether Ignatius implies that the social meal had already begun to be separated from the eucharistic rite of hallowing such a meal, both together having constituted the primitive eucharist of the New Testament and the original 'Didache', and, if so, whether in his day the meal itself was being relegated simply to the domestic type of eucharist which came to be known as an "agape" or love-feast. From his words to the Smyrnaeans, "It is not allowable without the bishop either to baptize or to hold an agape"—reference to corporate "eucharist and prayer" having preceded[1]—it seems probable that the separation in question had already occurred, so far as the usage most familiar to Ignatius was concerned. Such was probably the case in his own church at Antioch, which may have been earlier than most others in making this change in Church-order, owing to the dangers of abuse of which it may have had special experience. Another factor would be the practical difficulty—bound to emerge sooner or later— of arranging a meal for so large a body of Christians at Antioch as at this period (about 100 A.D.) would wish to share in such fellowship. Yet I believe that the change was not yet universal, judging by the evidence of Pliny's letter to Trajan (112 A.D.), which I take to imply an evening eucharistic meal—in spite of the Emperor's edict against club-meals, which certain ex-Christians said had led them to cease attending the church's evening-meeting.

Here again it is needful not to misconstrue Ignatius's thought, as though it was of a legal or precisian cast. The whole tone and manner of his writing are those of a man of prophetic and enthusiastic gift, laying claim to special inspiration. He puts forward his rules with the accent of prophetic insight, arguing from first principles of mystical religion, like Paul—by whom he is primarily influenced in his piety and thought. To Ignatius love, not law—even Divine or sacred law (as in the Roman

[1] Ignat. *Smyrn.* viii. 2 and vi. 2.

church)—was still the master-principle of Church-life and -order. He was quite right in arguing that fellowship in the Divine life of love, which is one in nature with God Himself, was in principle being undermined by the Docetists, both in their theory and in their practice; that the best practical guarantee against such tendencies was loyal corporate consciousness and action; and that the bishop, as Ignatius understood the office, viz., a single pastor-in-chief of the local fellowship, was the true embodiment and guardian of such corporate unity. Beyond this he does not really go, apart from some enthusiastic incidental references to matters of actual fact and usage, e.g., that "the bishops that have been appointed throughout the farthest parts (of the earth) are according-to (ἐν) the mind of Jesus Christ".[1] If he means that bishops like himself already existed every-where, this is mere rhetoric; for not only does Ignatius himself take no account of any such bishop at Rome, but Polycarp's almost-contemporary epistle implies only a college of presbyter-bishops at Philippi, as Clement had implied for Corinth about 96 A.D., and as Hermas strongly suggests was still the case at Rome itself some years later.[2]

But in any case Ignatius, who is urging a seemingly-new theory of the position and powers of the single bishop in the churches addressed, as distinct from his own church at Antioch, implies simply a city-episcopate, analogous to that of the incumbent of a town-parish to-day where there is only one worshipping church. Yet he has had read into him by later interpreters a good deal more (of a quite anachronistic kind); and incidentally he has been turned into a rather formal-minded ecclesiastical theorist as to "valid" episcopal orders and Apostolic succession—an idea quite alien to his own ideas and mode of thought. This misjudgment illustrates the importance of understanding Church-order in vital relation to contemporary Church-life, if we are to reach truly-historical conclusions.

The Ignatian letters had, as remarked, a profound influence on the subsequent development of Church-order. Ignatius himself was, so to say, a charismatic bishop; i.e., he created an ideal type of bishop—one in whom was included ideally the

---

[1] Ignat. *Eph.* iii. 2 fin.
[2] [It should perhaps be mentioned that, while about 140 A.D. is the usually-accepted date for the completion of Hermas's work, there are some grounds for placing it in the last decade of the first century: cf. W. J. Wilson in *Harvard Theol. Review*, vol. xx, pp. 21–62 (Jan. 1927), and B. H. Streeter, *The Primitive Church* (1929), pp. 203–213. See below, p. 66, n. 1. C.J.C.].

function of prophet also, a man possessed of specially-inspired insight into the will and ways of God. It was this enlarged conception of the bishop which helped to reconcile the Church to the practical dying-out of the specially-prophetic function in its midst, a loss to which the gain in point of safety from certain abuses already referred to made it the less sensitive. Further, the change was less-vividly realized in that there were still recognized here and there isolated cases of prophets, both men and women, who seemed to keep up the line of continuity with the past, which in general the Christian consciousness was so anxious to maintain. One such instance, the last prophet really known to us with any clearness, will now demand our attention.

The situation was now changing rapidly, but obscurely; and so we are the more thankful for the vivid insight into the heart of a great church, that of Rome, which the prophetic writing known as 'The Shepherd' of Hermas affords us.

The book is nothing less than a specimen of the utterances of a Christian prophet in the full sense (analogous to those of an Old-Testament prophet like Amos or Hosea), and recognized as such by the great church of Rome, where the principle of regular order was as strong as we see it to have been from the letter of Clement. In fact, one of the features of greatest value in the ministry of Hermas, the brother (seemingly the elder brother) of the bishop Pius (about 140–154 A.D.),[1] is that it reveals the possibility of co-operation—to the great benefit of the whole Church—of these two types of servants of the one Spirit (as they were, on true Apostolic principles). For Hermas plays exactly the part of Hebrew prophet over against the regular or official ministry of the Law of Moses, only that he does it in relation to the current understanding of the Gospel of Christ. That part was one of reviving a due sense of the inward and spiritual meaning of the Divine Message, which familiarity with its letter and forms tends ever to rob of sufficient spiritual power in the personal life of nominal believers as evidenced by the character of their daily walk. Here lies the inmost meaning of Hermas's ministry, continued, like that of a Hebrew prophet, over a long period of years, and performed piece-meal to meet urgent needs at the time. In the end it was gathered up in a single organic whole under the title of 'The Shepherd', due to

[1] [See above, p. 49, n. 2, and below, p. 66, n. 1.   C.J.C.].

the form under which the inspirer of the message or "burden" of the Lord, to use the Old-Testament language, appeared to Hermas's imagination. Its general effect is to hold a mirror up to the outer and to the inner (or spiritual) situation of the Roman church, but also through it to the situation of the Church at large. For Hermas felt his special revelations to be intended for Christians generally; and to the churches abroad they seem to have been sent forth through the regular organ of church-life provided for the purpose, viz., the Church-Secretary, such as Clement (whom Hermas mentions by name) was at the time of the trouble at Corinth.

But what is most instructive, as casting light upon the reality and mode of the prophet's gradual illumination by the Spirit, is the progressive way in which he is brought to realize the full needs of the church. These needs came home to him, to begin with, in his own case and that of his own household; and therewith the radical nature of the remedy necessary to meet them.

The Church's salt had largely lost its savour; and the witness of Christians had little that was distinctive about it, owing to the loss of real spiritual vision and so of moral power.

The special reproach of the Church's present state was Mr. Facing-both-ways, to use the imagery of Bunyan, whose 'Pilgrim's Progress' gives perhaps the best idea a modern mind can form of the spirit, purport, and quality of the inspiration of this second-century prophet. Both start from the level and context of current Church-life and experience, and by the inward travail of a soul-searching experience of the Spirit, are brought to a fresh vision of the really-normal or thorough-going, or as Hermas puts it "simple" or "single-minded", life for God.

Here we have the abiding place of the Christian prophet in the Church, as an open fountain for the constant renewal of authentic religious vision through immediate personal experience of victory in the great issue, God versus self, love for persons (seen in the light of God's redemptive love for them) versus love for the world (i.e., for its material or sensuous pleasures as ends in themselves).

So viewed, the recognition given to Hermas and his prophetic ministry by the Church, both at Rome and generally, when contrasted with the same Church's suspicious and faithless attitude towards the prophetic function as a permanent one in the fully-equipped Divine order of the Church, raises grave doubts as to whether the later development of Catholic order did in this matter fulfil the real purpose of God or adequately recognize His work in inspiring men apart from the regular or routine ministry of Christ's People.

Irenaeus at least, who seems here as elsewhere to keep the middle way of inclusive truth, utters a warning against certain who "receive not the gifts of the Holy Spirit, and cast away from themselves the prophetic grace, watered whereby man bears the fruit of life unto God". Such men "receive not the Spirit, that is, they reject prophecy".[1] The liberty of prophesying, and the free provision of a place for it in ecclesiastical order, would seem to be necessities in a Church living up to its Divine calling in all ages, whatever the variety of forms which this may take.

There had, however, already begun to be the third Christian generation,[2] one with considerable experience behind it of the abuses to which such liberty was liable, but with less really-spontaneous and authentic inspiration, due to profound personal experience of the Christian facts and ideas in all their wonder of fresh revelation of the Divine, and sobered not a little by the non-fulfilment of the high hope of the near return of Christ and the full manifestation of the Kingdom, as the foretaste of which the diffused Spirit-experience and its "gifts" had been hitherto viewed. Hence there was a tendency to fall back all round upon the more ordinary or regular routine and methods for the conduct of fellowship or corporate life. And so office per se came to bulk more largely in men's thoughts and feelings as safer, and at any rate more decent and orderly in its smooth expert working, than an order which provided for the liberty of the Spirit-prompting of individual members to express itself for the common benefit. To people in this mood it early became natural to allow to or even press on the regularly-appointed representative ministry, itself based on spirit-gift recognized by the corporate consciousness, a more-and-more exclusive exercise of Church-functions.

---

[1] Irenaeus, *Demonstration of the Apostolic Preaching*, 99 f.: cf. *Adv. Haer.* V. vi. 1 (ap. Eusebius, *Church-History*, V. vii. 6).

[2] [This paragraph has been taken from another part of Dr. Bartlet's manuscript. The third generation would lie in the first half of the second century, prior, of course, to the time when Irenaeus wrote.   C.J.C.].

APPENDED NOTE ON

THE GROWTH OF THE 'DIDACHE'

The earliest sections of the 'Didache' are i-vi. I, i.e., 'The Two Ways' (except i. 3b–ii. I, and a few minor glosses), vii. I and parts of 4,[1] ix.–xi. 2 (mostly), and xvi. Ia, 2–7.[2] So much and no more, I believe, were the contents of the original 'Teaching of the Lord', to use what was perhaps its earliest title. It was written down and circulated in Syria, probably northern Syria, at the time when the leading Apostles were beginning to pass from the scene. This points to a few years before or after 70 A.D., i.e., about the same time that Mark's Gospel was written down (about 65 A.D.) from much the same motives, viz., in order to perpetuate the teaching of the primary Apostolic witnesses. Its lower limit of time is possibly given by its use in the so-called 'Epistle of Barnabas', which Lightfoot and Ramsay seem right in dating under Vespasian, about 75 A.D.[3]

The revision of the 'Didache' referred to above (p. 36) as having apparently been effected about 80–90 A.D. affected several different parts of the treatise. Perhaps it was at this stage that the full title, 'Teaching of the Lord through the Twelve Apostles to the Gentiles', was prefixed to it, under the influence perhaps of Matt. xxviii. 19.[4] To 'The Two Ways' were added some more-distinctly Evangelic precepts, parallel to some of those in the Sermon on the Mount.[5]

---

[1] [A pencil-note indicates that Dr. Bartlet regarded vii. 2, 3, and a part of 4 as clear interpolations. C.J.C.].

[2] [I am not quite clear how this is to be satisfactorily reconciled with Dr. Bartlet's earlier intimation (p. 35, n. 2) that πάντα τὰ προειρημένα in *Did.* xi. I indicated clearly that the *Didache* "once ended at this point". C.J.C.].

[3] In 'Barnabas' *The Two Ways* appears in a form in which certain of its more Jewish conceptions of piety are modified in a Christian sense (on the lines followed by St. Paul and the author of the Epistle to the Hebrews), so as to suit the thought of its author, a "teacher" of the inspired kind referred to in Acts xiii. I. There need not, however, necessarily be any literary relation between our *Didache* and 'Barnabas', for the latter seems to quote only the oral form of *The Two Ways*, as used in his own home-region, and probably in his own constant practice as a teacher. If there *is* any literary dependence at all (cf., e.g., *Did.* xvi. 2 with *Barn.* iv. 9), it is probably on 'Barnabas's' side. [Dom R. H. Connolly, however, in *The Journ. of Theol. Studies*, vol. xxxv, pp. 113–146, 225–248 (Apl. and July 1934), argued strongly that 'Barnabas' could not have been dependent on the *Didache*; and this conclusion has been accepted as cogent by the late Drs. B. H. Streeter (in *op. cit.*, vol. xxxvii, pp. 369–374 [Oct. 1936] and J. M. Creed (in *op. cit.*, vol. xxxix, pp. 377–380 [Oct. 1938]: but —as the two last-named scholars maintain—it does not follow that the *Didache* borrowed directly from 'Barnabas': it is equally possible that both drew from a common source. C.J.C.].

[4] Cf. the use of the Matthaean Trinitarian formula in *Did.* vii. I. [In a pencil-note, Dr. Bartlet seems to suggest that *Did.* xv. 3 may echo Matt. xviii. 15–17. See below, p. 54, n. 3. C.J.C.].

[5] These are introduced in i. 4 by what seems to be an echo of I Peter ii. 11: "Abstain from fleshly and bodily desires", on which follows, "If any one give thee a blow on the right cheek, turn to him the other also: and thou shalt be perfect" (see Matt. v. 39, 48: and note the continuation in *Did.* i. 4b, 5a).

In the latter part of the 'Didache' the Trinitarian formula, as used in Matt. xxviii. 19, was perhaps substituted for the title "the Lord" or "the Lord Jesus" in the rule for baptism (vii. 1; cf. ix. 5). Following up in thought the allusions to fasting in connexion with baptism (vii. 4) and to prophets (x. 7) at the end of the section on the eucharistic meal, there were added certain precepts touching fasting and prayer (viii), the confinement of the eucharistic food to the baptized (ix. 5),[1] and the visits of Apostles and Prophets to local churches (xi. 3–12); also touching the support of the latter, if wishful to remain (xiii).[2] At the same time, probably, the rules for the corporate eucharist on Sunday (xiv) and for the mutual discipline needful to keep its worship pure (xv. 3)—possibly also the general rule as to prayers, almsgiving, "and all your actions" (xv. 4), as well as fresh Gospel-echoes in the last section, dealing with watchfulness for the Lord's Return, were inserted.[3]

CHAPTER III

EARLY CATHOLICISM

THIS matter of the freedom of prophesying, and the place accorded by the Church to the prophetic function as an abiding gift of the Spirit, is so crucial for our subject, the development of Church-life and -order—particularly in their mutual relations, both in idea and practice—that we must at this point sketch its history for the two generations following the publication of Hermas's prophecies.

This period, from about A.D. 150–225, was one of the most momentous known to Church-history. In it, largely by processes which we cannot trace in detail, but as to the causes and nature

---

[1] [If so, there was a failure to see that the baptismal formula was up-to-date, in conformity with that now inserted in vii. 1. C.J.C.].

[2] See xiii. 1, 3. The reference to Teachers in xiii. 2 and the supplementary details in xiii. 4–7, especially the precept as to the poor, in case the local church has no prophet, seem—like the kindred sections xv. 1 f.—to belong to a later and third stage in the *Didache's* growth. To that revision may belong also i. 3b, 5b.

[3] It is to be noted that in all these sections, as in the addition to the first part, there are echoes or adaptations of what we find in our Gospels of Matthew and Luke, particularly the former. [The little that Dr. Bartlet has to say about the *third* enlargement of the *Didache* will be found in the preceding footnote and in a paragraph on p. 36 above. C.J.C.].

Further justification of this theory of the gradual development of our *Didache* may be seen (though in a somewhat less-exact form than here) in my article in *The Journ. of Theol. Studies*, vol. xxii, pp. 239–249 (April 1921).

[For the convenience of readers in studying Dr. Bartlet's suggested analysis,

of which we have good evidence at various points, ecclesiastical temper and ideals underwent—to say the very least—profound change of emphasis. It was now that the characteristic forms of Catholicism, as distinct from primitive Christianity, assumed their first definite expression. That expression was hastened, and in part determined in its actual emphasis and form, in opposition to certain extreme or one-sided tendencies, operative first within the Church, and then outside its borders. This opposition meant that henceforth the common mind of the Church became antagonistic to certain ideas for which these extreme movements had stood, and to which they had for the time-being given an all-too-compromising expression. In order to estimate this antagonism aright, two principles of general application need to be in our minds throughout: on the one

and not as furnishing a complete and final solution of the problem, I append here a tabular summary of the foregoing comments.

First Stage 65–75 A.D.	Second Stage 80–90 A.D.	Third Stage ± 100 A.D.
Title: "Teaching of the Lord"	Enlarged title: "Teaching of theLord through the Twelve Apostles to the Gentiles."	
i. 1–3a		i. 3b
	i. 4–5a	i. 5b
ii. 2–vi. 1 (except a few minor glosses).		
vii. 1 (but with "the Lord" instead of "the Father and the Son and the Holy Spirit").	In vii. 1, the Trinitarian formula was substituted.	
vii. 4 (parts)	viii	
ix. 1–4 (mostly)	ix. 5	
x–xi. 2 (mostly)		
	xi. 3–12	
	xiii. 1, 3	xiii. 2, 4–7
	xiv	
	xv. 3–4	xv. 1–2
xvi. 1a	xvi. 1b and other	
2–7	"fresh Gospelechoes".	
	xvi. 8	

The unallotted portions are i. 6, ii. 1, vi. 2f., vii. 2f. and parts of 4, and xii. Dr. Bartlet perhaps intended that these should be included in his Second or Third stage. Unfortunately his article in *The Journ. of Theol. Studies* does not make his view on these details quite clear.

[The *Didache* presents so many peculiar marks of primitiveness—features hard to reconcile with our customary views, based on the ascendancy of Pauline and Johannine teaching, of what all early Christian belief and practice must have been—that not a little controversy has arisen in regard to its date and significance. There has been an unconscious tendency on the part of

hand, "The corruption of the best is worst", in its practical results; and, on the other hand, "The abuse does not do away with the use" of a thing.

The first of these more-or-less aberrant developments was Gnosticism. Gnosticism represented in one-sided forms the instinct, in itself a mark of vitality, to try to relate the fresh life in Christ to the ultimate conceptions reached by reflective thought in the circumstances of pre-existing culture. The effort itself was warranted in principle by Christ's own law of life, viz., that new wine must be put into new wine-skins, if harm on both sides is to be avoided; and it was in fact due to the vital pressure of the Spirit, active in what was often a genuinely-Christian experience. But that experience was conditioned intellectually, and to a lesser degree morally, by prior training

scholars who hold a high view of the antiquity and essential importance of the episcopal system as it developed in later centuries, to overvalue the arguments for relegating the *Didache* to as late a date as possible, and for stamping it as the peculiar product of some little hole-and-corner and semi-judaistic Christian community in northern Syria, which was not in any way representative of Christendom at large. Among the more recent contributions to the discussion of the date, I may mention the articles of J. A. Robinson and R. H. Connolly in *The Journ. of Theol. Studies*, vol. xxxv, pp. 113–146 (Apl. 1934), 225–248 (July 1934), B. H. Streeter in *op. cit.*, vol. xxxvii, pp. 369–374 (Oct. 1936), R. H. Connolly in *op. cit.*, vol. xxxviii, pp. 165–167 (Apl. 1937), 364–379 (Oct. 1937), and in *The Downside Review*, vol. lv, pp. 339–347, 477–489 (July, Oct. 1937), J. M. Creed in *The Journ. of Theol. Studies*, vol. xxxix, pp. 370–387 (Oct. 1938), and W. Telfer in *op. cit.*, vol. xl, pp. 133–146 (Apl. 1939) and 258–271 (July 1939). Dr. Bartlet's own published contributions were made in the 'Extra Volume' (1909) to Hastings' *Dictionary of the Bible*, pp. 438–451, and in the art. in *The Journ. of Theol. Studies*, referred to by him earlier in this note. A substantial monograph entitled *The Riddle of the Didache* was produced by F. E. Vokes in 1938: most unaccountably, it contains despite its fullness no allusion to Dr. Bartlet's two valuable discussions.

[It would not be practicable for me to attempt even to summarize the arguments here. I must limit myself to saying that I find the late Dr. Creed's plea for an early date (round about 100 A.D.—except for the almost-certainly interpolated passages [i. 3b—ii. 1] which may be dependent on Hermas) convincing.

[What, however, may be said with emphasis is that the opinion that the *Didache* was in any way a hole-and-corner production is completely mistaken. The vogue which it enjoyed in the Church shows that this idea is the reverse of the truth. It was apparently quoted as "Scripture" by the orthodox writers Apollonius (Eusebius, *Church-History*, V. xviii. 4—196–200 A.D.) and almost certainly by Clement of Alexandria; several other fathers quote it as authoritative though uncanonical; it was liberally used by the author of the Syrian *Didaskalia* before the middle of the third century; was drawn on by the compiler of the *Apostolic Church-Order* early in the fourth century; and was actually taken as the basis for the first thirty-two chapters of the seventh book of the *Apostolic Constitutions* about 375 A.D. To suppose that a writing known to be the unrepresentative production of a backward and semi-orthodox circle could ever have been accorded such recognition is very unreasonable. And the very fact that it was so-highly honoured tells in its turn on the question of date: it is most unlikely that a document produced after 150 A.D., especially one emanating (as some have recently suggested was the case) from Montanist circles, could ever have enjoyed such credit with the orthodox. C.J.C.].

of a kind very alien to that Hebraic and theistic outlook which was the proper setting of the Gospel and the true key to its understanding. This alien world-view, and especially its dualistic theory of evil as related to matter and to demonic powers in control of matter, sadly warped the perspective and details of most Gnostic systems, both in theory and practice.

The net result was that the common Christian consciousness, as it held fast to the historical tradition which could really claim continuity with Apostolic teaching, and to the Apostolic writings in general use throughout the Church, recoiled instinctively from the various Gnostic systems as arbitrary and seemingly-wilful innovations. But when challenged to justify this attitude, most Christians would have been hard put to it in argument with subtle thinkers like the leading Gnostics, but for the steadying part played by their own normal leaders, the college of presbyters, men of years and experience—and particularly the bishop, their spokesman and the chief official depository of each local church's tradition. This was true alike as regards the exact group of Christian Scriptures which was to be taken as the standard authority for the original Apostolic testimony, and as regards the body of traditional principles in the light of which they had been continuously read. In the last resort, indeed, it was the existence of such a normal type of interpretation which afforded the readiest answer for the plain believer to the plausible readings of this or that Scriptural passage in a new Gnostic sense.

Hardly[1] less influential at this date than Gnosis, but at the opposite pole of thought and feeling, was the tendency which finds its extreme expression in Montanism—the tendency, namely, to over-emphasize the "holy-Spirit" quality or inspired aspect of Christian experience, so far as this was immediate and spontaneous in its forms of expression, and to belittle or treat as "worldly" the intellectual and common-sense side of the soul's life. Montanism is the more important for our subject in that it laid stress upon the holy Spirit in the Church as related

---

[1] [I insert these few pages (57–62) on Montanism at this point, because the allusion on p. 56 to Gnosticism as "the first" of a number of fresh developments suggests that at least a second was in contemplation; and this expectation is confirmed by the pertinence of these pages to the whole theme. They were not, however, apparently included in the typescript; and I have accordingly transcribed them from the rough manuscript sheets. I trust that the section will read as an integral part of the whole chapter, even though the transition to what follows (p. 62) may seem a little abrupt. C.J.C.].

to Christian practice rather than to Christian theory, and particularly upon the Spirit's function of revealing fresh "truth for the times", bearing upon the ordering of the Christian life both personally and corporately. While it appealed to the Spirit as the source of Divine and prophetic revelation concerning the proximity of the Parousia (or personal Return of the Church's Lord), it appealed to the Spirit as also the guarantee and authority for fresh rules and methods of Church-order, to suit the new era of stricter claims upon Christian holiness corresponding to the maturer stage now reached in the Church's life. It came, however, in the end to regard the existing Church-officers, and particularly the bishops, as hopelessly bound up with—and indeed largely responsible for—a too lax and worldly practice in the Church at large. It therefore rested its own hopes for the realization of the higher ideals, of which it believed its own prophetic leaders to be the inspired media, on the first place in the Church's practical policy being entrusted once more, as had been the case in the beginning, to men endowed with the prophetic charisma.

This, and nothing else, was the essence of the Montanist claim to be conservative, not innovating, in regard to Church-principles of life and order. The contents of its prophetic message were indeed new—yet only in degree. The novelty consisted in the measure of ascetic rigour now enjoined on the Church in respect of "fasting to the world" on set occasions, as fostering the habit of constant prayer. These two together, prayer and fasting, were prescribed as forms and conditions of spiritual "watching" for the returning Lord, in the temper in which primitive Christianity, as reflected in the New Testament, had prayed, fasted, and watched. Thus even the Montanist "truth for the times", now being put forth in the name of the Paraclete, the Spirit-Vicar of Christ Himself among His People, was itself new in degree and specific form rather than in principle—nay, was profoundly conservative in its purport. And the like was true also of the medium of its communication. It was, as fresh revelations from God had ever been, and most of all in the New Covenant of the Gospel, prophetic rather than official in the personal organs chosen by God for the further enlightenment of His People or Church. It was not through the established or normal hierarchy of executive officials, but through the freely-chosen "prophets" of His will for the hour, that God's voice of authority was claimed to be specially audible for all who, as sensitive to the same Spirit, were expected to recognize His fresh utterance as such.

Thus, in this Montanist Church-order, the Christian " prophet", who still enjoyed in most circles a leading place of authority in the ministry of the Word—that due to manifest personal inspiration as distinct from representative official authority conferred by ordination—played the leading rôle in practice as well as in theory. It was, therefore, in the present case, no less than in that of Hermas's prophetic message some generation or more earlier, the duty of the ordinary, executive ministry to carry out the Divinely-inspired injunctions of the prophets, as being God's organs of utterance in the Church. Particularly was it so in this the last and supreme hour of her history, when her Lord was "at the door", uttering to her more clearly and authoritatively than ever His message, " Watch and pray, that ye may be counted worthy to escape the judgments coming on the earth, and to stand before the Son of Man".[1]

Here lay the fundamental issue between the Montanists and the Great Church of the bishops, namely, their attitude to fresh, direct, prophetic inspiration through the special charisma claimed for the "New Prophecy" (as it came to be called by its foes). The Montanists charged the Church of the bishops with "blasphemy", because it came ultimately to reject the Spirit as spurious. The latter fixed on the novel features, as it was objected, of its external forms, of which ecstasy was the chief. But really the difference went deeper than this. It turned, in the last resort, upon the practically-subordinate significance of "prophecy" as something quite exceptional in the Church-ideal of the one (the Catholic) side, and upon its primary and normative function in that of the other. Even as regards the exception taken in the end—though not at first, as it seems—to ecstasy as a true form of Christian prophecy, it is really not at all clear that a good deal of New-Testament and primitive prophecy was not of this type.

The whole issue, then, turned on a matter of spiritual value-judgment, namely, whether the Montanist message and its prophets themselves were self-evidencingly true or false to the spirit of Christ's own teaching, and so to be regarded as inspired by His spirit or by evil daemons.[2] Here the Montanists argued

---

[1] [A loose paraphrase of Luke xxi. 36. C.J.C.].
[2] [Dr. Bartlet's manuscript contains a marginal reference a little higher up to Eusebius, *Church-History*, V. xviii. In V. xvi–xviii Eusebius preserves for us a

that the new explicit teaching meant only that the Church, as now more mature than at the first, was able to receive and use to advantage stronger food in the way of self-discipline or asceticism of life, and further that the new teaching came, as was natural and fitting, not through the ordinary official ministry, but through special "prophets", speaking as the organs of Christ's own Spirit. This comes out clearly in what a most typical Catholic of the central region of Asia Minor (that most affected by Montanism), Firmilian, bishop of Caesarea in Cappadocia, says in 256 A.D. on the matter.[1] Adherents of the Phrygian heresy, he says, in claiming to make use of "new prophecies", show themselves thereby to be heretics. For "if we ask them what Christ they preach, they will answer that they preach Him Who sent the Spirit that spoke through Montanus and Prisca. And when we observe that in them there has been the spirit not of truth but of error, we realize that they who champion their false prophecy against the faith of Christ cannot possess Christ".

Firmilian's argument, as we see, appeals simply to spiritual perception, as resting on sound spiritual experience and living, and—in the writer's mind—had a self-evident conclusion; for to him number and quality alike were against the Montanists, and he felt that Catholic authority, in the sense of the later classic phrase "Securus judicat orbis terrarum"—

valuable collection of extracts from the writings of two leading Churchmen who wrote treatises against Montanism in the last decade of the second century. These illustrate vividly the indignant and contemptuous animosity with which representatives of the "Great Church" repudiated the new movement. I append immediately below a note inserted by Dr. Bartlet a little lower down in this chapter. C.J.C.].

Rome itself seems, however, to have been very loth to give a definite ruling against the New Prophecy: and this fact may well be due to regard for the recent prophetic ministry and the current prophetic writings of Hermas. In the end Montanism was repudiated by the Church generally, though not before Tertullian had given it his weighty support as a needful complement to the growingly-official kind of order of a more-autocratic type, represented by the monarchical episcopate. Certain rulings of the latter on questions of moral discipline seemed to him to imperil the purity of the holy Church.

[1] See section 7 of his letter to Cyprian of Carthage, included as no. lxxv in the collection of Cyprian's *Epistles* (ed. Hartel, *Cypriani Opera omnia*, vol. ii, p. 814).

[In leading up to the words quoted from him in the text above, Firmilian argues that to deny (implicitly, by one's heresy) any one of the three Persons of the Trinity is equivalent to denying them all. "Those accordingly who are called 'Cataphrygians' " (i.e., the Montanists), "and who attempt to employ new prophecies, cannot possess either the Father or the Son, because they do not possess the holy Spirit. If we ask them what Christ they preach, . . ." C.J.C.].

the virtually-universal consent of those competent to judge—was on his side. But to the Montanists, who knew that in spiritual matters minorities are often in the right—witness the Christians generally, at the first and at that very time—this was a mere begging of the whole question. The case of Tertullian, again, shows that the matter of spiritual discernment was not so simple as it is here represented by Firmilian.

The fact is that "truth" and "error" are not quite such clear-cut and mutually-exclusive things of intellectual and moral value, where men on both sides are sincere, as the argument used by both took for granted. Identity of religious spirit, and identity of such religious experience as could prove itself by the fruits of loyalty to Christ, even to the point of martyrdom, were really at bottom common to both sides, though neither of them yet understood the essence of Christianity clearly enough to perceive the fact, and so to credit the other with sharing "the fellowship of the Spirit" despite secondary diversities in its visible operation. It was a hard lesson to learn for those who had so great a zeal for Church-unity, alike for its own sake and on account of its practical value to Christians and non-Christians alike.

To identify spiritual unity with an excessive degree of uniformity in thought and practice, under the noble name of the faith of Christ and the only order that accords therewith—the order of brotherly love—was and is a natural tendency of human nature, limited as it is in its conceptions and experience of what God can approve and tolerate in His human children. Yet few Christians to-day, in the light of the long record of Church-history and of their own personal experience, can doubt that the "Great Church", the federated community of the vast majority of churches, which in the second and third centuries felt itself to be co-extensive with the one Church Universal on earth, to the exclusion of minorities separated by its action or their own, came far short of the truth of God and the ways of Christ, in its judgment of and attitude to the Montanists, Novatianists, and other dissentient groups. True, indeed, it is, that this error was shared also by the minority-groups themselves. The case was almost exactly parallel to that in English religious life in the sixteenth and seventeenth centuries, when the Puritans of various kinds, Congregational and Presbyterian, emphasized somewhat the same principles as the Novatianists, while the Quakers had most in common with the New Prophecy of the Montanists.

It was during the testing period which culminated in the latter half of the second century—a period of perplexing cross-currents of thought, and of tendencies to disunion which these fostered—that the full potential value of the regular administrative ministry became more-fully realized and prized. Most of all was this the case with the bishop, the single and most-specially qualified channel of tradition, both as leading teacher and as chief minister in public worship. And along with such an episcopate, now seen in an enhanced light as the prime guardian of an historically-continuous tradition, there were associated two other yet more objective guarantees of its fidelity to type. The one was the body of specially-inspired Scriptures—those of the Old Testament (taken over from the first at the valuation of the preparatory Jewish Church and of the Apostolic founders of the Christian Church itself) and those of the New (the test of which was now more and more felt to be Apostolic authorship, direct or indirect). The other guarantee was the Baptismal Creed, the traditional formula used in the preparation of candidates for membership in the Church, and confessed in the act of baptism. This formula was somewhat expanded in the actual explanatory instruction given; and in this expanded form it was styled "the Rule" or Standard "of the Truth" for faith. Its contents are alluded to by Irenaeus, in his 'Demonstration of the Apostolic Preaching' (3) as follows:

"First of all it bids us bear in mind that we have received baptism for the remission of sins, in the name of God the Father, and in the name of Jesus Christ, the Son of God, Who was incarnate and died and rose again, and in the Holy Spirit of God; and that this baptism is the seal of eternal life, and is the new birth[1] unto God, that we should no longer be the sons of mortal men, but of the eternal and perpetual God; and that

---

[1] Here is suggested one of those profound changes of conception as to the nature and conditions of the new Christian life which have far-reaching effects in the end upon Church-order, and are traceable to change in the Gospel's mental environment from Hebraic to current Hellenistic mentality. The relation of the seal of baptism to the new birth unto God, which to Paul was (as the word "seal" suggests) one of ratification to prior psychological fact—like that of circumcision to Abraham's faith (Rom. iv. 12; Col. ii. 11 f.)—was now more realistically conceived. It was as though the quickening of faith dated only from the consummating act of baptism, whereas for Paul man in baptism confessed (Rom. x. 9 f.), and God "sealed" with "holy Spirit", an already-living faith (Eph. i. 13 f.). See above, pp. 12 f.

what is everlasting" (i.e., the regenerate Christian) "and continuing is made Divine,[1] and is over all things that are (merely) made, and all things are put under him[2] . . .; and that all things are God's, and that therefore God is Almighty and all things are of God".[3] Further in his closing words Irenaeus returns to the baptismal formula itself, as the essence of the Rule of Truth or Faith, saying: "So then, in respect of the three points" (lit. "heads") "of our seal, error has strayed far from the truth. For either they reject the Father; or they accept not the Son and speak against the dispensation of His incarnation; or else they receive not the Spirit, that is, they reject prophecy".[4] The first of these deviations from the baptismal faith was clearly Gnostic dualism, as already described. But we have yet to see what is meant by the other two. For while Irenaeus evidently regards their representatives as less deadly to Christian life and fellowship than those who are "blasphemers against their Creator and against the Father", those who err as to the Son rank also as "lacking in faith"; while the third, who "receive not the gifts of the Holy Spirit, and cast away from themselves the prophetic grace (in the Church), watered whereby man bears the fruit of life unto God, . . . are in no wise serviceable to God, seeing that they cannot bear any fruit".[5] The moral, then, is that "of all such must we beware, and shun their ways", on pain of displeasing God[6]—words which suggest that they are all alike to be refused Catholic communion.

Now this is a very grave attitude for Christians, and especially for one so typical of the Church of his day as was Irenaeus, to take up in relation to any one sincerely claiming to be loyal to the Christian faith, and even to its baptismal confession, as they understood it: it goes right to the roots of Church-life and -order, since it means the dissolution of the tie of brotherhood in Christ, and of the Church-unity binding on all His disciples

---

[1] A favourite thought of Irenaeus, Hippolytus, Origen, and many later theologians, one echoed by Athanasius in a classic phrase of his treatise *On the Incarnation* (liv. 3), "He (the Logos or Son) himself became human, that we might become Divine" ($\theta\epsilon o\pi o\iota\eta\theta\tilde{\omega}\mu\epsilon\nu$).

[2] Cf. Psalm viii. 5 f.

[3] Not, as Gnostic dualism so strongly held, only *some* things, i.e., those of the mind or spirit, as contrasted with matter or body. In this connexion also there probably came in the resurrection of the body (or flesh), as part of the last stage of catechetical instruction. Cf. the early Egyptian Church-Order (about 250–300 A.D.), commonly but probably wrongly called "Hippolytean" (see below, pp. 105 ff.).

[4] Irenaeus, *Demonstration of the Apostolic Preaching*, 100.

[5] *Ibid.* 99.

[6] *Ibid.* 100.

on that basis. We may set aside the Gnostic dualists, because their attitude to Christ was one of divided allegiance. But was this so with the other two types Irenaeus has in mind, and with some others who also took a different view from that of the Church at large on "the gifts of the Holy Spirit", such as the Montanists?[1] To this question, as it affects the meaning and place of prophecy, as a function of the Spirit side by side with other and more-regular forms of operation in the Church—in ministry, in discipline, and in the sacraments—we must now devote serious and careful attention. Further, in trying to face it fully and frankly, we must raise the further oft-ignored question, whether prophecy did not in the course of time, as the Christian experience matured, assume different specific forms. And if so, we must surely allow for this fact, while claiming that the genus "prophecy", as a personal gift of the Spirit that "bloweth whither it listeth", i.e., apart from any human appointment or ordination, is an abiding element in the Church, according to the mind of its Founder and of His Apostles.[2]

What Irenaeus had in mind in referring, as above, to those who "reject prophecy", is made clear by what he had written in his earlier work 'Against Heresies'. There he says that some reject the Gospel according to John, where the sending of the Paraclete is promised, and so "repel the prophetic Spirit. Unhappy they, in good sooth, who wish indeed to be pseudo-prophets" (as claiming to utter truth in God's name), "but repel from the Church the grace of prophecy, being in like case with those who on account of those who come forward (as Christians) hypocritically, hold aloof even from the fellowship of the brethren".[3] Such people set aside apostolic authority:

---

[1] [Dr. Bartlet seems for a moment to overlook the fact that, whereas Irenaeus (as he himself notes—see above, pp. 52, 63) condemns those who *reject* prophecy, the Church-fault here noticed is the precise opposite, viz., a condemnation of those who *retain* prophecy. In other words, Irenaeus is *in this particular matter against* the growing tendency in the Church, not a participator in it. But see just below. C.J.C.].

[2] The Catholic writer Miltiades, in twitting the Montanists on the fact that their original prophets had no successors during the fourteen years which had elapsed since Maximilla's death, justly remarks that the Apostle (Paul) assumes that "the prophetic charisma ought to be in all the Church until the final Advent" (Eusebius, *Church-History*, V. xvii. 4.). [The writer, however, was not Miltiades, but the anonymous Anti-Montanist, whom Eusebius describes as having referred to him. C.J.C.].

[3] Irenaeus, *Adv. Haer.* III. xi. 9. [It was suggested by the late Dr. F. C. Burkitt and others (*Cambridge Ancient History*, vol. xii [1939], p. 456 n.) that we should read "pseudo-prophetas" instead of "pseudo-prophetae" in this passage, translating "who wish indeed false prophets to exist", the reference being to Montanism. C.J.C.].

for Paul spoke carefully of prophetic "charismata", and referred to both men and women prophesying in Church. In fine, Irenaeus regards them as sinning against the Spirit of God.

Here he is describing not Montanists, but anti-Montanists, who, going to the opposite extreme, denied the continued place of "prophecy" (specially-inspired utterance by non-official persons) in the Church. The Church as a whole, on the contrary, at this time accepted it in principle, like Irenaeus, who says "we hear of many brethren in the Church having prophetic gifts".[1] What its leaders charged against Montanism was that it was "New Prophecy", in a bad sense, not, as its adherents claimed, prophecy of a higher order than that of the Church's less-mature past. To the Montanists it was in fact the true fulfilment of Christ's promise of the Paraclete—the final form of the Spirit's function as revealing the Divine Will—in that it taught for the first time certain things of Christ which, as He himself had said (John xvi. 12), His disciples were not able to bear in the days of His presence on earth.

By [2]Irenaeus's day, the single episcopate, which had emerged from the collective pastoral oversight of the official presbyteral council of the church by a process more gradual in some places than in others, had assumed an established position almost everywhere. Curiously enough, at first sight, the differentiation of the bishop par excellence—first as primus inter pares, and then as permanent president of the church, occupying a special chair in the centre of the presbyteral bench—was at Rome itself a very slow process. There is in Hermas no reference to a single bishop, distinct from "those who occupy the chief seats"[3] —a phrase which seems to exclude any single officer above them in rank—though in later tradition his brother Pius is referred to as such a bishop.[4] The explanation seems to be that it was only by a very-gradual and almost-insensible process that one of the presbyters, entrusted by the church (acting perhaps in conjunction with the other presbyters) with the chief duty of oversight—that of eucharistic presidency, came to

---

[1] Irenaeus, *Adv. Haer.* V. vi. 1, ap. Eusebius, *Church-History*, V. vii. 6.

[2] [This is clearly the best place to insert (pp. 65–67) the contents of Dr. Bartlet's few written sheets dealing with the development of the monarchical episcopate. Not only is some allusion to this subject desiderated, but the sheets I here transcribe, although not included in the typed copies, were clearly intended to be used in the lecture itself. See below, p. 67, n. 1. C.J.C.].

[3] Hermas, *Shepherd, Vis.* III. ix. 7: cf. *Mand.* XI. 12.

[4] [See n. 1 on next page. C.J.C.].

9

hold this as his standing position, presumably on the basis of special gift in solemn prayer, and so was appointed definitely to it by a special and additional service of ordination. At what date this occurred at Rome it is difficult to say, possibly in the case of Pius himself or his predecessor Hyginus. What contributed greatly to the final stage of differentiation or distinction of the bishop from his colleagues was no doubt the growing need for a single channel of the Church's doctrinal tradition, at a time when divergent theories were meeting in competition at Rome, especially since the arrival of leading Gnostics there from about 135 A.D. onwards.

When Irenaeus refers to the Apostolic tradition of the faith as handed down through an historical line of "elders", by which he means specially the presbyters presiding over the churches, he is no doubt basing his theory of the true test of orthodoxy on actual experience and practice in the churches in his own day. This would carry us back to about the date of Pius's episcopate (usually put 140–154 A.D.).[1] Here then we have a natural development of the single episcopate in terms of developing Church-life and its needs, just as in the case of the prophetic ministry, which was its complement thus far.

But by the end of the second century, or early in the third, all the higher and once distinctly-charismatic functions were

----

[1] [This seems *formally* inconsistent with the fact, noted on the previous page, that Hermas makes no reference to a single episcopal head of the Roman church. Dunin-Borkowsky refuses indeed (in *The Catholic Encyclopedia*, vol. vii [1910], pp. 328a, 340a) to draw the inference that Hermas knew of no monarchical bishop at Rome. His explanation is, "Just because he was the brother of the Head of the Church, he must have thought it more advisable to be silent concerning him and to antedate the abuses which he reprehends". This is very unsatisfactory, for Hermas makes it clear throughout that he is speaking to the Church of his own day; and to have spoken as freely as he does of the "bishops", "elders", and "leaders" (προηγούμενοι) of the church, and said nothing about their responsible chief, would surely have been very unreal. The only authority for dating Hermas's *Shepherd* during the monepiscopate of his brother Pius is the Muratorian Fragment: but (1) the author of this Fragment was anxious to reduce the *Shepherd's* credit in comparison with canonical Scripture, and may have leaned to a late date for this purpose (so Streeter, *Primitive Church* [1929], pp. 206 f.): moreover, (2) Hermas himself writes (*Vis.* II. iv. 3) as a contemporary of Clement, the church's "foreign secretary", thus apparently dating himself about 100 A.D. (see above, p. 49, n. 2). The evidence of the *Muratorian Fragment* must in any case be regarded as an exaggeration, for the reason already indicated, namely, that, if the Roman church had had a single president when Hermas wrote, he would certainly have referred to him. Dr. Bartlet was clearly inclined to date at least the completion of Hermas's work as late as 140 A.D., doubtless out of deference to the evidence of the *Fragment*. On this view, however, we can hardly claim Pius, and certainly not his predecessor Hyginus, as a monarchical bishop: the first bishop of that kind will then be Pius's successor Anicetus (154–165 A.D.), who is in fact guaranteed to us as such by other evidence. If Pius *were* monarchical bishop, Hermas must have written before he became such. C.J.C.].

concentrated in the single bishop, with his teaching and liturgical primacy; and the position of the prophet, where it was
recognized at all, was of the exceptional or special kind, analogous to that of the martyrs. These latter also shared an honorary
position alongside the presbyterate in the formal disposition of
the assembled church. "Gifts of healing" were still recognized in
some, as we learn from our earliest formal Church-Order, later
than the 'Didache' and resting upon the work of Hippolytus,
the disciple of Irenaeus and a leading churchman at Rome of
the period 190-235 A.D. His περὶ χαρισμάτων ἀποστολικὴ παράδοσις,
which reflects both the older idea of χαρίσματα and the newer
(i.e., χαρίσματα as conditioned by the formal ordination-prayer),
closes the chapters of primitive Christianity and early Catholicism, and opens the next and long chapter concerned with a series
of written "Church-Orders".[1] Our study of these will involve
much detailed literary analysis: yet throughout we shall try to
keep to our clue of the correlation of Church-life and Church-order
as having the last word in our historic construction.

The[2] moment Church-order came to rest on written precepts
and precedents, associated with the spiritual prestige of
Apostolic names in one degree or another, it took on an objective
fixity and authority, which tended more and more to check or
arrest the process of change or revision, and at the same time
to favour literalism of interpretation according to new categories of racial or cultural mentality. In this way the growth of
the Canon of the New Testament came to be of crucial import,
both positively and negatively, for the idea of Church-order, as
compared with the freedom of the Spirit in this sphere. While
the Canon was a valuable safeguard against rapid change or
wide deviations from the forms framed when the impression of
the historical Christ was most fresh and vivid, it could not
guard against the subtler danger of unconscious misinterpreta-
tion, due to alien mental categories and instincts brought to the
written words from outside. In a yet-higher degree, too, the
danger of the misuse of written forms of order in a religion of the
Spirit, even though they were its own creations by means of

---

[1] [Dr. Bartlet's manuscript indicates that at this point he was originally
terminating the fourth and last of his lectures during the Lent term of 1924.
He says that with these Church-Orders "the rest of this course will be mainly
concerned, when it is resumed in the Michaelmas term". I have, however,
included his next and closing observation in the text above. C.J.C.].

[2] [This paragraph originally stood at an earlier point in Dr. Bartlet's manuscript; but a pencil-note intimates that he intended to transfer it to the end of
the second century. C.J.C.].

precedents and methods approved by corporate Spirit-experience, was as real as it was inevitable. Conditions of the greatest practical efficiency may, nay must, in course of time and as a result of change in the total vital context, cease to be those most favourable to the due expression, and particularly the progressive and educative expression, of such a religion.

A good transition from the older type of Catholicism, of the age of Irenaeus and Hippolytus, to that of the middle of the third century and onwards, is afforded by the letter of Firmilian, bishop of Caesarea in Cappadocia. It was written about A.D. 256, but represents the outlook also of some quarter-of-a-century before that date. To begin with, he well represents the current view of "the Catholic Church" as the exclusive home of the Holy Spirit. This is how he puts it:

" . . . heretics, if they have severed themselves from the Church of God, can have no power or grace, since all power and grace is established in the Church, where preside seniors who possess the power both of baptizing and of laying on the hand (in confirmation) and of ordaining. For as a heretic may not lawfully ordain nor lay on his hand, so neither may he baptize or do any act holily and spiritually, since he is alien from spiritual and deifying holiness. All which we some time ago confirmed in Iconium, which is a place in Phrygia" (no doubt à propos of Montanism), "when we were assembled together with those who came from Galatia and Cilicia and the rest of the regions hard by" (i.e., within Asia Minor), "as to be held firmly against heretics and to be vindicated, seeing that there was doubt in certain minds on that point".[1]

Yet, as the closing words suggest, this conception of the Church of the federated bishops, or of Catholic orthodoxy, as the exclusive sphere of grace as well as of moral holiness or god-likeness, was not a matter on which there had hitherto been one mind among the orthodox. And in fact the very object of this letter, addressed to Cyprian of Carthage, was to support his view of baptism administered among heretics against that of the Roman bishop, Stephen, who had laid down his theory on the subject in an over-bearing manner.

The Roman theory in question was that baptism in the name of the Trinity, as being a sacrosanct formula of Divine efficacy per se—a view congenial to the Latin mentality, as seen also

[1] See above, p. 60, n. 1.

in the old Roman religion—actually conveyed the grace proper to that sacrament. That is, it gave "washing away of the defilement of the old man, remission of ancient mortal sins, heavenly regeneration to Divine sonship, renewal to eternal life. . . ." This position, says Firmilian, Stephen, arrogantly confident in the locality of his episcopal office, as being himself the successor of Peter, the Church's foundation-apostle, laid down "by his own authority".[1] But it was in fact an innovation, alien to the older tradition of the churches at large, both in the East (which Firmilian knew well) and in the West (for which Cyprian was an equally good witness).[2] For it allows that "the Church exists there", i.e., among heretics who receive and give baptism. "Nor does (Stephen) understand that the verity of the Christian Rock is obscured by himself and in a way abolished, when he thus betrays and deserts unity".[3] For if the reality of baptism be conceded to heretics (the worst kind of schismatics), as regards its fundamental grace of cleansing from sin and regeneration— simply on the strength of the true formula, even when ex hypothesi used outside the Church—the principle that the one Church is the sole home of the Holy Spirit is logically undermined. It is, then, vain to try to save the situation by restricting the gift of the Spirit in confirmation to the laying-on of hands by a Catholic bishop: for this virtually makes a dualism between the action of Christ (the use of Whose sacred formula, the triune Name, is efficacious outside the Church) and that of His Spirit (assumed to be active only within it). The fact that, in face of this logic, urged alike by Cyprian and Firmilian and other weighty Churchmen of the day, this dualism in Divine Grace was in the end generally accepted (especially in the West), is a striking proof of the degree to which the formal type of thought of which the Roman Stephen was the protagonist gradually leavened ancient Catholic Christianity and moulded its ideas of Church-order. Allowance must be made for this fact in our reading of the developments which will meet us in successive stages of the Church-Orders, which we are next to study.

Thus far Firmilian is a typical witness of the general tendencies of Christian thought in his day, especially in the East. But in other references in his letter he shows us certain more-special

---

[1] C. 17 of the same letter of Firmilian (Hartel, vol. ii, p. 821).
[2] And we may add that Novatian also, like Hippolytus before him, agreed with Cyprian on this point, though applying the principle differently to the actual conditions.
[3] *Ibid.*

phenomena of the generation before his date of writing (about 256 A.D.). Some of these belong to the common element in the Church's developing life and order, and some to the element, whether of usage or of conception, proper to one region rather than another, for instance to Asia Minor, and particularly its eastern parts, such as his own Cappadocia and the adjacent Cilicia, lying between it and northern Syria. And as the two latter regions are the probable homes of most of the Church-Orders which will form our prime witnesses henceforth, his evidence as to local modes of thought and feeling, in part related to racial and social conditions, is particularly to our purpose.

Such differences are referred to broadly in what Firmilian says incidentally in speaking of the Roman church under Stephen. "As to the days for keeping Easter and many other sacred forms of Divine matters . . . there exist among them certain divergencies; and there are not observed there all things in like manner as at Jerusalem; just as in very many other provinces many varieties exist in keeping with the diversity of places and persons. And yet there has not on that score ever been any departure from the peace and unity of the Church universal, such as Stephen has now dared to make, breaking the peace against us. . ." (i.e., Firmilian, Cyprian, and others).[1]

Here we may note that, with an eastern Christian like Firmilian,[2] Jerusalem is assumed to be the chief standard of Apostolic tradition in Church-order, although difference even from it in such matters did not lead its bishop or others to withdraw from communion with the churches of any divergent region. In contrast to this he sets the action of the Roman bishop, who had thus sown "strifes and dissensions throughout the churches of the whole world", and, in declaring so many flocks cut off from his communion, had in fact "cut himself off"; since "he is truly a schismatic who has made himself an apostate from the fellowship of the Church's unity".[3]

As preliminary to our study of the extant Church-Orders (written bodies of rules for the ordering of Church-life, the earliest of which go back to the first part of the third century),

---

[1] See section 6 of the same letter (Hartel, vol. ii, p. 813).

[2] Compare his statement that the false spirit (*daemon*) who was believed to speak through the Cappadocian prophetess (section 10: Hartel, vol. ii, p. 817), in order to gain more authority, pretended to have come from Judaea and Jerusalem.

[3] Section 24 (Hartel, vol. ii, p. 825).

we must recall their general features and the conceptions connected therewith, which we know from other sources to have then prevailed. The situation issuing from the movements of life and thought within the Church was broadly as follows. Church-life and -order were "regulated[1] by a *Canon* or *Rule* (κανών, *regula*), a general traditional custom or 'common law' ... This *Canon*" of regulative principles, constituting a standard by fidelity to which a usage or theory was judged sufficiently normal or conforming-to-type to be allowable, either generally or locally, "includes three departments. (1) 'The Rule of Faith' or 'of Truth'. . . . prescribing the essential faith of the Church.[2] (2) 'The Rule of the Church' . . . , regulating the disciplinary administration (e.g. the conditions of ordination, Nic. *can.* 2, 6, 9, 10, and of reconciliation, *Ep. Clem. ad Iac.* 2, Nic. *Can.* 5, 13; . . .) and liturgical procedure (the worship of the Church generally, Origen *in Ioan.* xiii 16; the use of the interrogations in Baptism, S. Firmil. ap. Cypr. *Ep.* lxxv 10, and of Confirmation following Baptism, Cornelius ap. Eus. *H.E.* xi. 43, § 15; of the mixed chalice, Clem. Al. *Strom.* i 19 [96. 1] and the Invocation, S. Firmil. *u.s.*, in the Eucharist: cf. Tertullian's 'obseruatio inueterata', 'consuetudo', *de cor. mil.* 3). (3) 'The Rule of Discipline'. . . . , regulating the personal moral life and conduct of Christians. (4) The 'canonical' (*canonizati*, ...) books belong to the second department of 'the Canon', being so called probably as being prescribed by 'the Rule of the Church': . . . . but when, in the second half of the 4th cent., they come to be called collectively 'the Canon of the Scriptures' . . . , this may be considered to form a fourth department of 'the Canon'. Conciliar decrees (ὅροι Conc. Nic. *can.* 15, 17, 19: afterwards called

---

[1] I am availing myself here in the immediate sequel, when dealing with what is common ground for most historical students, of a scholarly summary in Dr. F. E. Brightman's essay on 'Terms of Communion' in *Essays on the Early History of the Church and the Ministry* (ed. Swete [1921], p. 358 f. note). From that essay I differ as a rule only in the perspective in which it sets its facts, particularly as regards the too-universal scope, both in place and time, which its author's manner of exposition seems to lend to some of them.

[2] So in Irenaeus, *Demonstration of the Apostolic Preaching* (i.e., of the message preached), 3: "We must needs hold the Rule of the Faith without deviation, and do the commandments of God. . . Now this doing is produced by faith. . . . And faith is produced by the Truth; for faith rests on things that truly are" (i.e., spiritual or Divine realities). ". . . Now faith occasions this for us; even as the Elders, the disciples of the Apostles, have handed down to us". Here there is something like a real balance between the two aspects of faith—the objective truth of the Gospel, and the subjective apprehension of it by the soul. The former aspect, however, viz., faith as formulated in an authoritative standard of belief or orthodoxy, "*the* Faith", or "*the* Truth", came more and more to predominate as the third century wore on.

κανόνες) are particular applications or enforcements of 'the Canon' . . . . It goes without saying that the contents of the *regula disciplinae* and the grounds of excommunication were largely determined by the Holy Scriptures: . . . ."

Such, then, was the general notion of Church-order which came to prevail increasingly in the third century, when Firmilian wrote. But even down to the close of the century there were no such things as "conciliar decrees", in the fourth-century sense, i.e., decrees binding on all bishops either in a given area or throughout the Church at large.[1] Until the alliance between the State and the Church in the time of Constantine, the very conditions of general or world-wide councils were lacking. But even local synods from the third quarter of the second century onwards were still exceptional and occasional features in Church-life and -order, though we do begin to hear of them in connexion with the special problems of Montanism and (rather later) of Easter-observance. They were no part of the regular order of Church-organization; and even when they did occur, sporadically and ad hoc, the decisions of the majority of their representing members were not strictly binding on a minority, or even upon a single church, if they did not commend themselves to its representatives as true to the analogy of faith and order, as already fixed by Scripture and tradition.[2]

No one was more emphatic in reserving this right of each bishop, on behalf of his own local part of the Church, than Cyprian of Carthage—the great advocate of the theory of a united episcopate as "the cement" of Church-unity—when the issue in question was not one already manifestly settled by the Church's traditional "Canon" of creed or discipline. On matters not already so settled, a synod "was only a deliberative and advisory body, and possessed no coercive power".[3] Not only is there no "bishop of bishops", such as Stephen, the Roman

---

[1] Cf. Dr. Brightman, on p. 362 of the work quoted above: "In the first quarter of the 4th century, Councils were assembled at Eliberis . . . at Ancyra . . . at Arles . . . and Nicæa . . .; and each of them enacted a series of disciplinary canons. These enactments formed the beginnings of a *Ius canonicum* in which the 'canon of the Church' was reduced to a written law, and the occasional decisions of local churches were replaced by rules valid over wide areas or over the Church at large".

[2] The members of Synods were not at first exclusively bishops: and even as late as the fourth century, presbyters were not only present and took part, but also appended their signatures to the findings agreed on, thus showing that their voice still counted as helping to represent their church.

[3] So Dr. J. H. Bernard in his essay on 'The Cyprianic Doctrine of the Ministry', in *Essays on the Early History of the Church and the Ministry,* pp. 241 f.

bishop, virtually claimed to be in his single capacity as Peter's successor; but "there are no 'bishops of bishops'. In a case where the bishops assembled in Council cannot agree on a point of discipline, they must be content to differ". Surely, that is the true corollary of the Christian principle of love in fellowship, where conscience towards God forbids compliance with the dictates of the corporate conscience of fellow-bishops. "Thus, on one occasion" (before Cyprian's own day) "there was some disagreement among the African bishops as to the admission of penitent adulterers to communion, and Cyprian explains that" the minority (with whom he disagreed) did not withdraw from the assembly of their fellow-bishops, so that "their divergent action must not be interpreted as a breach of the Church's unity. 'So long as the bond of concord remains, and the sacrament of the Catholic Church continues indissoluble, each bishop orders and directs his own proceedings' ".[1]

This is a purely-congregational theory as to the limits of synodal authority, viz., as stopping short of that coercive power to which presbyterianism and diocesan episcopacy alike advance, in the interests of ecclesiastical unity as later understood. In Cyprian's day most bishops were in fact pastors of local churches each of which was able to meet, as a self-sufficing congregation, for worship and all other normal Church-functions. And yet "Cyprian is careful to insist that the vote of each bishop is as weighty as that of his neighbour, all bishops being in theory equal".[2] This was not an outcome of his own special theory of the integral episcopate as a mystical corporate unity, the nucleus and cement of that of the whole Church Catholic;[3] for the logic of that theory, seen also in its later practical effects, was to favour the coercive subordination of conscience, on the part of each constituent bishop with his church, to the collective conscience of the synodal majority. Rather was it due to the persistence of the older genius and custom of the Church's immemorial past, putting a check upon the logic of his new theory of "Catholic" unity. That theory, indeed, finds a place in

---

[1] J. H. Bernard, as before, p. 242. [The closing sentence is loosely translated from Cypr. *Ep*. lv. 21 (Hartel, vol. ii, p. 639): the "sacramentum" mentioned probably means the Church's Creed, and the passage concludes with the significant words "rationem propositi sui Domino redditurus". C.J.C.].

[2] J. H. Bernard, as before, p. 241.

[3] J. H. Bernard, as before, pp. 243 f., especially p. 244, where "the cement of concord"-reference is made to the spiritual principle of the Church's "unity amid variety of discipline", while the concord of "the College of bishops provides the best security for this" in practical working.

the Church-Orders and acts of councils only in the course of the fourth century, *after* the union of State and Church, and at a time when the influence of the State's methods upon those of its spiritual ally had had time to tell. And even then, who can say how much its application to the sphere of discipline was helped by the fact that "the indivisible sacred symbol" of spiritual solidarity, the Creed, itself assumed in that century newly-formulated expressions, which were coercively imposed on minorities by the joint action of Church and State.

The restriction of synodal authority to purely-spiritual influence during the third century, especially in matters of Church-order, left wide liberty for local variety and tentative experimentation in Church-life. It was under these conditions that the writings of various kinds dealing with Church-order took shape in the third century. The very fact that they had to rely for such authority as they sought to carry, especially beyond the immediate circle of their composition, upon sanctions other than those of a legal or coercive nature, may help to explain the fictitious claim to Apostolic origin, and so to spiritual authority, which plays a growing part in them as the century proceeds.

" The idea"[1] had thus far "created the organization" for the fuller corporate expression of itself as a fellowship of love. But already there were not lacking signs that the organization might react unfavourably on the idea, hampering its creative power by casting out the widespread and pervasive liberty which had been the very atmosphere of moral personality in the earlier days. How far would this process go?

The personal and institutional elements in Christianity— as respectively the absolute (in idea) and the relative (conceptual) factors—come to typical expression in the life-experiences of Cyprian and his opponents, Novatian and Stephen. All three share an institutional conception of the Church which was

---

[1] [The two closing paragraphs of this chapter represent detached jottings not woven into the continuous discourse, but relevant enough to the general theme to deserve reproduction. The first was added to the typescript by Dr. Bartlet at the bottom of p. 73, with no precise indication as to where it was to go in. The second is written in ink indeed, but on both sides of a notice announcing a meeting of the Society of Historical Theology for 14th Feb. 1924 —as it were, some "villain fancy fleeting by", but labelled at the top "For the Birkbeck (Age of Cyprian)", and clearly therefore *intended* to be used in the lecture. C.J.C.].

too absolute, and which made even the less-strict doctrine of baptism adopted by Stephen and by later Catholicism illogical and unjustifiable. Even Augustine's theory, which started from the more personal side of Christian experience, yet fell short, because it made the attitude of the individual to the institution too sure an indication of his personal relation to Christ and to God as the Father of love and spiritual unity. The characteristic Christian idea of personality and conscience as sacred, because directly related to God, was too new and supernatural to be patient of being treated in terms of an institutional conception derived from sub-Christian or sub-personal types of religion, whether Roman or Jewish. Here is an antinomy never resolved thus far on Catholic lines. This is the problem left over to the modern world, with its appreciation of individuality—an aspect needing to be reconciled with the corporate idea, the principle of personality at large.

CHAPTER IV

THE SYRIAN DIDASKALIA

AMONG Church-Orders, or bodies of instruction in Church-life, which belong in whole or in part to the third century, the most important for our purpose is the so-called 'Didaskalia'. It is so for two reasons at least. Setting aside for the present the question as to the purity of the oldest form in which it survives to us, it presents the most living and detailed picture we possess of Church-life in that century; and it does so in such a way as to enable us to define to ourselves with fair precision the period and region which it represents. It affords, therefore, the best historical standpoint from which to look both backwards and forwards, and in particular to consider the contents of other Church-Orders which belong more-or-less to the third century. For we can thus best appraise their historical relations, and also distinguish, if needful, the primary and secondary strata which often occur side-by-side in them. It happens, moreover, to belong to much the same region as the 'Didache' on the one hand, and the 'Apostolic Constitutions' on the other. It forms, in fact, the chief basis for the first six books, of the eight in all, which go to make up the latter corpus or composite collection of Church-regulations, dating from the latter part of the fourth century. All three represent Syrian, probably north-Syrian,

Christianity. They stand in a sense on the same line of development, though at very different points. In fact we may say that the 'Didache' is the germ, both in idea and in some of its matter, of the whole growth seen in the other two. Each of these aims in some sense at superseding its predecessor, by supplementing or bringing up to date what had come to be felt to be too archaic or rudimentary.[1]

As a longer interval of time separated the 'Didaskalia' from the first than from the third of this series, the difference both in form and contents between it and the first is correspondingly greater than that between it and the third. The underlying continuity, however, is also considerable. This is suggested by its original title, which seems to have been (as at the end of the Syriac version) "Teaching (Διδαχή) of the Apostles": and in this connexion we may recall Eusebius's description of a work or works as "the so-called Teachings of the Apostles".[2] To this perhaps was prefixed later-on the briefer heading, 'Didaskalia', which also occurs in the same ending of the Syriac Version. The latter title may well have come from the text itself. We read, for example, at the close of the Preface, the words "Hear ye sacred teaching";[3] and to this there are later parallels.[4] The

---

[1] [Dr. Bartlet's typescript contains, at the commencement of this chapter, a reference in pencil to C. H. Turner, *Catholic and Apostolic*, pp. 252 ff., where it is argued that the early Church-Orders, in particular the *Didache*, the *Apostolic Church-Order*, the *Didaskalia*, and the *Apostolic Constitutions*, are not only Palestinian (Syrian?) in provenance, but predominantly though decreasingly Jewish-Christian in tone and character. C.J.C.].

[2] Eusebius, *Church-history*, III. xxv. 4.

[3] Ἀκούσατε διδασκαλίαν ἱεράν . . . [It should be explained at this point that the *Didaskalia* is extant in its entirety only in a Syriac version, of which an English translation is given by R. H. Connolly in *Didascalia Apostolorum*, Oxford, 1929. The Syriac, from a Mesopotamian manuscript, had been edited by Mrs. M. D. Gibson in *Horae Semiticae*, No. I (London, 1903): she also published an English translation of it in *Horae Semiticae*, No. II (same year). The text of the original Greek can for the most part be recovered from the *Apostolic Constitutions*, a work of which the first six books are an expanded version of the *Didaskalia*, the seventh is a greatly-enlarged reproduction of the *Didache*, together with other matter, and the eighth and last is thought to be based on the Church-Order of Hippolytus. The best edition of the *Apostolic Constitutions* is that of F. X. Funk, *Didascalia et Constitutiones Apostolorum*, two volumes, Paderborn, 1905. Fragments of the Latin version of the *Didaskalia* were published by E. Hauler at Leipzig in 1900. They are printed both by Connolly and by Funk. The former puts them opposite the corresponding sections of his English version of the Syriac. The latter embodies them in his own Latin version of the Syriac, which he prints continuously opposite the Greek of the *Apostolic Constitutions*: he distinguishes sufficiently but not very clearly between his own Latin and the old Latin. For purposes of quotation, I have used Funk's section-numbers, as these are more detailed than Connolly's; but I have added the page-number in Connolly for the sake of convenience. C.J.C.].

[4] E.g., VI. xiv. 11: τήνδε τὴν καθολικὴν διδασκαλίαν . . . . . (Connolly, pp. xxviii, 214 f.).

continuity in religious spirit between the two works is remarkable, particularly as regards the highly Hebraic and ethical cast of their piety. Both are eminently biblical in their type of religion, but on the lines of the Old-Testament Prophets, the Synoptic Gospels, James, and 1 Peter, rather than of distinctively Pauline or Johannine teaching.[1] This continuity is most pronounced in the case of the first Book of the 'Didaskalia', where it is traversing much the same ground as the first part of the 'Didache' (which deals with "the Two Ways" of Life and Death), probably with the intention of substituting for it a fuller and more-positively Christian ideal of the conduct befitting members of God's Church. Indeed, when we fix our attention on this first Book by itself, the probability presents itself that this part (perhaps in an even more primitive form than that which it now possesses in our 'Didaskalia') was originally an independent whole known as 'Didache', and was afterwards taken as the basis of a work of enlarged scope, which adopted the longer term 'Didaskalia'. Such a theory has in its favour the fact that it explains the otherwise-strange anomaly—that it is only in the last of the six books of our 'Didaskalia' that the historical occasion of its origin is set forth. For if the bulk of the whole, viz., Books II–VI, was grafted on to an earlier work, addressed to Christians generally—both men and women successively—such a phenomenon becomes more natural.[2]

As it is our purpose to use the 'Didaskalia' largely as a criterion for dating other Church-Orders, and, where needful, for distinguishing stages in their growth, it will be convenient to have before us a fairly-clear conception of its contents.

The work was once a single unbroken body of instruction and exhortation. But for convenience of reference we shall use the division into six books which appears in its later form as part of the 'Apostolic Constitutions'.

Book I deals with the Christian ideal of conduct for all.

Book II sets forth the qualifications of the Church's pastor or bishop, and his duties in various concrete cases; especially his duty towards those needing discipline, one in which the Church as a whole has its part to play, and which it should discharge with loyalty both to the Gospel and to the bishop.

[1] Contrast the degree to which the Fourth Gospel enters, by way of formal quotation, into the matter added by the later hand or hands which contributed to the *Apostolic Constitutions*.

[2] See below, pp. 93 ff.

Book III gives directions as to widows and the ministry of those officially so styled.

Book IV prescribes the proper treatment of orphans, and deals with the subject of almsgiving.

Book V speaks of confessors and martyrs, then of the doctrines of Resurrection and Judgment, and incidentally of the Paschal Fast.

Book VI discusses heresy and schism, the former being the chief occasion of the work.

Coming now to a fuller account of the matter falling under some of these headings, we have to note that the form of the work is, like that of the 'Didache', hortatory. Indeed it is more freshly and prophetically so, being a sort of Christian prophetic manifesto, like the Epistle of James. It opens with an impressive address to its readers, Christians at large, as follows:

" God's plant and His chosen vineyard,[1] ye who have believed in His error-free religion, who through faith are in process of enjoying His eternal Kingdom, having received His power and participation in holy Spirit, armed by means of Him and having your breasts girt with His fear, sharers in sprinkling of the precious and innocent blood of the Christ;[2] ye who have received confidence to call the Almighty God 'Father', fellow-heirs and joint-partakers of His Beloved Servant (παιδός); listen ye to sacred teaching, ye who keep fast hold on His promise by injunction of the Saviour, in conformity with His glorious utterances.

" Take heed, ye sons of God, to do all in obedience to God, and become well-pleasing in all things to the Lord our God. For if any one pursue lawlessness, and do the things that are opposite to God's will, such a one shall rank with God as a lawless heathen. Abstain then from all greed (πλεονεξίας) and injustice: for in the Law it is written, 'Thou shalt not covet . . . aught that is thy neighbour's' "; for so to covet is to be already guilty of the sin in question, and to be "condemned by our Lord and Teacher Jesus Christ—to whom be glory for ever. Amen".[3]

---

[1] This is the common element to which our sources witness. The different position of the words "the Catholic Church" in the Syriac and the Latin (so also the *Apost. Const.*), as well as their differing grammatical constructions, point to their being a later addition.

[2] I suspect that this long-drawn-out description, largely in terms of 1 Peter (e.g., i. 2, 17, 19: cf. ii. 9 as echoed in *Didask*. II. xxvi. 1), was added in the *Didaskalia* to its original basis, which appears clearly in the words "His Beloved Servant", here alone found in the *Didaskalia*.

[3] *Didask* .I pref., i. 1–3 (Connolly, pp. 2–5).

The law of the Christian life is "the Decalogue of the Law", as contrasted with the secondary element (δευτέρωσις) of ritual rules given after Israel's lapse into idolatry through the Golden Calf.[1] This it is which Christ, as Lord and Teacher, sums up, confirms, and—by spiritualizing it yet further—fulfils. Thus "for men who obey God there exists one Law of God, simple, real, living—to wit, 'What thou hatest to be done to thee by another, thou shalt not do to another' " (the negative form of the Golden Rule with which the 'Didache' opened).[2] And so the writer goes on to expound this simple Law, as it is called, very much as is done in the 'Didache'.[3] He then proceeds as follows: "Bear, then, slaves and sons of God, with each other"; and he works out this law of mutual consideration, in terms first of men's and then of women's behaviour. Men are to treat their wives considerately, and avoid all that might ensnare other women.[4] Let them also shun gadding about the streets in idle curiosity concerning the evil ways of the world, but pay attention to their craft and work, seeking to please God and pondering constantly the sayings of the Christ.[5] If rich, and so in no need to work at a craft, let them seek the company of believers of like mind, sharing with them the life-giving words, or sit at home reading the Law, the Books of the Kings, and the Prophets, and the Gospel their fulfilment.[6] By reading the Scriptures, then, a man will grow greatly in faith and be edified. But he is to keep aloof from all heathen books, as permeated with an ideal of conduct alien to that of Christian fellowship.[7]

The section addressed to men ends thus: "And, not to draw out unduly our exhortation, and in case we have omitted aught, do ye select, as wise men, for yourselves the fair things out of the Sacred Scriptures, and confirm yourselves, refusing

[1] *Didask*. I. vi. 7–12, VI. xv–xxiii (Connolly, pp. 12–15, 216–259). It looks as though this teaching as to the δευτέρωσις, which is a very interesting form of early "higher criticism" of one style of biblical revelation by another and a later one, is part of the additions made to an earlier basis in this portion of the *Didaskalia*. Cf. Connolly, pp. xxxiv–xxxvi, lvii–lxix, lxxxi f., lxxxix.

[2] *Didask*. I. i. 7 (Connolly, pp. 4 f.): cf. *Didache*, i. 2.

[3] *Didask*. I. ii (Connolly, pp. 6 f.): cf. *Didache*, i. 3.

[4] Here, as in the section addressed to women, there is a noteworthy touch of the full Christian sense of responsibility for others' safety, in the injunction to avoid causing temptation to those of the opposite sex by self-adornment and display.

[5] *Didask*. I. iii f. (Connolly, pp. 8–11).

[6] *Didask*. I. v (Connolly, pp. 11–13): cf. Harnack, *Bible Reading in the Early Church*, pp. 58 ff. In *Didask*. I. vi. 5 (Connolly, pp. 12 f.), the Law is called τὸν ἔνδοξον τοῦ Κυρίου Νόμον.

[7] *Didask*. I. vi f. (Connolly, pp. 12–21).

all evil things, in order that ye may be found holy in life eternal with God".[1] Similarly, the corresponding section addressed to women[2] ends with a kindred passage.[3] This injunction is remarkable,[4] as leaving so much to lay folk to learn for themselves by the use of Scripture; and it points to an early date for the original work, of which it was probably the close.

In all this we see the intensely Hebraic and ethical nature of the writer's religious ideal.

Passing on now to consider the 'Didaskalia' proper, as distinct from its possibly-older starting-point (the assumed basis of its first part, addressed to Christians simply as such), we notice the way in which its author dwells on the need for Christians to discriminate between the moral and the ritual elements in the Old Testament, and to attach authority only to the former as of abiding validity, because confirmed by Christ. This grave duty is confidently entrusted to the average educated Christian. Here is a fact which, while consonant with the thought and practice of the ancient Catholic Church all along,[5] implies a high notion of the spiritual competence and responsibility of the members of the Church generally, and so indicates the general attitude taken up towards them in the 'Didaskalia'. The work is in fact addressed to the Church as a whole, and not primarily to its officers, the clergy. This feature is, indeed, partly obscured by the large place filled, especially in Book II, by special directions to bishops as such, a feature which seems to have been considerably enlarged by a revising hand even before the revision effected by the author of the 'Apostolic Constitutions'.[6] But the general fact holds good, after all deductions, that the ecclesiastical attitude revealed inter alia in its normal mode of address, namely to "the Brotherhood" (a phrase found in Irenaeus and in the first stage of the 'Apostolic Church-Order') of the Church catholic, is characteristic of the third century, and of its opening rather than of its close. This attitude becomes significant in the light of the clerical tendency seen in the changes effected by the late-fourth-century compiler

---

[1] *Didask.* I. vii. 17 (Connolly, pp. 20 f.).
[2] *Didask.* I. viii–x (Connolly, pp. 20–29).
[3] *Didask.* I. x. 4 (Connolly, pp. 28 f.)
[4] It seems echoed in the *Apostolic Church-Order* (xv in the Greek and Sahidic texts), yet to be studied.
[5] As Harnack has well shown in his *Bible Reading in the Early Church*.
[6] Traces of this earlier revision are noted from time to time in this chapter and in ch. viii. More detailed proof will be found in an appendix to this chapter on the revised *Didaskalia* called *Diatax(e)is* (see below, pp. 93 ff.).

of the 'Apostolic Constitutions'.[1] Thus, whereas the latter begins the next part with the words, "Now touching bishops thus have we (the Apostles) heard from our Lord", the 'Didaskalia' originally ran, "Now touching the office of bishop, hear as follows"[2]—still having in mind as the body addressed the Church generally.

" The pastor", it continued—using a term characteristic of the light in which the office is described in Book II—"who is installed in oversight of the presbytery[3] in every church and parish,[4] must be blameless, . . . a man of not less than fifty years, because he will (then) have (already) escaped in some fashion the disorders of youth,[5] . . . educated, if possible; but if unlettered, then experienced in the Word, as befits his age.[6] But if", owing to the smallness of the parish, such a one be not found of ripe age, then "let a young man, if witnessed to by his associates as worthy of oversight (ἐπισκοπῆς)—since under the conditions of youth he was wont to exhibit in gentleness and ordered conduct" (not "the disorders of youth" above referred to) "the temper of age, be duly tested to see whether he has such witness from all, and be installed in office in peace" (like the youthful Solomon and other leaders of Israel).[7] "Hence, even if young, let him be gentle, . . . merciful, . . . a peacemaker, . . . purified from all malice, wickedness, and injustice".[8] "Thus then let him be tested, whensoever by receiving ordination he is installed in the place of oversight (τῷ τόπῳ τῆς ἐπισκοπῆς), to see whether he be grave, whether he (had or)[9] has a grave and believing wife, whether he has reared his children piously and

---

[1] *Apost. Const.* II. i. 1.

[2] *Didask.* II init. in the Syriac (Connolly, p. 28).

[3] So the Old Latin Version, with some support from other witnesses.

[4] "Parish" (παροικίᾳ) means first the people, then the area, of a local church, the sphere of a primitive bishop.

[5] *Didask.* II. i. 1 (Connolly, pp. 28 f.).

[6] *Didask.* II. i. 2 (Connolly, pp. 30 f.).

[7] *Didask.* II. i. 3 f. (Connolly, pp. 30 f.)

[8] *Didask.* II. i. 5–8 (Connolly, pp. 30–33). What comes next, largely in terms of 1 Tim. iii. 2–6, may be secondary. "Accordingly, let him be also soberminded, 'temperate, orderly', stable, not easily upset, 'not given to wine, no striker, but gentle, uncontentious, no lover of money, no new convert . . .' Such 'ought the bishop to be, husband of one wife, ruling well his own house'" (*Didask.* II. ii. 1 f. [Connolly, pp. 32 f.]. It seems probable, indeed, that the whole of the matter after the reference to the young candidate's installation " in peace", being uncalled-for, is probably secondary, since his case is only an incident in the description of a normal candidate's qualifications; and these are resumed (from before "But if . . . in peace") with "Thus then let him be tested . . . to see whether . . ." (*Didask.* II. i. 3 [Connolly, pp. 32 f.]).

[9] The Syriac omits this, and the order of the words "had" and "has" differs in the Latin and in *Apost. Const.*

has by discipline led them forward; whether his domestics all revere, honour, and obey him": else what hope that others will do so? "Let him, then, be tested, to see whether he is spotless touching worldly affairs. . . ."[1]

Then follows a long list of other moral virtues,[2] ere the writer passes to the bishop's special qualifications for the teaching-office. "Let him be forbearing, patient in exhortations, much given to teaching, giving care and zeal to the Books of the Lord, devoted to (the public) reading (of them), that he may interpret the Scriptures carefully, interpreting the Gospel in keeping with the Prophets and the Law", and vice versa.[3] "Above all let him become a good discriminator, distinguishing Law and 'Deuter-osis', . . . lest any fall into the bonds. Do thou, then, take charge of the Word, O bishop,[4] that, if possible to thee, thou mayest interpret all things word for word, and in much teaching ($\delta\iota\delta\alpha\chi\widehat{\eta}$) feed and water thy people richly with the illumination of the Law".[5]

" But let not the bishop be given to base gain, especially as regards the heathen. . . ."[6] In a word, "Whatsoever fair virtues exist among men, these let the bishop possess in himself. Be-cause, if not taxable with iniquity, a pastor shall constrain his own disciples even by his behaviour . . . to become worthy imitators of his own acts, as said the Lord in the Twelve Pro-phets, 'And it shall be, like priest, like people'. For ye ought to be watchmen to the people, because ye too have a watchman, the Christ".[7] For the Lord through Ezekiel (xxxiii. 1–6) bids His servants watch and warn His People against the coming of the Sword. "The 'sword' is the Judgment; the 'trumpet' the Gospel; and the 'watchman' the bishop, appointed for the Church, who must by preaching testify and assure as to this Judgment".[8]

Here we have the essential idea of the bishop in the 'Didas-

---

[1] *Didask.* II. i. 3 f., ii. 1 (Connolly, pp. 32 f.). Lat. and Syr. add "and in body", with reference to the Old-Testament citation which follows (Levit. xxi. 17)— a clear case where their text of the *Didaskalia* is different in type from that used in the *Apost. Const.* and secondary to it.

[2] *Didask.* II. iii. 2–v. 3 (Connolly, pp. 32–34).

[3] *Didask.* II. v. 3 (Connolly, pp. 34).

[4] The first case of such apostrophes or asides, directed to a particular element in the church (in the course of the writer's address to it generally), and marking this and later parts of his work.

[5] *Didask.* II. v. 4 f. (Connolly, pp. 34 f.). The *Apost. Const.* (II. v. 7) then quote Hosea x. 12 (LXX), while the Syriac quotes Proverbs xxvii. 23–26—seem-ingly a case of independent lines of textual development.

[6] *Didask.* II. vi. 1 (Connolly, p. 35).

[7] *Didask.* II. vi. 4–6 (Connolly, pp. 35 f.). The passage quoted is Hosea iv. 9.

[8] *Didask.* II. vi. 6–11 (Connolly, p. 36).

kalia', as simply the faithful leader of his people in the Christian type of life, going before it as "scout" or "watchman" (σκοπός), himself showing the way and giving the alarm, where needful, by his preaching and testimony to the Word. From this Hebrew prophetic conception flow the principles of pastoral oversight and discipline—a topic very prominent in the writer's thought and no doubt in the actual situation of his day. If, says he to bishops, ye keep repeating the message, the sin of ignorant ones will not be yours: for so an impression will be made—though Israel has not heeded, "not yet those others who think themselves to have heard, being dragged down into deadly and awful heresies, as to which we shall yet speak.[1] For we do not believe, brethren, that anyone, after having washed, does any more the abominations of the lawless, since if any man has sinned after baptism, he will be condemned to hell".[2]

"If anyone is convicted of having done any lawless deed, such a one is no Christian, but rather by hypocrisy a liar to God"; and it is the bishop's duty to hold apart from such, if he is to be free from blame and partiality.[3] But if for self-interest and partiality he suffers the lawless sinner to remain in the Church, he has smirched his church before God and men, and will ruin many new members and enquirers under instruction, and also the young in years, along with himself.[4] If, on the other hand, the sinner sees the bishop and deacons[5] without blame and the flock pure, in the first place he will not dare in defiance to go to church, being conscience-stricken: but if he does, he will be censured by the bishop, and having nothing to fix on in bishop or people he will go forth weeping and abashed, and the flock will remain pure. Further, the sinning member himself will turn penitently to God "and so have hope (of God's forgiveness); and the whole flock, seeing his tears, will get an admonition that he who sins perishes".[6] We observe here the primitive emphasis on the idea of the "holy" Church, in the sense of its being free from patent, recognizable sin of a grave type in any of its members, and along with it, it seems, the unprimitive though early view that there were sins of a certain gravity—short of the apostasy contemplated in Heb. vi. 4–8—

[1] *Didask*. II. vi. 16 f. (Connolly, pp. 37–39). The promise is redeemed in VI.
[2] *Didask*. II. vii (Connolly, pp. 38 f.).
[3] *Didask*. II. viii. 3 f. (Connolly, pp. 38 f.).
[4] *Didask*. II. ix, x. 1 (Connolly, pp. 38–40).
[5] I.e., the full pastorate, as in *Didask*. II. xliv (Connolly, p. 109).
[6] *Didask*. II. x. 3–5 (Connolly, pp. 40 f.).

called "mortal" (πρὸς θάνατον—I John v. 16f.), because unforgivable on earth. These involved ipso facto the withdrawal of God's holy Spirit; and while there was with God a door of forgiveness for them by true contrition, yet there was no door of readmission to the full communion of the Church, since it could not infallibly know the heart's renewal from its state of deadness to the Christian life, after having once tasted its distinctive good. This attitude, implied already in Hermas, and extending the principle of apostasy dealt with in Heb. vi. 4–8 to adultery and even fornication, as well as homicide, became a burning issue at Rome between the majority under bishop Callistus and the old-fashioned minority under Hippolytus—each claiming to be the true church under the legitimate bishop of Rome for the time-being. It looks as if the 'Didaskalia' shared Hippolytus' view that the Church was not warranted in actually restoring mortal sinners to its full communion, and as if in fact it represents his side of the controversy at Rome. This would suggest that the 'Didaskalia' was written between about 217 A.D. and the Decian persecution in 250 A.D.

The moral for the bishop himself, which it goes on to draw, is one of zeal to be pure in his own actions, recognizing his position "as having God's stamp" (ὡς Θεοῦ τύπον ἔχων), i.e., as virtually representing God Almighty.[1] "And so in church utter thy word seated, as having authority to judge, on God's behalf, those who have sinned; because to you bishops it has been said in the Gospel, 'Whatsoever ye shall bind on earth, shall be bound also in heaven'.[2] Judge, then, O bishop, with authority, as God; but those who repent take to thyself with love, even as God (does), and chide and admonish and exhort; for the Lord God has sworn to grant remission to sinners, even as He said by Ezekiel: '. . . As I live, says the Lord, I desire not the death of the sinner, but that he turn from his evil way and live. . .'[3] Here, then, He has given hope to sinners, that, if they repent, they may attain salvation by their penitence, lest in despair they yield themselves over to their transgressions and add to them, but may rather turn and weep over their sins and repent from the heart".[4]

---

[1] *Didask.* II. xi. 1 (Connolly, pp. 40 f.). We may compare Ignat. *Magn.* vi. 1: . . . προκαθημένου τοῦ ἐπισκόπου εἰς τύπον Θεοῦ.

[2] *Didask.* II. xi. 2 (Connolly, pp. 40 f.).

[3] *Didask.* II. xii. 1 f. (Connolly, pp. 40–42), quoting Ezek. xxxiii. 10 f.

[4] *Didask.* II. xii. 3 (Connolly, p. 42). The words "by their penitence" are significant. They seem to imply the possibility of God, as the Knower of all hearts, forgiving the penitent, but not the authority of the Church to pro-

Here we have an austere view of the possibilities of Divine forgiveness, as regards the assurance of it in this life. It is felt as a matter between God and the sinner's own conscience, and is unconfirmed by the Church's judgment. The living nature of this issue is proved by the fact that, after a warning to those who have not thus sinned to be watchful (since none knows if he will have time granted for penitence),[1] the author returns at great length to the subject, to argue against a totally-aloof attitude on the part of the bishop to a penitent—such as some urged, lest men be defiled by condoning and so sharing the sinner's sin and lot. He quotes the Old Testament, especially Ezekiel, in extenso, in order to show this fear to be groundless, especially on the part of the laity, some of whom were apt to take this line and demand a more-severe policy than the cautious one outlined, which latter at least meant holding out a friendly hand to the penitent sinner, though without promising him restoration to Church-fellowship.[2]

Thus far[3] all that has been said relates to the teaching and pastoral ministry exercised by the bishop, without any reference being made to the administration of the sacraments as bearing upon his qualifications. This silence is striking in any case, especially when compared with the different emphasis in the other Church-Orders of the third and fourth centuries. But it does not mean that the ministry of sacramental acts did not now belong specially to the bishop, just as it had from the time of his first emergence early in the second century as a distinct official in whose hands the various functions of oversight, once diffused throughout the presbytery as a whole, were in practice concentrated.[4] It is only that these sacramental acts

nounce forgiveness in His name. *Apost. Const.*, which throughout implies the Church's power on God's behalf to restore the penitent sinner after discipline to its fellowship, omits the words (II. xii. 3). Conversely, in II. xi. 2 (Connolly, pp. 40 f.), the *Didaskalia*, in quoting Matt. xviii. 18, omits the clause about loosing, while *Apost. Const.* inserts it. This situation points to a date earlier than 250 A.D. for the *Didaskalia*.

[1] *Didask.* II. xiii. 1–3 (Connolly, p. 42).

[2] *Didask.* II. xiii. 4–xv (Connolly, pp. 42–52), quoting Ezek. xiv. 12–14, xviii. 1–32, xxxiii. 12–20.

[3] [The three following paragraphs, with a reference to the quotation constituting the fourth (i.e., pp. 85–87), are inserted here from Dr. Bartlet's rough notes, because they bear on the very important topic of the bishop's sacramental functions, regarding which the typescript is otherwise practically silent. C.J.C.].

[4] Thus it was as "the president of the brethren"—so Justin (*Apol.* I. lxv. 3, lxvii. 5) gives us to understand—that the bishop voiced "to the best of his ability" the eucharistic prayer of the local church, which in its turn signified approbation of it as its own prayer by the solemn "Amen" characteristic of this act of worship in particular.

are not thought of in connexion with the personal qualifications
for the episcopal or pastoral oversight over a local unit of the
Church's life. With such qualifications alone have the Christian
men in their local churches to do—for it is they who are primarily addressed—when they choose one of their number for the
"place of oversight", seemingly by acclamation after "testing".

Sacramental qualifications, on the other hand, were now
thought to depend on something other than personal virtues
and gifts—namely, upon solemn initiation (κατάστασις—used also
of civil office) or ordination by the laying on of hands.[1] The term
used for "ordination" (χειροτονία) does not, indeed, mean originally "laying on of hands":[2] yet by this time it had already
gained that specialized sense in connexion with the rite of
ordination. That rite was now often thought to convey not only
authority—a commission or jurisdiction for the exercise of
representative functions—but also special sacramental grace.
By the third century at latest, ordination was apparently
viewed as a Divine-human act, in which God was thought to
convey to the ordained person—through certain men as special
organs of Christ's Body, the Church—actual Divine power,
both as authority (ἐξουσία) and as energy (δύναμις), to perform
certain sacramental acts. These acts in turn were themselves
thereby guaranteed to convey, like material channels (because
not essentially conditioned by the conscious or subjective state
of the recipient), certain forms of "grace" or Divine power, not
otherwise to be received. Of these forms of grace, baptismal
regeneration and the body and blood of Christ as food for body
and soul were the chief. Further, these forms—as well as the
more-characteristic grace of orders, associated with the laying-
on of hands—were by this time usually confined to the rites
as administered by bishops, though with certain qualifications
in favour of presbyters, as the colleagues of the bishop in the
superior order of ministry if not of office. But broadly speaking,
the sacramental as well as the teaching ministry was now
concentrated in the bishop's hands.[3]

As regards the nature of the bishop's teaching, it may be

---

[1] Cf. *Didask*. II. ii. 3: τὴν χειροτονίαν λαμβάνων καθίσταται ἐν τῷ τόπῳ τῆς
ἐπισκοπῆς (Connolly, pp. 32 f.).

[2] That is χειροθεσία, as in *Didask*. II. xli. 2, III. xii. 3 (Connolly, pp. 104, 146).

[3] [I am not clear how Dr. Bartlet would have harmonized the statements in
this paragraph with what he says below on pp. 92 f. Possibly he does not mean
to say there more than that the mechanical aspect of the conveyance of sacramental grace is comparatively undeveloped in the *Didaskalia*, or more here
than that at least the germs and promise thereof are visible in it. C.J.C.].

noted here in passing, that the teaching in mind was of a practical rather than of a doctrinal sort: it dealt with Christian duty
rather than with theology proper. There is no suggestion in the
'Didaskalia' that the bishop enjoys any ex-officio grace of
illumination qualifying him to perceive and hand on the true
purport of any dogmatic deposit of faith—if that be the real
meaning of Irenaeus' phrase about the "charisma veritatis
certum" which went along with historic succession from the
Apostles.[1] It is only in the sphere of sacraments that a special
official grace is assumed to be attached to the episcopate. It is
here accordingly that we may reasonably look for the main
cause of those changes in perspective and emphasis in the
conception of the office which are reflected in the relevant
sections of the later Church-Orders—changes which may be
roughly described as leading in the direction of authoritarian
hierarchy. Without further anticipating here the forms taken
by this later development, we may note how the change in
question might have been suggested and fostered by the
assumption that supernatural power was conferred through
episcopal ordination. A foreshadowing of what was likely to
come can be discerned in a passage like the following, in which
—unlike what we have hitherto seen in the 'Didaskalia' and
elsewhere—the bishop is not simply conceived as the typical
disciple of Christ, the great Exemplar, but is placed by himself
upon an official pedestal, as God's vice-gerent over His elect
People:

" For they" (i.e., the bishops) "are your high priests, . . . But
your high priest and Levite is the bishop: he it is who adminis-
ters the Word to you and is your mediator: he is your teacher
and, after God Who regenerates by water, your father: he is
your chief and leader: he is your mighty king. Let him, reigning
(as he does) in God's place, be honoured by you like God, since
the bishop presides over you in the pattern of God. . . . Just as
it was not lawful therefore for a stranger, who was not a Levite,
to offer anything or (even) to approach the altar without a
priest, so do not ye do anything without the bishop. But if
anyone does anything without the bishop, he does it in vain:
for it will not be accounted to him as a work, because it is not
fitting to do anything without the (high) priest".[2]

[1] Irenaeus, *Adv. Haer.* IV. xxvi. 2.
[2] *Didask.* II. xxvi. 3 f., xxvii. 1 f. (Connolly, pp. 86–89). [Dr. Bartlet's manuscript contained only the jotting "xxvi ff." at the bottom of the preceding
paragraph. I have selected and translated the clauses which I imagine he had in

writer's training, if not his profession in ordinary life, was that of a doctor.[1]

Placed[2] in this setting the 'Didaskalia' assumes the greatest actuality, because of its close relevance of meaning and emphasis. How relevant it was felt to be to actual conditions one may already judge from its apology for the severity of its criticisms of the heresies it deals with.[3] Its relevance has appeared again and again, as we have gone rapidly through some of its contents, in such a way that life and order might be seen in their real relations. For what is most distinctive of the 'Didaskalia' as a Church-Order is its interest in Church-life as a whole, so that each separate institutional element appears in its vital and organic relation to the great common end of the Church—the creation and fostering of the Christian type of living, according to the will of God as seen in Jesus Christ. In this sense it is more concretely religious in spirit and tone than any of our other and later Church-Orders—though it is only fair to add that the similar work of Hippolytus (of about the same date, but from the opposite quarter of Christendom), in so far as it still shines through the re-mouldings which it has undergone in its historical use, approximates most clearly to the 'Didaskalia' in this respect. Compared with them, the other Church-Orders are abstractions, though significant even as such.

When we look at the mentality implied in the language, style, and texture of the characteristic contents of the 'Didaskalia', we find them markedly Jewish—so much so that it is easiest to suppose that the writer had a Jewish element in his blood or training or both, and that this was typical of the region in which and for which he wrote. This, along with the fact that its Scriptural citations include matter from the Jewish Apocrypha—even if already interpolated in his Old-Testament text, e.g., the Prayer of Manasses in his Book of the Kings, suggests that he largely shared the standpoint of a Hellenist Christian like Stephen. With Stephen's view of the Law and of the significance of the idolatrous apostasy through the Golden Calf, in the history of Israel's relation to God's living oracles

---

[1] Cf. Connolly, p. xci.
[2] [I here insert as apposite at this point a paragraph containing a few sentences from some rough notes on the *Didaskalia* found among Dr. Bartlet's papers. C.J.C.].
[3] *Didask.* VI. xxiii. 3–7 (Connolly, pp. 256–259).

given by Moses, he has a deep underlying affinity of spirit as well as of form.[1]

But if he had Jewish or semi-Jewish mentality working under the forms of his Greek culture, we have here the best key to the pseudo-Apostolic and fictitious form under which he sets forth his earnest and prophetic "tract for the times"— times of serious and subtle dangers to faith and practice—and also the key to his emphasis on Church-order, especially the episcopal office, as a prime safeguard against these dangers. As a Syrian Christian, he naturally takes over the idea of Apostolic origin embodied in the 'Didache', as an established traditional mode of thought: and to him as a prophetic teacher of Hebraic mentality it takes on imaginatively and realistically the form of a sequel and supplement to the Apostolic Conference, where the Apostles were said to have "gathered together" at a certain historic crisis.[2] That gathering, however, is conceived in terms not only of the canonical book of Acts, but also of other and secondary writings, of the same period (as it was thought), under the name of Peter, whether his 'Preaching' or his 'Acts'. This view reduces the sense of fiction which to us Westerns and moderns hangs about the form of the 'Didaskalia', so tending to obscure its high significance both religious and historical. That form, just because it was of a piece with habitual convention in his environment, was natural enough to the generally-oriental and specifically-Hebraic mentality of its author. In view of the prophetic urgency of the situation, it was felt to be a legitimate and helpful piece of poetic rhetoric.

As time went on, however, and it was read with the growingly-literalistic Greek mentality of the Eastern Church, let alone the legal mentality of the Latin (into which at the end of the fourth century it passed in a translation recently brought to light), the practical results of the element of fiction in its form became more serious. Some of these results will come before us in certain of the Church-Orders yet to be examined. But what is so important to notice at this point is that the vital quality of the work, connected with its relevance to its own age and conditions, its spirit rather than its letter, tended to operate less and less, while its fictitious idea of quasi-legal Apostolic authority behind all its ecclesiastical allusions and prescriptions became ever more potent. They were read largely apart from that which

---

[1] *Didask.* VI. xvi (Connolly, pp. 218–224).
[2] Acts xv. 6; *Didask.* VI. xii f. (Connolly, pp. 204–211).

forms their context—the whole burning appeal for purity and fidelity to the ideal of religious and ethical holiness in each church and in all its members. It is that appeal which forms the real burden of this Christian prophetic Instruction in the name and—it was felt—in the spirit of primitive and Apostolic Christianity.

The appeal centred indeed in the pastoral function of the bishop, as chief pastor of the local flock on earth. The deacon stands to him as does Christ to the Father, or as Moses' prophet Aaron stood to Moses: he acts as medium of communication, both ways, between bishop and people. The bishop, then, is to be reverenced and obeyed as the human similitude of God the heavenly Pastor of His People, the Church (both conceived on the Hebraic lines of Old-Testament prophecy). This is high doctrine of an ideal sort. And, as in the case of the kindred letters of Ignatius of Antioch, the parallel is pushed even to the point of making criticism of the bishop's distinctive or ex-officio actions savour of sacrilege. Not only however was it balanced in its original context by an equal emphasis on the local church as in practice corporately sharing the bishop's responsibility for preserving its own purity in cases of discipline; but also the emphasis falls throughout on the religious aim of the whole treatise, viz., purity and love in each and all, as that which all methods and ministries in the Church's life were to subserve. That is its essential spirit; and it is one which admits of the flexibility needful for the progressive adaptation of all institutional elements and methods of Church-order to the paramount needs of the Christian life. Such adaptation can take place only under the continued guidance of the Holy Spirit, to Whose pervasive energy in each member of the Church the 'Didaskalia' so strongly appeals.

Further, just as the original spirit of the Ignatian Epistles contrasts so markedly with the spurious revision of them at the end of the fourth century, so does the 'Didaskalia' contrast with the later 'Apostolic Constitutions'. While there is in Ignatius and the 'Didaskalia' such stress on the bishop as the centre of the Church's working unity, and thus as God's image and earthly representative, there is no hint that this function of his —or indeed of any other representative of God's Divinely-given ministry in His Church—is in any way bound up with any special forms of appointment or ordination. This is in both writers the more noteworthy, since each definitely represents bishops as succeeding in certain respects to the primary ministry of Apostles in their day. The succession, however, such as it is, is due to the Divine idea of the office in either case, its relation to God—as was true also in the supreme case of the Christ. Nowhere is there any suggestion of the later conception of Apostolic Succession, in the sense of a share in specific Apostolic grace, communicated ex opere operato, as through material channels, from one bishop to another, in virtue of certain bodily acts and sacrosanct formulae. It is only later, in works of quite-different provenance, that we shall see the first traces and growth of this conception.[1] Meantime it is to another early-third-century writing, parallel to the 'Didaskalia' in its developing form, namely, the 'Apostolic Church-Order', that we must devote our next chapter.

APPENDED NOTE ON

THE REVISED 'DIDASKALIA' CALLED 'DIATAXEIS'

There exists in a group of manuscripts a series of chapter-headings taken from a work bearing the title 'The Ordinances' (αἱ Διατάξεις), no doubt 'of the Apostles', a title either identical with or akin to that of our 'Apostolic Constitutions' (Διαταγαὶ or Διατάξεις).[2] The 'Headings' seem at points to go behind this latter work (with the first seven books alone of which it affords parallels), to another and perhaps-earlier form, which we have other reasons to suspect once existed. They are arranged in three groups: 'On Bishops' (1–13), 'On Church-Constitution' (περὶ καταστάσεως ἐκκλησιαστικῆς, 14–27), 'On Oblations' (28–30). The most-noteworthy traces of knowledge of an older basis, in addition to the 'Apostolic Constitutions', are furnished by certain of the 'Headings' (κεφάλαια) in the first group, and particularly the first of them, which reproduces a prologue not belonging to the 'Apostolic Constitutions', though prefixed to its opening in one manuscript. This manuscript, like the chief one of our special group, is at Vienna; and the two perhaps came from the same region. The Prologue is summarized in the 'Heading' as follows. "That the Church is like a ship. The steersman is Christ, and the look-out man (πρωρεύς) is the bishop; the sailors are the presbyters; the overseers of the rowers are the deacons, the petty officers (ναυτολόγοι)

---

[1] [On the question of the consistency of this paragraph with what has been inserted above concerning the sacramental functions of the bishop (pp. 86 f.), see p. 86, n. 3. C.J.C.].

[2] See Funk, *Didascalia et Constitutiones Apostolorum*, vol. ii (1905), pp. XXXIII f., 137–143.

are the order of readers and servers" (ὑπηρετῶν τάγμα, assistant deacons). This simile is modelled on the one found in the 'Epistle of Clement to James' (14–16), prefixed originally to the common basis of the Pseudo-Clementine 'Homilies' and 'Recognitions', viz., the 'journeyings (περίοδοι) of Peter', the third-century nucleus of the story of Clement as the chief disciple of Peter, which suggested the very idea lying behind the form of our 'Apostolic Constitutions'. The conjecture that such a prologue once preceded the 'Didaskalia', at a stage later than that represented by our Latin and Syriac Versions, is confirmed by the preface found in the Mesopotamian manuscript used by Mrs. Gibson in her edition, as also in the Arabic and Ethiopic 'Didaskalia'.[1] There we have not indeed the simile of a ship, probably because it was not suited to the region in question, but a series of nominal similes which by their very lameness point to something more natural as having suggested the effort to seek such descriptions of functions at all. "The bishop is in the likeness of the shepherd of the sheep, and the presbyter in the likeness of a teacher", and so on with deacon, sub-deacon, reader, etc., "and the rest of the people as those who hearken to the word of the Gospel".

Further, the eighth 'Heading' makes the bishop the anti-type of Christ (τύπον φέρει Χριστοῦ), the presbyters of the cherubim, the deacons of the angels, the readers and musicians (ψάλται) of the prophets; while the tenth assigns to the readers a portion in the church's offerings in kind (τὰς εὐλογίας) and first-fruits, along with the bishop and the clergy (τοῖς κληρικοῖς, i.e., the presbyters and the deacons). When we compare all these features with the relevant sections in the 'Apostolic Constitutions' we find differences.

Thus while in the 'Didaskalia'[2] we find no comparison of the Church to a ship, in the corresponding section of the 'Apostolic Constitutions' the bishop instead of Christ has become the steersman; the deacons are the sailors, a status assigned above to the presbyters. The change is quite in keeping with the prominence of deacons in the 'Apostolic Constitutions', as a result of the further development of the general conceptions in the original 'Didaskalia'. In the earlier document the deacons are assistants to the bishop in the administrative ministry of the Church, while the presbyters are mainly the bishop's council of advice and share his dignity, seated on either side of his presidential chair. But it departs further than does the simile prefixed to the 'Apostolic Constitutions' in the Vienna-manuscript, and the 'Headings' based mainly on some manuscripts akin to the source whence that Vienna-manuscript came, from the probable fountain-head of this form of the simile of the Church as

---

[1] Cf. Funk, op. cit., vol. ii (1905), pp. XXVIII–XXXII, 120–122; Connolly, Didasc. Apost., pp. xiii f. See above, p. 76, n. 3.

[2] Didask. II. lvii. 2 (Connolly, p. 119).

God's ship, as seen in Hippolytus's 'Exposition concerning Christ and Antichrist' (lix), where it is found in quite-another form.

The above-quoted Syrian form, as we may style it, first emerges in the 'Epistle of Clement to James' already cited. The only difference between it and the first 'Heading' is that the 'Epistle' compares catechists to those whose task it is to assign their places and duties to the passengers (οἱ ναυστολόγοι), while the 'Heading' likens to the ναυτολόγοι "the order of readers and servers"—where "servers" are apparently those later known as "sub-deacons". In marked contrast with both these views stands out the representation in the 'Apostolic Constitutions'. There the presbyters have a purely-honorary function in the church as assembled for worship, whereas the deacons are to be charged "like sailors to assign their places to the brethren as to passengers (καθάπερ ἐπιβάταις)", so combining the functions of both presbyters and deacons as given in the first 'Heading'. Here, too, in the word used to describe the latter (τοίχαρχοι), we have the very same term emerging as is applied to deacons in the Prologue, which we saw reason to connect with a form of the 'Didaskalia' intermediate between our extant form and the 'Apostolic Constitutions', and in which we may reasonably infer that a like description of the Church occurred. This inference is borne out by the emergence a little further on in the 'Apostolic Constitutions'[1] of another function, that of the "passenger-officers" (ναυστολόγοι), i.e., door-keepers and female deacons, who regulate the entrance of men and women respectively, in place of the "readers and servers" (i.e., the sub-deacons) of the 'Heading'. This change means also a change of conception as to what was meant by the entrance and the mode of its regulation. For while in the Prologue, as in the Pseudo-Clementine 'Epistle', it was entrance to the spiritual ship of the Church by instruction of would-be members in the Word, in the 'Apostolic Constitutions' it refers simply to admission to the material church and direction to one's proper seat—a function for which "readers" of the Scriptures would not be required. To such "readers" two lessons from the Old Testament ("the Prophets", generically) were attributed, followed by the singing to music of the Psalms of David by the "singers";[2] and thereafter a lesson from the Apostolic Epistles, also—as it seems— by the reader. But the Gospel-Lesson is now[3] reserved to a deacon or presbyter, followed by exhortation from several presbyters in succession, and finally from the bishop, as befits a "steersman". This title had hitherto been reserved for Christ; and now that it was transferred to the bishop, the latter's old title of "look-out man" (ὁ πρωρεύς) passes, in a new and material rather than a spiritual sense, to the bishop's deputy or assistant, the deacon, in his function of seeing that each sat in his own proper place.[4] The addition of this whole

---

[1] *Apost. Const.* II. lvii. 10.
[2] The ψάλται of *Heading* 8.
[3] In *Apost. Const.* II. lvii. 5–9.
[4] *Apost. Const.* II. lvii. 11.

fresh simile of the Church as a ship to that proper to the original
'Didaskalia' (the simile, that is, of a flock) is seen in the next sen-
tence: "for not only to a ship, but also to a sheep-fold, has the
Church been likened".[1]

It has seemed worth while going into this detailed evidence for the
existence of an intermediate 'Didaskalia', as the immediate basis of
our 'Apostolic Constitutions' I–VI, for two reasons. First because it
is highly important to be able to allow for such an intermediate
stage in using the 'Constitutions' for historical purposes, in order to
distinguish from their author's own touches (which hold good only
for about 375 A.D.) matter which may belong rather to the first half
of the fourth century; and next because incidentally our argument
has meant some exposition of the morphology of Church-life and
-order at both stages. Both of these results will be of use to us in our
final attempt at a synthetic picture of the historical development
during the first four centuries.

APPENDED NOTE ON

EARLY FRAGMENTS CONCERNING (a) FASTING AND EUCHARIST, AND (b) THE BRINGING-IN OF LAMPS

The same Vienna-manuscript as contains the 'Diataxeis' includes
also a small fragment, which has parallels in the 'Egyptian Church-
Order' and the 'Canons of Hippolytus', but is clearly more original
than either of these.[2] It runs as follows: "Let widows and virgins
often fast and pray for[3] the Church. Let presbyters fast whensoever
they will, and laymen likewise. A bishop cannot fast, save when the
whole people also does so: for it happens sometimes that some one
wishes to make oblation,[4] and it is not possible to refuse him; but
having broken bread (for him), he (the bishop shall) by all means
taste (thereof)". Here the 'Egyptian Church-Order' paraphrases
"make oblation" by "take something (to eat) to the Church", i.e.,
to have it offered to God's uses in a meal of brotherly love
(ἀγάπη).[5] This becomes plainer from what follows. "And when

---

[1] *Apost. Const.* II. lvii. 12.

[2] See Funk, *Didascalia et Constitutiones Apostolorum* (1905), vol. ii, p. 112,
and Dix, *The Treatise on the Apostolic Tradition of St Hippolytus of Rome*
(1937), pp. 44 f.

[3] ὑπέρ, not " in," as the later versions read.

[4] [The Greek term here used is προσενεγκεῖν, one often used in a eucharistic
sense. The eucharistic sense is not, however, invariably in mind; and the
probability is that in this passage the term should be rendered simply "to bring
something" (i.e., as a charitable contribution). In that case the bread-breaking
mentioned in the immediate sequel would not be eucharistic, but somewhat
in the nature of a private agape.   C.J.C.].

[5] As is observed in the notes of Cooper and Maclean to their edition of *The
Testament of our Lord* (p. 230), the oblations of the people in kind "were
originally made for the purposes of the Agapé as well as for the Eucharist.
The name εὐλογία was afterwards used for bread formally blessed (though not

he eats it, and other believers with him, let them receive from the bishop's hand a piece of the bread (offered by him with prayer), before each one breaks his own bread. For this is (bread of) blessing,[1] but not eucharist, like the Lord's body".

Here we have a "Lord's Supper", as it is called a little further on, preserving most of the features of the eucharistic meal of a domestic type in the 'Didache'; and the 'Egyptian Church-Order' assumes that it should be taken in church. But this is not said in what was probably the original Greek of the Old-Syrian Church-Order[2]—to which we may safely assign our fragment; nor was it probably so meant, at least, in its original home in Syria. Such special oblation or consecration to God could take place in a Christian house not less than in church, as we see from what follows. Here all Christians present at a meal, by invitation of an individual, are bidden, "before eating and drinking anything" to "take a cup and give thanks,[3] and so feast".[4] This is how the original read according to the combined witness of the Latin and Ethiopic. In what follows the Latin has: "Moreover at every oblation (of this sort) let him who offers[5] (i.e., utters or joins in the prayer of blessing or consecration) remember him who invited him; because for this cause (i.e., for such remembrance) he besought him to come under his roof". The references to such Christian communion which follow (where the Latin preserves the oldest form of thought and usage) are vivid and interesting, including the reference to benediction of a Lord's Supper by a presbyter or even a deacon, from whose hand the piece of blessed bread is to be received as from the bishop's. No mere layman may say the benediction, representatively or ministerially for his fellows, when thus gathered together.

But specially striking is the long section peculiar to the Ethiopic form of the 'Egyptian Church-Order' on "the bringing-in of lamps at the supper of the congregation", i.e., at a corporate agape. It reads:[6]

consecrated) and distributed at the end of the Liturgy. This custom, which is still common in both East and West, is thought by Dr. Keating to have dated from the time when the Agapé died out". In the Latin and in the Coptic of the *Egyptian Church-Order*, but not in the Ethiopic and Arabic, which here preserve the original text, "the bread of blessing" which is to be given (afterwards) to catechumens also—who are not allowed to join the faithful at their sacred meal itself—is styled "bread of exorcism", which is quite another thing.
    [1] Cf. "pain bénit"—the phrase used even to-day.
    [2] [For the meaning of this phrase, chapter VI below should be consulted. C.J.C.].
    [3] A Jewish usage of Jesus' day.
    [4] Our authorities all add a parenthetical injunction to give a portion of the blessed bread and a cup of drink to the catechumens, who are not allowed " to sit down at the Lord's Supper" as being a meal of full Church-fellowship. This shows how sacred such fellowship in the name of God was in all its forms.
    [5] The *Egyptian Church-Order* has "eats" instead of "offers", and, at the end of the sentence, "them" for "him".
    [6] See Horner, *Statutes of the Apostles* (1904), pp. 159–161; and cf. Dix, *The Treatise on the Apostolic Tradition of St Hippolytus of Rome* (1937), pp. 50–52.

"When the evening has come, the bishop being there, the deacon shall bring in a lamp; and standing in the midst of all the faithful, being about to give thanks, the bishop shall first give the salutation, thus saying, 'The Lord (be) with you all'. And the people also shall say, 'With thy spirit'. And the bishop shall say, 'Let us give thanks to the Lord'. And the people shall say, 'Right and just! Both greatness and exaltation with glory are due to Him'. And he shall not say, 'Lift up your hearts', because that shall be said at the time of the oblation. And he prays this, saying, 'We give Thee thanks, O God, through Thy Son Jesus Christ our Lord, because Thou hast enlightened us by revealing the incorruptible light. We therefore having finished the length of a day, and having come to the beginning of the night, and having been satiated with the light of the day which Thou hast created for our satisfaction, and now since by Thy grace we have not been deficient of the light for the evening, we sanctify Thee and we glorify Thee through Thine only Son our Lord Jesus Christ, through whom to Thee with Him (be) glory and might and honour with the Holy Spirit now and for ever and world without end'. And they shall all say, 'Amen'. And having risen up therefore after supper, the children and virgins having prayed, they shall say the Psalms. And afterwards the deacon, holding the mingled cup of the oblation shall say the Psalm from that in which (is) written 'Hallelujah', after the presbyter has commanded, 'And likewise from those Psalms'. And afterwards the bishop, having offered the cup, as is proper for the cup, shall say the Psalm 'Hallelujah'; and all of them, as he recites the Psalms, shall say 'Hallelujah', which is to say, 'We praise Him who is God most high: glorified and praised is He Who founded all the world with one word'. And likewise, the Psalm having been completed, he shall give thanks over the cup, and shall give of the fragments to all the faithful. And as they are eating their supper, the believers shall take a little bread from the hand of the bishop before they partake of their own bread, for it is eulogia and not eucharist as of our Lord.

"And when the bishop speaks, let every one be silent. And if the bishop is not present, they shall receive the bread of blessing from the presbyter or from the deacon. And when the bishop speaks let all be silent, nor shall one answer another a word, for the bishop shall ask them. And if (not) the bishop but only the faithful are present at the meal, they shall take the eulogia from the hand of the presbyter if he is there; and if the presbyter is not there, they shall take from the hand of the deacon; and the catechumens also shall take their portion of the mystic bread. And if there are laymen only they shall eat quietly; and for the laymen it is not proper that they should make the eulogia".

This passage seems to describe a full Church-agape of the kind implied by Tertullian in his 'Apologeticus' (39). Perhaps, too, what we read of in the 'Church-History' of Socrates as customary in certain parts of Egypt (though not in Alexandria itself) on Saturday evenings —when, according to the Jewish reckoning, Sunday was about to begin—was not really the eucharist proper, as he supposed, but rather a benediction of the coming Lord's day over a cup of wine (and water), in continuity with the Jewish Kiddush-ceremony on the eve of *their* sacred day, the Sabbath.[1] This would explain why this archaic practice was tolerated by the Alexandrian Church, which did not itself observe it; for it would hardly have allowed the custom, had it been a matter of eucharistic usage proper. That the section in question, however, was not added to the 'Egyptian Church-Order', but was part of its original form, is shown by the traces of it still found in the Syriac 'Testament of our Lord', one of our most conservative witnesses to that Church-Order. On the other hand, it is typical of the drastic way in which the compiler of the 'Apostolic Constitutions' dealt with what was not to his mind, according to the changed ideals and practices of his own day and place, that it omits altogether not only this archaic service, but also the other and more domestic kind of agape, with its eucharistic type of preliminary blessing of God over a broken loaf and a cup of wine.

Thus the comprehensive and compilational sort of Church-Order which marks the end of the fourth century, and a little later, was formed not only by the blending of earlier bodies of rules but also by larger or smaller omissions of parts of their contents, as no longer congenial to current ideas and usages. This aspect of the case may be illustrated by further examples from almost every aspect of Church-life.

CHAPTER V

THE APOSTOLIC CHURCH-ORDER

THE special feature of the Syrian 'Didaskalia' among writings of its class—writings, that is, which deal with Church-order as an element in corporate Christian life—is the manner and degree in which it addresses the Church itself, and particularly each local church-unit under the paternal supervision and rule of its pastor or bishop. It is the holy People of God as such and the conditions of its maintaining in practice its vocation as

---

[1] Socrates, *Church-History*, v. 22: "The Egyptians in the neighbourhood of Alexandria, and the inhabitants of Thebaïs, hold their religious assemblies on the Sabbath, but do not participate of the mysteries in the manner usual among Christians in general: for after having eaten and satisfied themselves with food of all kinds, in the evening making their offerings they partake of the mysteries".

"the holy Church" of God and of His Christ, that are primarily
in mind; and various specific classes in it—whether laity (men
or women), widows, bishop, or bishop along with his assistant
deacons—are separately apostrophized, according as the general
course of the exhortation requires. There is no sustained address
to the clergy, or to the bishop as most responsible of all, over
the head as it were of the rank and file of the Church, whether
general or local. But it is otherwise, in increasing measure,
with most of the ancient Church-Orders, which are as they
stand of later date than the 'Didaskalia'. They treat Church-
order, that is, more than does the 'Didaskalia', in abstraction
from Church-life in its concrete, vital aspects; so that it is
harder to appraise the spirit or ideal of the Christianity as
working personal and even corporate experimental religion in
the various places and times which gave them birth. This we
have henceforth to bear constantly in mind.

The first of this later type of Church-Order, which may be
fitly called such in form and substance alike, is the work styled
'The Apostolic Church-Order' or 'The Ecclesiastical Canons'.
It has come down to us, however, in a later recension which
largely obscures its original genius and relatively-early date,
when it stood far nearer in spirit to the 'Didaskalia'. That our
Church-Order belongs to Egypt and to the first half of the fourth
century is generally agreed; but here agreement for the most
part ends. The date and provenance of the earlier work on which
the Egyptian edition was based are open questions, which it
will be our task to attempt to narrow down as far as possible
on the strength of the existing data.[1] The 'Apostolic Church-
Order' consists of two clearly-distinguished parts, one containing the Two Ways, which forms the first part of the 'Didache' also, the other the body of Church-rules proper. The
latter seems to have been meant to replace the latter part of
the 'Didache' by something more in keeping with current conditions and ideals. Our extant authorities are rather varied and
scattered. The original Greek is represented by one late manuscript covering the whole work.[2] Its text is fairly pure, as is

---

[1] I must warn some of my hearers that we shall be breaking fresh ground at
some points, and that I shall be glad of friendly criticism from all as to any
matter in which I seem to be outrunning the evidence or failing to carry conviction in the construction attempted. [Note interpolated by Dr. Bartlet at
this point in the manuscript. C.J.C.].

[2] A manuscript of about the twelfth century, now at Vienna. For the first
part there are other Greek manuscripts, one of the tenth century at Moscow
(entitled *Extracts from the Diataxeis of the holy Apostles*), and a group of three,

proved by a Latin version of the end of the fourth century, preserved for most of the second part in a very early but incomplete manuscript of about the sixth century, and by the Syriac and Coptic versions, also of early origin.

As an example of the sort of internal criticism which is recognized by all experts as needful in the case of our Church-Order, we may here cite Dom Connolly's remarks on its date and nature: "In attempting to find its age two points deserve special notice. (1) The author prefers that a bishop should be unmarried (ἀγύναιος): though he is willing to acquiesce in one who is ἀπὸ μιᾶς γυναικός (xvi 2)—whatever may be the force of the ἀπό. Presbyters, again, are to be elderly, and so τρόπῳ τινὶ ἀπεχομένους τῆς πρὸς γυναῖκας συνελεύσεως (xviii 1). Nothing is said in either case of duties in regard to the upbringing of children, though I Tim. iii and Titus i are under contribution. . . . This is all in a different region of ideas from the *Didascalia*, the author of which has nothing to say about celibacy, and does not even mention virgins: he assumes that the bishop will have a wife and children, . . (2) There is another passage which may well arouse suspicion. In ch. xxv Peter is made to say περὶ δὲ τῆς προσφορᾶς τοῦ σώματος καὶ τοῦ αἵματος ἀκριβῶς μηνύσωμεν. This is decidedly not early eucharistic terminology: references to the Eucharist as 'the body *of Christ*' or 'the body and blood *of the Lord*' are familiar enough in early Christian writings; but can any parallel be brought from an ante-Nicene document to this absolute use of 'the oblation of the Body and the Blood'? It seems more

---

edited by Th. Schermann, *Eine Elfapostelmoral* (Munich, 1903), which also use the division of the 'Two Ways' between the several Apostles, but apply it to the text as it stood in the earlier form of the *Apostolic Church-Order*. [A still-better edition of the Greek text was published by Schermann in 1914 under the title *Die allgemeine Kirchenordnung des zweiten Jahrhunderts* (Paderborn), pp. 12–34. C.J.C.]. The Latin Version (L), forming part of the Verona manuscript which contains also large parts of the *Didaskalia* and the "Hippolytean" Church-Order, also of the third century (with which our next chapter will deal), has been edited by E. Hauler in *Didascaliae Apostolorum Fragmenta Veronensia Latina* (Leipzig, 1900). The Syriac version (S), along with the variant readings of the Coptic, was published by Dr. J. P. Arendzen, in *The Journ. of Theol. Studies*, vol. iii, pp. 59 ff. (Oct. 1901). This edition, with its notes, is the best and most convenient form in which the text can be read, though for fuller study and criticism the older edition, with scholarly Latin commentary by F. X. Funk, entitled *Doctrina Duodecim Apostolorum* (Tübingen, 1887), is still needful. Harnack's study in the *Texte und Untersuchungen*, vol. II, v (1886), which contains text and notes, is also valuable and stimulating, but is marred by the untenable theory of two separate early written sources as pieced together in the second part of the document. There is an English translation of this by J. Owen, entitled *Sources of the Apostolic Canons*, published by A. and C. Black in 1895.

likely that the use of earlier sources in the Apostolic Church-Order has lent a false air of antiquity to it as a composition, and that 'Egyptian and monastic' would be a fair description of it".[1]

Here we have the judgment of a learned Roman Catholic scholar (based on reasons regarding which he cannot be suspected of a bias to see in them evidence of later date than seems needful), to the effect that the 'Apostolic Church-Order' "can hardly be placed so early as even the end of the third century". On the exact matter of date, indeed, required by the above two points, I shall make clear my own opinion in the sequel. But in any case Dom Connolly witnesses to the need of distinguishing between earlier and later elements in the work. When we apply such internal criteria, and others of a more-formal nature, particularly the different series of Apostolic speakers in the first and in the second parts, as well as the confused order in which the names occur in certain sections of the latter, we shall, I believe, be able to get far back behind the later features—some of which are really Egyptian and belong to the fourth century —to a considerably earlier and simpler picture of Church-conditions. In fact we reach a stage not far removed from that revealed in the 'Didaskalia', which seems (in some form) to be known and used by the author even of the original form of our work. This would point to a period about 225–250 A.D.; but as the region represented by the two works is not quite the same, though perhaps adjacent—as, for example, Cilicia and Cappadocia are to northern Syria—it is not possible to draw exact chronological inferences from their different types of organized life.

One special and interesting feature of our Church-Order, which has to be borne in mind throughout, is that it belongs to a region where the Church was largely in a missionary-stage, throwing out fresh outposts beyond the churches already in being, and so the more requiring such a directory as this for the guidance of new groups of Christians desirous of being organized as self-contained churches on normal lines. This appears clearly from the opening words of the second part, where a group of less than a dozen male adult Christians is in question. It is altogether probable, then, that the Church-order here sketched,

---

[1] Connolly in *The Journ. of Theol. Studies*, vol. xxiv, pp. 155 f. (Jan. 1923). He observes in a footnote that "Harnack places it between 300 and 350, Bardenhewer at the close of the third century (later than the *Didascalia*)".

in the first instance, should present only the simplest and most general outlines, and so would seem to stand in need of supplementation—before the close of the third century. But the work becomes the more interesting in this light, as directing our attention to the things felt to be most essential (alike in the ministry and the qualifications for it and in the type of Christian life), which determined first the original forms and then the changes made in them. And this becomes the more instructive, if we are able to compare the fresh things which were felt to call for emphasis in more than one later recension. Thus the sacerdotal conception of the ministry seems to emerge only at the stage after 300 A.D., while concern lest the ministry of women should be too far-reaching—so as to include even liturgical ministry at the eucharist—appears perhaps rather earlier. We have referred already to a recension which arose, as Dom Connolly holds, some century or so later than the original nucleus, and on the different Church-soil of Egypt. But there are, if I mistake not, clear traces also of an earlier revision, adapting it to later ideas in its own native regions, probably Cilicia or Cappadocia, somewhere about 275–300 A.D.[1]

The following typical sections will illustrate the working of the above literary and historical analysis and show in each case the homogeneity of the secondary and tertiary matter characteristic respectively of the periods A.D. 250–300 and A.D. 300–350, as distinct from 200–250 A.D.

"Peter said, 'If there exist a paucity of men, and there be not yet to hand a full complement of those able to vote about a bishop—less (that is) than twelve men, let them write to the

---

[1] [There follow, at this point in Dr. Bartlet's manuscript twenty-one sheets of written matter, bearing upon the literary problems connected with the *Apostolic Church-Order*. Some of this material was apparently used in or for "Lect. V. Ap. C.O.": but it is not in finished form, nor does it constitute a unity, being in three distinct sections, not easy to relate to one another. I shrink from omitting from my printed edition of the lectures so large a portion of what Dr. Bartlet had apparently written for one of them; but there seem to be three good reasons for doing so. (1) It would be extremely difficult, if not impossible, to transcribe and present the matter in a form that would be readily intelligible to the reader. (2) The discussion of the literary phenomena and their interpretation is very complicated and evidently highly conjectural. (3) What weighs most is that Dr. Bartlet, in having clearly excluded these pages from his typescript, seems not to have wished to publish or perpetuate them. The rest of the chapter as printed above is introduced on the typescript by an insertion ("The following typical sections", etc.) in Dr. Bartlet's own hand, and thus seems unmistakably to be the whole of what he wished to substitute in the published form of the work for the twenty-one sheets here omitted. His numbering of the typed pages points to the same conclusion. C.J.C.].

neighbouring church(es), where it[1] chances to be planted, in order that thence may come three chosen men and test carefully him that is worthy—if any one has a fair repute with the heathen, [if he is free from sin, a friend of the poor, self-controlled, not a drunkard, not a fornicator, not over-reaching or abusive, or a respecter of persons, and such-like]. [[It is a fair thing indeed that he be without wife: but otherwise, having had (but) one wife, cultured, able to interpret the scriptures; but if unlettered, let him be of a meek disposition, and let him abound in love towards all]]; lest perchance a bishop becomes convicted by popular opinion of any fault' ".[2]

"John said, 'The appointed bishop [knowing the devotion and love for God of those about him] shall appoint whomsoever he shall have tested, as presbyters, two in number'. [[All replied to this and said, 'Not two but three. . . ' "]].[3] " . . . 'The presbyters, then, must be men already of long time in the world [[in some fashion abstaining from sexual intercourse]], generous towards the brotherhood, not respecting a man's person, [[fellow-initiates of the bishop and supporters of his, assembling the congregation together, zealous for the pastor]]' ". The functions of the (twenty-four) Elders are next differentiated into two groups in the worship of the Church, while in discipline they were all to unite and act corporately.[4]

" James said, 'Let a reader be appointed, after first having been carefully tested, [not a tongue-wagger, not a drunkard nor yet a jester, seemly in bearing, persuasive, of good sense, first to hasten to the gatherings on the Lord's Day], easy to hear, good at exposition ($\delta \iota \eta \gamma \eta \tau \iota \kappa \acute{o} s$), [knowing that he is performing the office of an Evangelist], [[For he who fills the ears of one who does not understand (the Scripture as read) shall be accounted as written down (for good) before God]]'."[5]

"Kephas said, 'Let widows be appointed, three in number—two of them persevering in prayer for all those in trial and with a

[1] This singular suggests that originally the antecedent was "church" not "churches", which latter would be an easy correction when the rule came to be that *three* bishops were needful.
[2] *Apost. Ch.-Order*, xvi.
[3] *Apost. Ch.-Order*, xvii. The second emendation must contain a primitive textual error, namely, "three" for "twenty-four", for the text goes on to cite in support the twenty-four Elders of the Apocalypse.
[4] *Apost. Ch.-Order*, xviii.
[5] *Apost. Ch.-Order*, xix.

view to revelations touching whatsoever is needful, and one attending upon those tried by sicknesses. [Let her be fit for ministering, sober, reporting to the presbyters what things are requisite, not a lover of filthy lucre, not addicted to much wine, so that she may be able to be soberly fit for night-services and for any other sort of good deeds she may desire to do. For these things are the Lord's chief good treasures]' ".[1]

CHAPTER VI

THE "HIPPOLYTEAN" CHURCH-ORDER

THE subject lying behind this title is one of the most complicated, and until quite-recently one of the most enigmatic, of those connected with Church-Orders as a branch of ecclesiastical literature. It was opened afresh, more than thirty years ago, by Dr. Hans Achelis in his study of what he called 'Die Canones Hippolyti',[2] a body of Church-rules extant only in Arabic, but having an older basis in common with several other Eastern Church-Orders, particularly the so-called 'Egyptian Church-Order', extant in Coptic, Ethiopic, Arabic, and partly in Latin, and parts of the eighth book of the 'Apostolic Constitutions', which date from the last quarter of the fourth century. But while Achelis's careful comparative study of these, exhibited in parallel columns, showed that in much of its contents the so-called 'Canons of Hippolytus' were earlier than this last, and in a smaller number of points earlier even than the 'Egyptian Church-Order', it was evident that in not a few it was later than both: so that scholars differed widely as to the exact relations of the three inter-connected documents, and were at a loss to account for them fully and satisfactorily.[3]

[1] *Apost. Ch.-Order*, xxi. [For the penultimate sentence Dr. Bartlet apparently adopted a conjecturally-emended text. The Greek seems to mean : "And (so too) if any other woman desires to do good deeds". C.J.C.].

[2] In *Texte und Untersuchungen*, vol. VI, iv (1891).

[3] [This section of Dr. Bartlet's work will perhaps be somewhat more readily understood if certain items of the relevant data are clearly stated here.

It is known for certain that Hippolytus of Rome (born about 160 A.D., martyred about 238 A.D.) wrote περὶ χαρισμάτων ἀποστολικὴ παράδοσις. What is not certain is whether these words designate one work or two, and in what extant documents, if any, it (or they) survive.

The view held by Dom Connolly and by many other scholars along with him is

(a) that *two* works are indicated by these four words:

(b) that the treatise περὶ χαρισμάτων was lost:

(c) that the discussion of χαρίσματα in *Apost. Const.* VIII. i f. was written with-

Lightfoot, indeed, in the great essay on Hippolytus appended
to his second volume on Clement of Rome, had already a year
before Achelis's book appeared pointed in the right direction
for a solution of the problem as to the nature of the work to
which, as to a nucleus, the common element in the above-
mentioned works really went back.[1] 'The Canons of Hippolytus'
were right as to the name of the author of that work, but the
word 'Canons' was misleading in the suggestion as to its nature.
It was in fact something less formal, something more-closely
bound up with Church-life, namely, a treatise 'on Gifts of Grace'—
περὶ χαρισμάτων ἀποστολικὴ παράδοσις, to quote the title included
in the list of Hippolytus's writings carved on the base of the
episcopal chair, in which he was represented in stone a few
years after his death, and which was discovered in situ at Rome
in the sixteenth century. Traces of this treatise Lightfoot found,
not only in the Arabic Canons, but also in the title of a collection
of 'Ordinances' (Διατάξεις), closely related to the eighth book of
the 'Apostolic Constitutions', and labelled 'Ordinances of the
holy Apostles touching Ordinations (χειροτονιῶν), through the
medium of Hippolytus';[2] further, the matter which this collection immediately follows was styled 'Teaching of the holy
Apostles touching Gifts of Grace'.[3] This is practically identical
with the first two chapters of the eighth book of the 'Apostolic
Constitutions', which deal with such Divine gifts, imparted

out a source, and was put where it was because *Apost. Const.* VIII. iii (for
which see below) begins with an allusion to a foregoing treatise on
χαρίσματα:

(d) that the so-called *Egyptian Church-Order* (see Dr. Bartlet's first paragraph) represents fairly-closely the actual work of Hippolytus entitled
ἀποστολικὴ παράδοσις.

In opposition to this view, Dr. Bartlet believed

(a) that the four words represented but one Hippolytean treatise, *The
Apostolic Tradition concerning Grace-gifts:*
(b) that it was not a "Church-Order" (Hippolytus never having written one),
but dealt mainly with orthodox belief:
(c) that it was transported from Italy to Syria, and was there re-edited, and
also expanded by the substitution, for its latter part, of a set of Church-
regulations:
(d) that the section on χαρίσματα became embodied in *Apost. Const.* VIII. i f.:
(e) that the expanded section on Church-regulations was later embodied in
i. The *Egyptian Church-Order*, about 250–300 A.D.
ii. The *Testament of our Lord*, about 350 A.D.
iii. The *Apostolic Constitutions*, about 380 A.D.
iv. The *Canons of Hippolytus* (edited by Achelis), about 400 A.D. (?).
C.J.C.].

[1] Lightfoot, *The Apostolic Fathers*, Part I, vol. ii (1890), pp. 400–403.
[2] Funk, *Didascalia et Const. Apost.* vol. ii (1905), pp. XI–XIX, 77–84. This
is the document otherwise known as *Epitome* or *Constitutiones per Hippolytum*,
and usually regarded as later than *Apost. Const.*
[3] *Ibid.* pp. 72–77.

both to worthy and unworthy recipients, as recorded in Scripture, and warn men against pride in the possession of such, particularly as this possession is no guarantee of personal acceptance with God.

Lightfoot held that the full title of Hippolytus's work underlying these chapters was 'Apostolic Tradition concerning Gifts of Grace', and that the four Greek words representing this on the chair did not refer to *two* separate treatises, entitled respectively 'Concerning Charismata' and 'Apostolic Tradition'. He suggested that "Hippolytus, starting from the discussion of the χαρίσματα generally, might have been led to speak about some of the special gifts" (qualifying for Church-ministry) "mentioned in S. Paul's two lists (1 Cor. xii. 28, Ephes. iv. 11), and that some later editor, working up the material of Hippolytus and others, would give to it the name of this father"[1]—as was done in the case of the 'Apostolic Ordinances' just referred to, as handed down 'through Hippolytus'. This was an attractive hypothesis; and as regards its first part, probably near the truth. But in the light of the fresh evidence made available since Lightfoot wrote, its second part no longer seems to hold good.

The chief new factor is that afforded by the discovery and publication of the precious Verona-fragments of a Latin version, not only of the 'Didaskalia' and the 'Apostolic Church-Order', but also of the "Hippolytean" Church-Order conjectured by Lightfoot, and that in a form purer in text and nearer to the original form of the treatise than any of our hitherto-known authorities.[2] The available material had a year before been increased also by the publication in Syriac by Rahmani of the 'Testament of our Lord' (accompanied by a Latin translation).[3] This, which forms the first two books of the Syrian 'Octateuch', or eight books of Church-order, claiming to come from the Apostles through Clement, the special disciple of Peter, was almost unknown to scholars, though most of it had been published already in 1856 by Lagarde, with a Greek rendering, from a manuscript (Codex Sangermanensis 38), which gave it only in a series of full extracts.[4] Later there came a critical

---

[1] Lightfoot, as above, p. 402.

[2] E. Hauler, *Didascaliae Apostolorum Fragmenta Veronensia Latina; accedunt Canonum qui dicuntur Apostolorum et Aegyptiorum Reliquiae*, Leipzig, 1900.

[3] I. E. Rahmani (Uniat Syrian Patriarch of Antioch), *Testamentum Domini nostri Jesu Christi*, Mainz, 1899.

[4] A. P. de Lagarde, *Reliquiae Juris ecclesiastici antiquissimae*, Leipzig, 1856.

edition by the Rev. G. Horner (with an English Version) of the Egyptian 'Statutes of the Apostles', as found in Sahidic, Arabic, and Ethiopic translations.[1] Finally the full Syriac version was published in a French translation by F. Nau;[2] and this enables us to check and correct at certain vital points the witness of the Latin version, since it goes back in places to the original form of the "Hippolytean" matter contained in the preface to the 'Ordinances of the holy Apostles touching Ordinations, through the medium of Hippolytus'. At one important point, too, it is supported by the evidence of the Ethiopic text of this preface. By the aid of these we are now able to reach pretty clear and firm results.

The key to the situation is a preface to the matter in the Latin version (L) which is parallel to the common element in the 'Egyptian Church-Order', the 'Testament of Our Lord', the 'Apostolic Constitutions', the 'Canons of Hippolytus', and particularly the 'Ordinances of the holy Apostles touching Ordinations' to which Lightfoot appealed, and which is commonly called the 'Epitome' of the eighth book of the 'Apostolic Constitutions'. This last is really more than an epitome, since it goes back at certain points, behind the work of the compiler of the 'Apostolic Constitutions', to the "Hippolytean" Church-Order which he was using. Restored to its original form by the aid of these witnesses, and also of the form in which the eighth book of the 'Apostolic Constitutions' appears in the Syrian Octateuch, the preface ran as follows.

" The first points, indeed, of the discourse we have duly set forth, touching the Gifts of Grace—as many, that is, as God from the beginning according to His own will supplied to men, in bringing to Himself that image" (of Himself, i.e., man, cf. Gen. i. 26 f.) "which had gone astray—but also[3] how we have convicted the conduct of those who attempt to speak false-

---

[1] G. Horner, *The Statutes of the Apostles or Canones Ecclesiastici*, London, 1904.

[2] F. Nau, *La version syriaque de l'Octateuque de Clément*, Paris, 1913.

[3] From here to the end of the sentence the Syriac, where it diverges from the text of *Apost. Const.* (which it generally follows), restores for us the original wording of Hippolytus known to the copyist to whom the Greek text behind the Syriac goes back. Its absence from L and the Egyptian Church-Order is easily explained by the consideration that, once the actual text of the first part of Hippolytus's work *On Charismata* was omitted—as in the recension common to L and the *Egyptian Church-Order*—it was no longer ad rem to retain, in the section now used merely as preface to a Church-Order, a back-reference of this purely-negative nature to matter which was no longer felt to be worth preserving.

hoods or are moved by an alien spirit; demonstrating by argument, to those who either by ignorance or of deliberate will are
being driven to error, how God has often made use even of
wicked people for both prophecy and the doing of wonders.
But now, led on by love towards all the saints, we have been
carried forward to the climax of the ecclesiastical tradition, in
order that those who have been well taught may through our
exposition guard the tradition that has remained until now, and
may by its recognition abide more steadfast, in consequence of
that lapse which through ignorance has lately been invented,
and of those who are in ignorance, in order that, the holy Spirit
vouchsafing full grace to those who believe aright, they may
come to perceive how (they) ought to hand down and guard all
those which are established in the Church".[1]

Here we have, in the first sentence, obvious reference to a
discussion on Charismata such as occurs in the eighth book of
the 'Apostolic Constitutions'; and there is no reason to doubt
that the original Greek of the "Hippolytean" Church-Order (as
distinct from the version used for L) did contain the part of
Hippolytus's own work on Charismata proper, even if in an
earlier form than that now extant only in the first two chapters
of that eighth book. Certainly it did not claim to represent
apostolic authority, as the 'Egyptian Church-Order' does.[2]

When we compare the second half of this preface with what
follows in L and the related witnesses, we are struck by the
difference between what we should expect and what we actually
find. The sort of "tradition", from the first until the writer's
own day (compare the singular verb "I counsel", at the end of
L, already cited), to which the preface surely points, is one of
true faith, not of correct Church-order. And in point of fact the
Syriac version of the passage, the text of which goes here, as at
other points, behind that enshrined in the 'Apostolic Constitu-

---

[1] The materials on which this construction is based may be seen in Horner,
Statutes, etc., p. 162; in *The Journ. of Theol. Studies*, vol. xvi, p. 329 (Apl. 1915),
and vol. xxii, pp. 358 f. (July 1921); and in Dix, *The Treatise on the Apostolic
Tradition of St Hippolytus of Rome* (1937), pp. 1 f. The grammar of the last
clause of the Latin version is lame. Perhaps it should run, "Omnia ea quae
ecclesiae prosunt" (not "omnia eos qui ecclesiae praesunt"), which would
bring it closer to the Ethiopic, and to the idea of "Haec itaque si cum gratia
et fide recta accipiuntur, *praestant aedificationem in ecclesia* . . ." at the close of
the Latin.

[2] "It is the work of one person, who 'counsels', but does not 'command',
those who are 'bene sapientes' to keep the 'apostolic tradition' as he has
essayed to set it before them" (Dom Connolly, in *Texts and Studies*, vol. VIII,
pt. iv, p. 146).

tions' to the common Hippolytean basis, actually has "the faith which is proper in the churches" as its paraphrase for "tradition", the word used in the Latin, and for "outline-picture" (διατυπώσεως) which appears in the 'Apostolic Constitutions' and which made the reference to its own sequel more definite and so departed more-widely from Hippolytus. What was in the mind of the original writer was to secure the fidelity of "those who have been well taught" to a tradition not of sound discipline but of true doctrine. And this interpretation is fully borne out by the peroration in L, corresponding to its preface. For there we read: "These things, then, if they are received[1] with grace and right[2] faith, afford edification in the Church and eternal life to believers. That these things be guarded by all those of good mind I counsel. For if all hear the apostolic tradition[3] and keep it, no heretic, nor yet any man at all, shall cause them to err. For so the numerous heresies increased, because they who were leaders would not learn the purpose of the Apostles, but after their own pleasure do what they like, not what is fitting".

Here the reference to "heretics", rather than schismatics or simply to those who held erroneous views of Church-order, makes fairly clear the kind of "error" which was in Hippolytus's mind and must have run through his whole treatise. It was error of the kind common to "the numerous heresies" to which he here refers, and to the refutation of which he himself devoted so much of his energy. It was fundamental error, striking at the root of "right" belief such as he himself traced to the action of the holy Spirit in the soul, and such as he classed with "charismata"—nay, such as he made the chief "charisma", the root of all others in their true or Divine form. So, too, what he set over against error was "Apostolic tradition" on this crucial issue, or, as he styles it, "the crowning point of the ecclesiastical tradition", such as was embodied in the Rule of Faith taught to candidates for membership in the Church at baptism. This fits in completely, as the other type of "tradition" does not, with

---

[1] The *Egyptian Church-Order* in the eastern versions has "Ye receive . . . ye will . . . be graciously granted"—a change of person due to taking the sentence as referring to the immediately-previous context rather than, as it really does, to the whole foregoing work.

[2] I.e., "orthodox," a rendering which, in one of the two distinct forms of this passage in L, Dom Connolly (p. 145, n. 2) brilliantly restores from its servilely-literal form "recta gloriosae"=Greek ὀρθοδόξου. Cf. the words in the preface: "the holy Spirit affording full grace to those who believe aright" ("recte", i.e., orthodoxly).

[3] Here the Latin breaks off; and for the rest we have only the eastern versions of the *Egyptian Church-Order*.

what Hippolytus says above as to the comprehensive purpose of God's gifts of grace,[1] namely, that they were means whereby God restores to Himself man, as made in His own image, after man had lost this by going astray into sin. It was, then, with the further development of this theme—and that at its crowning point, the gift of grace par excellence, God's unspeakable gift in the Incarnation of His Divine Son, that the sequel in Hippolytus's 'Concerning Charismata' originally dealt.

This suggestion finds further support in the forms under which the preface appears in the 'Canons of Hippolytus'. That work, while late and interpolated in its present Arabic form, at times preserves traces of the common basis of the group of documents we are considering as witnesses to an "Hippolytean" Church-Order. Its first section is entitled 'On the holy Faith', and is as follows.[2] "Before all we speak of the holy, true faith in our Lord Jesus Christ, the Son of the living God. We have formulated it in the creed, in which we agree with all steadfastness. Thus we say then in truth . . . that He (is) the Word (Λόγος), the Son of God, Who is the creator of all creation [visible and invisible]. This we have formulated, and we in truth agree in it. But to those who err and speak what is unlawful (Unerlaubtes) about the Word of God, it will turn out as our Lord Christ has spoken of them. Therefore have we united together all the closer in the power of God, and have separated them, because they agree not with the Holy Scriptures, God's Word, nor with us the disciples of the Scriptures.[3] Accordingly we have separated them from the Church and referred their case to God, Who will judge the whole creation in righteousness. But to those who are unaware[4] we make this known without malice, lest they fall like the heretics into an evil death, but that they may be deemed worthy of eternal life, and may teach their children and successors this one and only Faith".

Here, apart from two intrusive clauses near the beginning[5] on

---

[1] A clause significantly omitted by the compiler of *Apost. Const.*, as though it alluded to what was made plain only in the part of Hippolytus's work which he does not use.

[2] I follow the text used in W. Riedel's German Version in *Die Kirchenrechtsquellen des Patriarchats Alexandrien* (Leipzig, 1900), pp. 200 f., which improves on the Latin version given in Achelis, *op. cit.*, pp. 38 f.

[3] This sentence is quite in Hippolytus's style throughout, as in fact is most of what precedes and follows, judging particularly by his attitude and language to the party of Zephyrinus and Callistus, the bishops of Rome about A.D. 198–222.

[4] This sounds like a manifesto addressed to Christians everywhere, like Hippolytus's great work on Heresies.

[5] One of which upsets the grammar, "the Trinity" being followed by "He".

the Trinity, which is not here in question, there is not a line which might not have come from the pen of Hippolytus, in his polemic against the Monarchian theory of Christ's nature, to which he opposed the Logos-type of Christology. It was relative to this doctrine of the Logos, as God's proper image even before the creation of man, that Hippolytus thought of man as derivatively "the image of God", ere he fell away by sin from that high estate, and so needed gifts of Divine grace to help his restoration to God. But the climax and crown of this process of restoration was the Incarnation and the gifts of the Spirit flowing therefrom.

Let us now, in this light, look more closely into the discussion on charismata which precedes this preface and which is found in the first two chapters of the eighth book of the 'Apostolic Constitutions', to see if it is of a piece with such a line of thought —even though its form there may not be altogether the same as what Hippolytus wrote in the first part of his work 'On Charismata', and whether, in that case, it casts any light forward upon what might be needful to complete the whole argument which Hippolytus had in mind, so far as we can judge of that argument from the hints in the preface and from the further extract which underlies the opening of the 'Canons of Hippolytus'.

It opens with the fact that "our God and Saviour" (an expression of Hippolytus, found for instance in a fragment 'On the Theophaneia'),[1] Jesus Christ, when "handing over to us the great mystery of godliness, furnished his followers for their work of witness to the world with Spirit-given charismata. These were bestowed (first on the Apostles, then on other believers), "not for the advantage of those who work them", but for that of those on whom they are wrought.[2] Thus ability to cast out demons is less a ground of joy for believers than the fact of having one's name written in heaven: for the former is a matter simply of God's power, but the latter implies human good-will and earnestness, aided, to be sure, by God. Further,

---

[1] [The Hippolytean authorship of this baptismal address is, however, gravely doubtful. A few detached pages of manuscript remain, written in Dr. Bartlet's hand, in which he brings out the genuine Hippolytean character of certain ideas in this treatise; but as the notes are incomplete and do not fit in easily, and are moreover labelled by Dr. Bartlet "cancelled", I have not included them.   C.J.C.].

[2] Here there seem to be echoes, as would be natural, of thoughts in Hippolytus's master, Irenaeus (*Adv. Haer.*, II. xxxi. 2 f., xxxii. 4 f., V. vi. 1: cf. the reference which follows to believers as "casting out demons, or raising dead persons, or speaking with tongues" (*Apost. Const.* VIII. i. 4).

even works of power do not convert all men, but only those whose souls are made ready or "worthy of salvation" by the inner working of the Spirit of Grace. Nor, again, are the signs themselves wrought by the strength of the worker, but by God's own will. Hence those possessing charismata should not be uplifted and look down on those who have them not;[1] since, after all, "there is no man who has believed through Christ upon God who has not received a spiritual charisma. For the very breaking with the impiety of polytheism and believing in God . . . is a charisma of God".[2] Similarly, right belief in the truths of the Incarnation of "the Divine Logos", when not mere irrational assent, but an act of judgment and full conviction, means the reception from God of a charisma, as likewise does the being clear of all heresy.[3] "For God's charismata, given by Him through Christ, are diverse"; not only those named by Paul but also foreknowledge of things to come, the word of teaching, endurance of evil, and lawful continence.[4]

Here the spirituality of the comparative assessment of the grace involved respectively in works of power and in spiritual states of mind is a striking feature, and one which points to a writer like Hippolytus. And the same also is true of the writer's view of official ministries in the Church, resting on special gifts, as compared with the fundamental grace involved in being a true Christian. For "to be a Christian, indeed, rests with us, but to be an Apostle or bishop or anything else rests not with us, but with the God who giveth the charismata".[5]

"So much then for those deemed worthy of charismata".[6] But further, charismata are no guarantee of piety or character, as is shown by many Biblical examples, alike in the Old and the New Testament, in which the prophet or exorcist had no "spark of godliness", but was "laden with ignorance owing to voluntary badness".[7] Thus it is evident that there are false prophets, and

---

[1] *Apost. Const.* VIII. i. 8. Here there may be reference to the attitude of Montanists to ordinary Christians at large. But we must also remember that the Roman Modalists, like Zephyrinus and Callistus, seem to have had more in common than had Hippolytus and his party in Rome with the charismatic side of Montanism.

[2] *Apost. Const.* VIII. i. 9 f.

[3] *Apost. Const.* VIII. i. 11.

[4] *Apost. Const.* VIII. i. 12. On the charisma of prediction, cf. Iren. *Adv. Haer.* II. xxxii. 4.

[5] *Apost. Const.* VIII. i. 21.

[6] *Apost. Const.* VIII. i. 22: the added words "or official posts" ($\dot{\eta}$ $\dot{\alpha}\xi\iota\omega\mu\acute{\alpha}\tau\omega\nu$) probably come from the compiler, whose hand is also visible in i. 19–21 and ii. 8–10. To Hippolytus charismata included $\dot{\alpha}\xi\iota\acute{\omega}\mu\alpha\tau\alpha$.

[7] *Apost. Const.* VIII. ii. 1 f.

those in office who forfeit their right to their title. "Neither an ungodly king is any longer really a king, but a tyrant; nor is a bishop laden with ignorance or evil-mindedness any longer a bishop, but is false to his name, being put forward not by God but by men. . .".[1] As false prophets in the Bible, so also false bishops and presbyters shall not escape God's judgments. In so saying, the writer explains, one does not set at naught true prophecies, but aims at restraining the overweening spirit of vainglorious men; and he adds that from such God takes away His grace.[2]

This last sentence seems to refer to the whole of the foregoing passage on false possessors of charismata and of offices resting thereon. It would lead on naturally, and at once, to the opening words of the transition to the second part of the original treatise, with its reference to charismata as furthering God's grand object (the bringing of erring man back to likeness to Himself) and to the urgent need—imposed by the dangers of the hour—of seeing clearly and holding fast by the Church's true faith as handed down from the first. The brief summary of that faith, as centring in a true view of the person of the Incarnate Saviour, which the 'Canons of Hippolytus' preserves (in preference to the general opening words of the preface), may well have come next. And then what? Here I venture to hope that I have lit upon an answer which at once completes and confirms my suggested solution of the problem as to the nature of Hippolytus's genuine work, which formed the nucleus of the later so-called "Hippolytean" Church-Order. It at the same time removes the difficulties which arise from the assumption that the contents of that work were almost wholly from the pen of Hippolytus, and so represent a circle at least of the Roman church early in the third century.

The true answer to the question as to what Hippolytus meant by "the climax ($\kappa o \rho v \phi a \iota \acute{o} \tau a \tau o v$ [$\kappa o \rho v \phi \acute{\eta} v$?])[3] of the ecclesiastical tradition", and by those things which, when "received with grace and right faith, afford edification in the Church and eternal life to believers"—as he says in his peroration—is to

---

[1] *Apost. Const.* VIII. ii. 4. Here we seem to hear the authentic voice of Hippolytus, in his attitude to Callistus, bishop of Rome.

[2] *Apost. Const.* VIII. ii. 5–7: the passage closes with a verbatim quotation of 1 Peter v. 5. What follows to the end of the chapter (8–10) seems to be due to the compiler of *Apost. Const.*, as it is in terms of supposed Apostolic authorship, and has marked parallels with other parts of his workmanship.

[3] See above, pp. 109 f.

be found, as is natural, in the mode of thought and speech characteristic of his master Irenaeus. With him that which is at once the crown and ground-plan of the Church's structure, as the living temple of God, is none other than her creed, otherwise compared to the standard measuring-rule (regula, Gk. κανών) by use of which the work of building is to proceed and be tested. This itself is the prime gift of grace from God, her Architect and Lord. It is this which Irenaeus describes as "the sure grace-gift of the Truth (charisma veritatis certum)", received "along with succession to the office of oversight, according to the Father's good pleasure", by "those presbyters who are in the Church", holding "succession from the Apostles", as distinct from "those who stand apart from the primary succession (principali successione)", and about whose possession of this grace-gift, the true tradition, one may therefore not be sure. This applies both to heretics and schismatics, lifted up and "pleasing themselves", rather than conforming to God's chosen order for handing on His truth securely.[1] "From all such therefore one ought to keep aloof, but to adhere to those who both guard, as we have already said, the Apostles' teaching, and along with the order of the presbyterate manifest healthful speech and conduct without offence".[2] Of this deposit of the true faith Christ is the sum and substance, being "the treasure hid in the Scriptures".[3]

This is exactly Hippolytus's idea. It is his duty (as a bishop), to which also God's "love for all the saints"—not only in Rome but throughout the whole Church—constrains him, to "expound" or explain authentic "tradition", over against lapse from it, due largely to "ignorance" or incompetence in thought. Such error he describes elsewhere[4] as having recently arisen both in provincial Asia and in Rome, under Zephyrinus, the mentally-untrained bishop of Rome (198–217 A.D.), but particularly under Callistus who succeeded him as bishop (217–222 A.D.). Hippolytus, after strenuously opposing this tendency in its confessed representatives—like Noëtus who came from Smyrna and formed what he calls a "school" outside the Roman church proper[5]—and their secret abetter, Callistus, under the

---

[1] Irenaeus, *Adv. Haer.* IV. xxvi. 2.
[2] Irenaeus, *Adv. Haer.* IV. xxvi. 4.
[3] Irenaeus, *Adv. Haer.* IV. xxvi. 1.
[4] *Refutatio Omnium Haeresium*, ix and x.
[5] [The widely-held view that Noëtus came to Rome is not supported by any ancient evidence. C.J.C.].

episcopate of Zephyrinus, felt forced, once Callistus became
bishop, to separate him and his adherents from the communion
of the true Church, as he esteemed it, namely, from the communion of those loyal to the true doctrine of the person of Christ in
particular, even though these formed only the numerical
minority. Of the true believers in Rome, then, Hippolytus
regarded himself as the bishop, the residuary trustee of the
function of pastoral oversight or episcopate[1] vacated by Callistus, who, on the principles laid down in the opening part of the
treatise 'On Charismata', had by heresy forfeited his right to the
title.

This work of Hippolytus, then, as a whole, in the light of the
universal form of its address, and also in view of its closing
words, with their strong personal note of grave advice to all
concerned, is now seen to be a general manifesto or appeal
from the local opinion in Rome—which for the time had gone
astray—to the Church at large. This fact explains not only its
language and contents, as here interpreted, but also the fact
that there is no other indubitable trace of the second part, with
its more-patent polemic against the majority of the Roman
church and its so-called bishop. That part of Hippolytus's work
contained matter critical of Callistus which the later Church in
all circles would gladly allow to die. And so the treatise as a
whole has failed to survive by not being copied in its original
form,[2] and that in spite of its author's high repute as an orthodox theologian. But the first part of the manifesto contained
matter too valuable to be allowed to suffer the same fate. It
was therefore adopted as leading up to and prefacing an
exposition of the Church's tradition in a certain locality,
touching the ground-plan of "Apostolic tradition" in another
and different sense from that intended by Hippolytus, viz.,
one of Church-order.

Towards the substitution of this other meaning of "tradi-

---

[1] The question as to whether and how Hippolytus was ordained to the
episcopal office is an open one, which must be reserved for the present.
[2] I suggest, with some confidence, that the bulk of "the ecclesiastical tradition" which Hippolytus went on to expound and justify in the larger part of
his *Apostolic Tradition touching Charismata*, does survive—without its polemic
against Callistus—in two known quarters. The *first* is the Pseudo-Tertullianic
treatise *Adversus Omnes Haereses*, generally recognized as based on a work
of Hippolytus. It opens abruptly, and ends with a brief section on Noëtus
[Praxeas? C.J.C.]. The full Hippolytean discussion of this important form
of error from Hippolytus's own standpoint, which may once have come here,
really survives in the *second* of the two quarters referred to above, viz., Hippolytus's *Homily against the Heresy of one Noëtus*.

tion", one element in the original contents of Hippolytus's treatise may well have contributed; and that is the element which has hitherto been urged as the chief argument for the Hippolytean origin of the great bulk of the Church-Order in question—the document which to-day is usually called, from one of the chief sources of our knowledge of it, the 'Egyptian Church-Order'. I mean the Baptismal Creed which is found, rather oddly, in the midst of the description of the various orders of ministry and of other classes and customs of the Christian community. It is perfectly natural that Hippolytus in his manifesto urbi et orbi should have quoted the Baptismal Creed, and have done so in the current Roman form, when dealing with the crowning part of the Church's traditional faith —the part connected with the true view of the Person of Christ, which he set himself to expound in terms of the Logos-doctrine as an element in the full doctrine of the Godhead. Confirmation of this suggestion may be found in the fact that it is as preface to a baptismal order of Syrian type that the extract found at the beginning of the "Hippolytean" Church-order in our other sources occurs in a unique part of the Ethiopic form of the 'Egyptian Church-Order'. Here the author of this fresh conjunction has kept closer to the nature of the original second part of Hippolytus's work.[1]

Some may feel that too much space has been spent in this rather formal and technical discussion of the nature of the true Hippolytean sequel to the first part of his treatise 'On Charismata'. But the issues hanging on the right view as to the region and the date represented by the Church-Order here in question are of the greatest historical moment. At not a few points the true theory of the development of Church-order, both generally and on specific matters, depends largely on whether this body of usages reflects conditions at the opening rather than the middle or close of the third century; and again, whether it applies primarily to West or East, be the date what it

---

[1] See Horner, *Statutes of the Apostles* (1904), pp. 162 ff. On the above view of the whole matter, it seems needless to argue against the theory at present prevalent among experts in this field, at least in England, to the effect that, contrary to Lightfoot's opinion, *two* treatises of Hippolytus, an *Apostolic Tradition* and a *Concerning Charismata* were used in the composition of the so-called "Hippolytean" Church-Order (or the 'Egyptian Church-Order)'. For the whole reading of the original meaning of Hippolytus's own words which preface the "Hippolytean" Church-Order is here called in question; and if rightly, the other theory, in every shape and form, simply falls to the ground as lacking any positive support.

may.[1] Much, then, of our construction of other evidence, before and after the third century as well as falling within it, is being virtually determined, one way or another, by the truth or error of our theory on what has thus far been occupying us in this chapter.

On this point, that of the importance of the issue we have been trying to settle, it may perhaps be well to cite the witness of Dom R. H. Connolly, the learned author of the fullest and most-thorough study of our subject, and the chief British advocate of the view here set aside as untenable. After expressing the hope "that the so-called 'Egyptian Church Order' . . . will yet find its place in an edition of the *Quae supersunt omnia* of Hippolytus, under the title *Ἀποστολικὴ παράδοσις*", he goes on to point out the need of a critical edition of the work,[2] on the ground that "the result would be a contribution of the very first importance for the study of early Christian institutions. 'Eg. C.O.', in the fulness and precision of its information as to the worship and regulated working of a Christian Church, is unique in the first three centuries; it supplements in this respect the *Didascalia*, unique on its side as a presentment of the religious life and ideas in an early Christian Community".[3] The last sentence is true on any theory; and it may be added incidentally that, on the view set forth above, the work which thus supplements the 'Didaskalia', while put further away from it in date, is brought nearer to it in place; and so, for purposes of mutual elucidation as stages in a strictly-historical, because local development, the value of these two precious early witnesses is enhanced rather than impaired.

That the text of the 'Egyptian Church-Order' preserves faithfully the original form even of the Church-Order which was attached to the Hippolytean preface is far from likely. It has against it, time and again, a consensus of the other parallel sources, or of two of them. In certain cases, too, the simpler form in the 'Canons of Hippolytus'—simpler in idea even more

---

[1] The absence of any influence of the assumed *Apostolic Tradition* of Hippolytus (whether or not a separate work from *Concerning Charismata*) upon the thought and language of the Western Church before the end of the fourth century, is a fact which seems to tell heavily against the Hippolytean origin of the matter in our Church-Order. And the like is true of the radical difference between the ordination-prayers in it and in extant Latin ordinals.

[2] [Since Dr. Bartlet wrote, this need has largely been supplied in the Revd. Gregory Dix's work, *The Treatise on the Apostolic Tradition of St Hippolytus of Rome* (S.P.C.K., 1937). C.J.C.].

[3] In *Texts and Studies*, vol. VIII, pt. iv, p. 149.

than in form—seems to carry us back to a stage earlier than any of the other witnesses, even though it has manifestly much late Egyptian matter.[1] Its value lies, probably, in the fact that it rests on an independent line of textual tradition (witness its form of the opening section, already quoted), which began its life in Egypt before the line represented by the 'Egyptian Church-Order' started on its course.

APPENDED NOTE SUMMARIZING

SOME RESULTS THUS FAR REACHED AND THEIR SIGNIFICANCE.[2]

. . . . I am of course setting aside the general belief that the so-called "Hippolytean" Church-Order embodies Roman materials from the pen of Hippolytus himself. Apart from some differences between those who hold this view (Dr. Frere,[3] for instance, seeing in the document less of Hippolytus's own work and more in the way of Eastern accretions than is allowed by Dom Connolly and others), I must reaffirm the result of my argument elaborated above to the effect that Hippolytus had nothing to do with the Church-Order in question. The point is one of primary moment for the reconstruction of ancient Church-order, since it affects not only the area of the evidence in question (leaving us without this witness for the West), but also its date (since it can no longer be assigned with any cogency to the first rather than the second half of the third century).[4]

Our other literary findings relative to locality and date were as follows. The earliest forms of the 'Didaskalia' and of the so-called 'Apostolic Church-Order' alike belong to the half-century before 250 A.D.; but both also received additions in the half-century following, though these are less important and also harder to identify in the 'Didaskalia' than in the 'Apostolic Church-Order'. The home of the former was not far from Antioch, that of the latter some distance north-west of it, on the borders of Asia Minor, where rather-different cultural conditions obtained, especially as regards the more-prominent position accorded to women.

Both of these documents dealt with the ministry mainly as regards

---

[1] For illustrations of the above, see my article in *The Journ. of Theol. Studies*, vol. xvii, pp. 248–256 (April 1916).

[2] [I think this is the best place and form in which to insert the passages here transcribed. They were originally found in the middle of Chapter IX; but they would be less suitable there (see below, p. 161, n. 1), as Chapter IX deals for the most part with general principles.   C.J.C.].

[3] See *The Journ. of Theol. Stud.* vol. xvi, pp. 323–371 (Apl. 1915).

[4] My own view would appear to be justified by the way in which it fits into the rest of the evidence on matters of detail. See, e.g., pp. 121, 123 below, regarding the place of the reader.

qualifications, functions, and relative dignity, and only to a lesser degree with its appointment. In the so-called "Hippolytean" Church-Order, which I prefer to style the Old-Syrian Church-Order, and assign to the period 250–300 A.D., we get for the first time definite rules as to methods of appointment and also ordination-prayers for those offices for which such prayers are felt to be fitting.

In the period 300–350 A.D., the 'Apostolic Church-Order', which originally dealt with conditions in Cilicia or Cappadocia, underwent revision in Egypt. The three stages of the development of this document, falling roughly as they do into the three periods 200–250, 250–300, 300–350 A.D., can be distinguished pretty-definitely by means of formal tests connected with the various Apostolic names to which the several ordinances in it are attributed. The results furnish a valuable analogy for the analysis of similar documents which have undergone revision for the purpose of keeping them in touch with developing ideas and usages, such as the 'Didaskalia' and the Old-Syrian Church-Order, each of which shows traces of similar revision between 300 and 350 A.D. Dr. Frere recognizes such a second edition of the latter, to which all beyond the part dealing with ministerial offices and certain special classes (like confessors, virgins, and healers, as persons with charismatic qualities) may well belong. To the same period may also be assigned the form in which the developed 'Didaskalia' was used (under the new title 'Ordinances of the Apostles') by the compiler of the 'Apostolic Constitutions' (about 375 A.D.).

In proceeding now to the more-general features characterizing these three periods and reflected in the Eastern authorities just described, we may start with the list of ministerial offices in Rome about 252 A.D., since it affords an exactly-dated standard of reference. The Church-roll of those entitled to support from the offerings of the faithful, besides 1500 widows and others in straitened circumstances (orphans, etc.), had on it the bishop, forty-six presbyters, seven deacons, seven sub-deacons, forty-two acolytes, exorcists (who were mainly occupied in treating those under preparation for baptism, on the assumption that they needed to be delivered from evil spirits), readers, and door-keepers—the last three being lumped together, as of quite minor importance, and totalling fifty-two.[1] Of the rest the first three were the clergy proper, being found in all churches; the others were the minor orders, and existed elsewhere in only rudimentary forms, if at all.

In the 'Apostolic Church-Order', drawn up originally for a church in process of organization out of a missionary group, there are no minor offices: but the clergy consists of bishop, presbyters, readers, official widows—female presbyters, as it were, seemingly three in number—and deacons.

---

[1] See below, p. 160

We note with interest the high place of the reader, as compared with the case at Rome, a point in which the other Eastern third-century Orders in various degrees support the 'Apostolic Church-Order'.[1] Here, however, we are shown the reason of his higher position; namely that his function includes not only reading the lessons, but also paraphrasing their meaning (like the methurgeman in the synagogue), and so sharing the ministry of the Word, which was still regarded as more-or-less charismatic.[2] Now Dr. F. E. Brightman observes that "in Africa too only the Reader occurs" (i.e., besides the three major orders) "before the middle of the third century",[3] while at Rome by 250 A.D. he is already classed below sub-deacons and acolytes, between exorcists and door-keepers. Surely this tells heavily against Rome being the source of a Church-Order[4] in which he comes above the sub-deacons, though below the widows—who, be it also noted, do not appear at all in the ministry at Rome in the middle of the third century.

The place of the official widows in the 'Apostolic Church-Order' is also noteworthy. In the non-Egyptian stage of the work, they come before the deacons. This, however, seemed to the feeling of its Egyptian reviser (about 300–350 A.D.) an anomaly; so he introduced an extra section on deacons before that on widows, but naïvely reveals the fact by leaving part of the section on deacons also after it. The functions, too, given to the widows are instructive. One of them is to abide in intercessory prayer for all tried ones and with a view to revelations as to anything needful (for them)[5]—a distinctly-charismatic touch: another is to attend to the sick, and be "apt to minister"—i.e., virtually act as a deaconess. The embarrassed way in which the 'Didaskalia' deals with the official widows in III. v f., where it is anxious to exclude any teaching-ministry from their

---

[1] Thus in the *Didaskalia* (II. xxviii. 4 f.) a reader, if there be one, receives the same share of the people's offerings as the presbyter and the deacon.

[2] We may compare with the position of the reader that of the catechist in the basis of the Pseudo-Clementine literature (probably of rather later date), where he (the catechist) comes next to the deacons: see, e.g. *Ep. of Clement to James*, 14.

[3] In *Essays on the Early History of the Church and the Ministry* (ed. 1921), p. 388.

[4] Represented by the *Egyptian Church-Order*, the *Canons of Hippolytus*, and the *Testament of our Lord* (i. 23—as distinct from i. 45 f.). "In (*Test.*) I. 45 the reader is to be 'with much experience'. This is not found in the other Church Orders, except in Ap. C.O. 19 (which, as we have seen, places the reader *above* the deacon). There the reader must have been 'proved by a great trial' . . . , words that are much more emphatic than those used of deacons" (Cooper and Maclean, *Testament of our Lord*, pp. 204 f.). Again in i. 19 "the reader *or* chief deacon" is to "name by way of commemoration" the benefactors who "offer the oblations, or those for whom they have offered [them], . . . when the holy things are offered by the bishop" (in prayer). This commemoration (by the help of the diptychs?) of the special offerers shows the "high place of the readers, which is a mark of early date" in the *Testament* (Cooper and Maclean, as above, p. 151).

[5] Cf. Horner, *Statutes of the Apostles*, p. 304.

functions, suggests that it is at pains to repress a usage which recognized some such function. This conjecture is borne out by the high place assigned to widows of the presbyteress-type in the 'Testament of our Lord',[1] even as it stands, and yet more by what it suggests had once been the case in the region which the passages represent. Thus such widows stand within the "veil", which divides the altar-precincts from the congregation, "immediately behind the presbyters on the left side" (of the bishop, who is in the centre of the presbyters), "and the deacons also behind the presbyters on the right hand side; the readers behind them, and the sub-deacons behind the readers, and the deaconesses behind the sub-deacons".[2] We do not seem here to possess the full first form of the Old-Syrian Church-Order, save perhaps as it is reflected in the 'Testament of our Lord', which alone gives a "Prayer of appointment ($\kappa\alpha\tau\acute{\alpha}\sigma\tau\alpha\sigma\iota\varsigma$) of widows who sit in front" (i.e., presbyteresses), while distinguishing it from ordination proper by the laying on of hands.[3] The presence of the prayer at all, however, is significant, since there is no such prayer over readers, but only a charge addressed to the candidate at his appointment.[4] When we turn to the Coptic form of the 'Egyptian Church-Order', we find the case reversed as between the order and the reference to prayer;[5] while the 'Apostolic Constitutions', going back, like the 'Testament', to the Old-Syrian Order (though itself putting the reader after the subdeacon), makes the reader receive ordination by laying-on of hands with prayer, and—what is most significant—includes in that prayer the words "give to him holy spirit, prophetic spirit".[6] Thus it supports the charismatic idea of the reader's office already implied in the 'Apostolic Church-Order', and at the same

---

[1] They really seem to be the female counterpart of the male presbyters, since the *Testament* (i. 34 fin.) reckons "thirteen widows who sit in front" (i.e., in the seats of the clergy)—a number answering to the bishop and twelve presbyters just named (cf. the prayer accompanying their formal appointment, cited below). These special features are perhaps peculiar to the region represented by the original Greek text of the *Testament*, viz., the borders of Cappadocia, rather than north Syria proper, the home of the Old-Syrian Order, which it embodies. But its order for such widows, next to confessors and before subdeacons (i. 39–44), holds good also for the Old-Syrian Order as seen in the Ethiopic and the Arabic (here older than the Coptic) versions of the *Egyptian Church-Order*.

[2] *Test.* i. 23 (init.). Cf. the Arabic *Didaskalia*, as quoted by Cooper and Maclean, *The Testament of our Lord*, p. 167, where reference is made to their "spiritual gifts", along with touches of a rather-later type.

[3] *Test.* i. 40–45. "With regard to the prohibition of laying hands on confessors, widows, subdeacons, readers, etc., Bishop Wordsworth justly remarks (*Ministry of Grace*, 286) that prohibition of a thing generally means that some one wanted to do it" (Cooper and Maclean, *The Testament of our Lord*, p. 205).

[4] At the institution of a subdeacon in the *Testament* (i. 44) (now put before a reader), the bishop prays over him, but there is no reference to laying-on of hands, and no prayer is cited, only an address to him. Cf. Cooper and Maclean, *The Testament of our Lord*, pp. 11 f.

[5] Cf. Horner, *Statutes of the Apostles*, p. 309.

[6] *Apost. Const.* VIII. xxii. 3.

times makes it likely that it here preserves part of the ordination-prayer which once stood in the original form of the Old-Syrian Order.

Thus, as regards the ministry both of widows and readers, the various witnesses which use the Old-Syrian Order, either in its third-century form (about 250–300 A.D.) or that of the first half of the next century, are seen to be involved, in varying local ways and degrees, in later prejudices. These all tended to lower the idea and rank of the reader below the later fourth-century office (as it was in the East) of sub-deacon,[1] and to reduce the status of widows, once the female counterpart of presbyters and deacons combined (as in the 'Apostolic Church-Order' and the Old-Syrian Church-Order)—except as regards the ministry of the eucharist. It is owing to this difference that the later form of the Old-Syrian Order, as reflected in the 'Egyptian Church-Order', denies to the presbyteress the laying-on of hands, "because she does not offer the oblation or conduct the public worship ($\lambda\epsilon\iota\tau\upsilon\rho\gamma\acute{\iota}\alpha\nu$), while ordination ($\chi\epsilon\iota\rho\upsilon\tau\upsilon\nu\acute{\iota}\alpha$) is for the clergy for the sake of public worship ($\lambda\epsilon\iota\tau\upsilon\rho\gamma\acute{\iota}\alpha\nu$)". This is the point on which a later edition of the 'Apostolic Church-Order', belonging to the time after its transference from its original Cilician or semi-Asian conditions of feeling and usage, shows anxiety to restrict the ministry of women, even of widows, which it still retains. For it puts into the mouth of John, its leading authority, a fresh rule evoked by Peter's suggestion for more-accurate definition of the ministry of women with relation to "the oblations of the body and the blood of the Lord"—a mode of phrasing which Dom Connolly connects with the fourth century rather than earlier.[2]

"Ye have forgotten, brothers, that when the Teacher asked for the loaf and the cup and blessed them, saying 'This is my body and blood', He did not allow them (women) to stand with us. Martha said, 'Because of Mary, for He saw her smiling'. Mary said, 'It was not because I laughed. The reason was because, as He had already told us in His teaching, that which is weak (and so the female sex) shall be saved by means of that which is strong' (the male sex)".[3]

Here we have a hint of one argument put forward against women's sharing in the central act of public worship—viz., her less self-controlled emotional nature—and also of another argument, viz., that there is a deeper and Diviner reason, connected with the very principle of redemption itself, that of the dependence of the weaker upon the stronger for salvation. That is, the weaker is to be repre-sented by the stronger in the sacrament of salvation. The moral of

---

[1] Called earlier, in the early fourth-century basis of *Apost. Const.*, "assistant" ($\upsilon\pi\eta\rho\acute{\epsilon}\tau\eta s$, III. xi. 1, 3).
[2] Cf. his note in *Texts and Studies*, vol. VIII, pt. iv, p. 131.
[3] Cf. Horner, *Statutes of the Apostles*, p. 305.

this view is expressed by John's brother, James, when he concludes
that the ministry of women was to be of a kind in which they could
fulfil, and not infringe, this very law—the ministry, namely, of
strengthening their weaker sisters in their need (xxiv, xxvi, xxviii).
It was along this line that the later development of the ministry of
women in the Church's order proceeded, i.e., that of the professional
"deaconess". The very name suggested (as "widow" or "presbyteress" did not) the subordinate type of service which it was theirs
to render. It was one limited also more than before to the privacy of
the home, rather than one which brought its holders before the eye
of the church as such by "sitting in front" among the clergy, "within
the altar-rails". Deaconesses of this type, called by that special name
(διακόνισσα, not διάκονος with the feminine article), first appear in
our group of Church-Orders in the 'Apostolic Constitutions', i.e.,
about 375–380 A.D.

The other group of minor clergy in the wide sense, i.e., persons of
rank on the older basis of the Church's custom, though not by formal
appointment (with or without ordination), consists, in the Church-
Orders we are studying, of confessors and healers, to begin with; and
later it comes to embrace professional celibates or virgins of both
sexes. The persistence of the charismatic idea in the first two is
interesting, particularly so in the case of the confessors, as bringing
into comparison and partial conflict the charismatic and ex-officio
principles of spiritual rank and authority in the Church. For of the
confessors who in the Old-Syrian Order come between deacons and
widows, we read that their Divinely-inspired courage of confession
confers ipso facto the title to sit among the spiritual aristocracy of
the Church, the presbyters, that is, "who sit in front".

CHAPTER VII

SERAPION'S PRAYER-BOOK[1]

CHURCH-ORDERS are of various kinds, differing according to the
aspect of the Church's corporate life which they emphasize.
For, like all early Christian documents, they were written down
with a practical end in view, namely, in order to direct Church-
ideals and Church-practice on matters of special moment at
the time and place of their origin. Thus the 'Didaskalia' was
concerned to set forth the ideal of Christian life, and as connected therewith the system of ministry and discipline thought
needful to maintain the character of the People or Church of
God as "holy", and free from heresies tending to impair its

[1] [See my note below, pp. 141 f., n. 1.   C.J.C.].

holiness. The 'Apostolic Church-Order' again, while also pre-occupied with the moral walk of Christians according to the Divinely-given "Way of Life", dealt more definitely with the ministry in its several grades, and the special qualifications proper to each. The ancient Syrian Church-Order, connected with the name of Hippolytus, was, even in its original form, more comprehensive in its scope than anything previously produced, including as it did some treatment of Church-worship. But in the 'Prayer-Book' of Serapion, we have a fuller and more-specialized representation of the liturgical forms of Church-worship and sacraments, as current, no longer in Syria (the part of the Church thus far in question), but in Egypt, and in the first half of the fourth century.

But, even so, we are still at the earlier stage, that of primarily-practical interests: we have not yet reached that of theoretic, much-less systematic, expositions of the whole subject of Church-order generally. The latter stage came after our period, or at least only towards its close, when vitally-creative growth had largely been replaced by codification. The beginnings of this process we shall study in our next lecture, when we find instances of the collection of older sets of Church-Orders as a "corpus" or body of Church-rules. Such collections usually claim, not simply the authority of immemorial tradition, but Apostolic authorship, as giving the whole a uniquely-Divine or absolute sanction. A claim like this transformed ecclesiastical precedents and rules into Canon-Law, so hampering for the future that very freedom of the Spirit which had in the first instance been their source. Dr. Hort closes his review of the organization of the Ecclesia in the Apostolic Age with the aphorism, that "the lesson-book of the Ecclesia, and of every Ecclesia, is not a law but a history".[1] Ere the end of the fourth century, as a result alike of formal and informal expressions of current Church-consciousness, of Councils and of Church-Orders, this largely ceased to be the case. But before we reach that stage, we meet with two[2] very-representative specimens of the older and more-spontaneous type of Church-Order, which cast light both backward on the past and forward on the more fixed and specialized forms to which the future was to belong for many centuries.

The first and more comprehensive of the two is the so-called

---

[1] F. J. A. Hort, *The Christian Ecclesia*, p. 233.
[2] [See my note below, pp. 141 f., n. 1.   C.J.C.].

'Prayer-Book' (*Εὐχολόγιον*) of Serapion, bishop of Thmuis in the Nile-Delta, a contemporary and friend of Athanasius, as also of Antonius, the great pioneer of Christian monasticism in Egypt. It was discovered in 1894 in a monastery on Mount Athos, in an eleventh-century manuscript of good quality, and in 1899 was made accessible in English by Bishop J. Wordsworth, in the series entitled 'Early Church Classics', published by the Society for Promoting Christian Knowledge.[1] In form it is like what was called at a later time a "pontifical", that is, a collection of prayers for the use of a bishop in his official capacity; and so it omits a good deal of the setting in which certain of the prayers were said in actual Church-practice. But, as observed by Dr. F. E. Brightman, to whom we owe the best edition of these prayers,[2] such a title would in this case be misleading, as being too specialized to apply rightly to so early a type of collection. He therefore prefers to call it a "sacramentary", in the wide sense descriptive of all sacred rites of the Church and not referring only to its sacraments in the strict sense. But even so it "is quite rudimentary as a Sacramentary: it is exclusively a celebrant's *libellus*", or service-book, "with no indication of the parts of the deacon and the minor orders, with only one at most of the standing formulae which form the permanent framework of the rites, and with no rubrics beyond two or three notes and what is implied in the titles of the several prayers".[3] Their proper setting, however, can as a rule be supplied by analogy, and so we can obtain a fairly concrete and living picture of certain aspects of Church-life and Church-order in a typical church in Lower Egypt in the first half of the fourth century.

But this is not all. In two places the manuscript connects certain prayers with the name of Bishop Serapion. It has no general title, but begins simply with "An Oblation-prayer (*εὐχὴ προσφόρου*) of Sarapion, bishop". Then about halfway through the thirty prayers which follow, we read "Prayers (*προσευχαί*)[4] of

---

[1] [A second, revised edition of this work was published in 1923. C.J.C.].

[2] In *The Journ. of Theol. Studies*, vol. i, pp. 88–113 (Oct. 1899), 247–277 (Jan. 1900). [They have also been edited by G. Wobbermin in *Texte und Untersuchungen*, N.F., vol. II, iii b (1899), pp. 4–25, and by F. X. Funk, in his *Didascalia et Constitutiones Apostolorum* (Paderborn, 1905), vol. ii, pp. XL–XLII, 158–195. For an English translation, see text above, and below, p. 143, n. 2. C.J.C.].

[3] In *op. cit.*, pp. 89 f.

[4] [The manuscript reads *προσευχ.*, which Wobbermin (p. 12) expands as *προσευχή*: but Brightman (p. 90) and Funk (p. XLI) hold that it really stands for *προσευχαί*. The prayer so introduced is no. 15. C.J.C.].

Sarapion, bishop of Thmuis". Now both the fuller description of "Serapion" by his see, and the use of a different word for "prayers", rather suggest that here we have really the original title of the whole collection, and that the order has been changed at some stage in its history, so as to bring to the beginning the primary or eucharistic prayer, perhaps the only one specified in the original form of the collection as specially Serapion's. Further, whilst in most of the prayers Serapion had probably contributed something of his own, in virtue of the liturgical (originally the "prophetic") freedom still enjoyed by a bishop, it was felt that he had put his special stamp most markedly on the great prayer of oblation or "anaphora". There is good reason to believe that the wording of most of the prayers, if in different degrees, represents the third century, and some of it even the second. This is exemplified not only by the prevalence of different strata of characteristic ideas and even language, but also by the existence of parallels in earlier authorities to certain features alike of the thought and of the basal structure of the services to which the bulk of the prayers plainly belong.[1] This is a most interesting and important aspect of the work, and deserves more definite notice than it has yet received. For, so far as the criterion of analogy can carry us, it thus becomes a witness also for the third century and even earlier. It is altogether natural that an oral body of Church-prayers should have grown up by gradual and repeated readjustment to changing ideals, more even than we have seen to be the case with several of the Church-Orders already examined. For these latter were in writing from the beginning of the third century at any rate, yet underwent more than one revision before reaching their present form. Accordingly in reading Serapion's Prayer-Book we must be prepared to go behind Serapion to the traditional basis, probably oral, which he was using. That original form, as I conceive the case, was not written down by Serapion himself, but rather by his

---

[1] Brightman (in *op. cit.*, p. 90), after saying that "it may well be that the whole collection" was meant to be attributed to Serapion, as being the prayers he was wont to use, adds that, "allowing for difference of subject-matter, there are no marked differences either of language and style or of character to be discerned in the several prayers". But the general uniformity of language and style would be sufficiently explained by the fact that Serapion was saturated with those of the time-honoured oral tradition of which he was the trustee; while as to the character of the conceptions, and of certain phrases to which Brightman himself refers as distinctive of given groups of prayers and their doxologies, the degree of difference is what will now be examined.

successor, who felt that it would be valuable to preserve in writing the usage of so great and inspired a man. Such a view seems borne out by the note appended to the last of the prayers in their present order, viz., "All these prayers (εὐχαί) are said through before the Prayer of Oblation", that is, they are an appendix to complete the original sacramentary. This fits on naturally to the special title of that prayer as given in our manuscript; so that the note was probably made by the original compiler, since it uses the same word (εὐχή) for "prayer" as occurs elsewhere throughout, save for the rubric which we have just alluded to, and which may have been the colophon of Serapion's part.

The Prayer-Book contains—(i) the eucharistic Anaphora or prayer of Oblation (1), followed by Communion-prayers (2–4), a prayer for a blessing on the oil and water offered in association with the central eucharistic oblation (5), and the benediction at the end of the whole service (6); (ii) baptismal prayers (7–11); (iii) ordination-prayers for deacons, presbyters, and bishop (12–14); (iv) an anointing-prayer for candidates for baptism, a prayer over the oil used after baptism, and one over the oil, bread, or water used for the sick, and a funeral-prayer (15–18); (v) pre-anaphoral prayers, i.e., prayers for the first part of the service culminating in the above-mentioned anaphora (19–26). This reversal of the actual order in use is significant of the feeling for sacramental worship (as contrasted with other worship), which came to exist at a later date.

Here we shall probably do best to start with those prayers which, as least connected with the public liturgy of the Church, and therefore most characteristic of the bishop's personal practice, would naturally reveal most of his own mentality and the full extent to which the development of current ideas had gone in his region. Then we can by analogy allow more confidently for the personal factor in his writing-down of the time-honoured public forms of his church's tradition—forms as to which the corporate consciousness tends to be most conservative. The special prayers in question are those of the kind called "occasional", used, that is, as occasion needed; and they form a group to which the rubric "Prayers of Bishop Serapion" is immediately prefixed. As to the oblation-prayer, where the word "oblation" (πρόσφορον, i.e., "a thing offered") denotes the material symbols expressive of the people's thanksgiving or eucharist, and taken from the sum-total of their gifts to God (gifts offered prior to the prayer in question), we can deal with it most advantageously later on, in its proper place in the service. For by that time we shall have before us the further criterion furnished by the analogies to those prayers supplied by earlier witnesses, from Justin Martyr onwards.

The four occasional prayers in question are:

15. "A prayer relative to the anointing (ἄλειμμα) of those being baptized".[1]

16. "A prayer relative to the anointing (χρίσμα) with which those already baptized are anointed (χρίονται)".

17. "A prayer relative to oil for the sick, or to bread or water".

18. "A prayer touching one dead and being carried out (for burial)".

Of these the first two relate to the office of baptism, and were used in the course of it. This is made the clearer by the words, "Guide him (Thy servant) to regeneration", which occur in the companion-prayer (10) following the rite of anointing before baptism. That the four occasional prayers, supplemental to the primary sacramental group (1–14), are not Serapion's own work throughout, but imply an older oral basis, is proved by one fact which is interesting and instructive in itself, viz., the peculiar psychology involved in the phrase "soul, body, spirit", occurring in that order in three of them. The prayer in which this psychology appears most explicitly is 18—that "touching one dead and being carried out (for burial)". This probably means "that 'soul' is set apart and distinguished from 'body' and 'spirit' ", as the concrete personality, consisting of the two elements which, in their Divinely-adjusted unity on earth, constitute the man, and will yet again by God's power do so at the resurrection.[2] That is on the lines of Old-Testament psychology, and suggests that Jewish mentality has moulded the prayer, though perhaps the kindred native Egyptian notion of body, soul, and "Ka", may be a factor explaining why it became prevalent only in Egypt. The influence of the Jewish synagogue on early Christianity in Egypt is certain; and it is

[1] To this answers 10, "A prayer after the anointing" (ἄλειψιν, according to Brightman's convincing emendation of ἀνάληψιν, in *op. cit.*, pp. 264, 271).

[2] We may illustrate this use by our description of a ship as "lost with all souls on board". This interpretation, put forward by Dr. Brightman, in *The Journ. of Theol. Studies*, vol. ii, pp. 273 f. (Jan. 1901) as one of several suggestions, seems to be rendered more probable by Dr. F. C. Burkitt in the same *Journ.* vol. iv, pp. 586 f. (July 1903), by the aid of Greek inscriptions on gravestones in Upper Egypt.

borne out not only by a reference here to the soul as at rest with Abraham and Isaac and Jacob, but also by the use of Hebraic phrases elsewhere, such as "O Lord God of the Ages" (23), which reminds one of the common use of "O King of the Ages" in Jewish prayers. In fact the traces of Old-Testament influence at the basis of the prayers recall the like features in the eucharistic prayer towards the close of the (so-called First) Epistle of Clement, to which Lightfoot directed attention. We have, then, in the prayers in Serapion's collection illustrations of the influence of local mentality at one stage. In contrast to this, the later influence of the non-Jewish thought, adding other elements to others of the prayers, becomes easier to discern.

In passing next to the order of public worship, and its prayers in particular, our surest starting-point is Justin Martyr's account, mainly in his '(First) Apology', soon after A.D. 150, of the Sunday-worship of Christians. Its order is as follows.

1. Lessons from the Gospels or "the Prophets" (i.e., the Old Testament), as long as time permits, read by one simply described as "him who reads".

2. The hortatory address of the presiding officer (the bishop or his delegate), based on the lessons or some part of them.

3. All rise and so offer prayers, for themselves and all others everywhere, in earnest tones, "in order that, having learnt the truth, we may also by means of deeds be counted worthy to be found good livers and keepers of the precepts, in order that we may be saved with the eternal salvation".

4. Mutual salutation with a kiss ("of peace").

5. Bread and a cup of wine and water, already mixed and brought to the presiding officer.

6. These he takes in his hands and sends up prayers like those of the people, and thanksgivings to the best of his ability, viz., "praise and glory to the Father of the universe through the name of the Son and the Holy Spirit", making thanksgiving at some length "for being deemed worthy of these things (i.e., earthly food) from His hand", and so leading up to reference to redemption and the offering of these samples of God's gifts in homage, as symbols of self-oblation, "in remembrance" (εἰς ἀνάμνησιν) of the supreme and redemptive self-oblation of Christ's Passion.

7. The people emphatically associates itself in this act with the "Amen".

8. The deacons hand round, and the people take, each his portion; and the participation extends to those not present, the deacons conveying their share to such.[1]

Here we have clearly the result of a fusion of the synagogue-type of worship with that distinctive of the Christian eucharist, now separated from the sacred meal of fellowship with which it was once associated. The point of original division is marked by the mutual salutation with the kiss of peace or of brotherly love, since any breach of this, as the 'Didache' had emphasized, smirches the purity of the corporate act of worship at its climax. Before this, however, there came in all later accounts at any rate—though we are not told by Justin that it was so in his day—the dismissal of all who were not full (i.e., baptized) members of the Church, ere its more distinctive prayers, beginning with intercessions, were offered up. This dismissal came after the Scripture-lessons and the sermon of exhortation based in part at least on some portions of these.

Let us now look at this prior stage—open to all comers—as it is represented by the prayers in Serapion's church in Egypt about the middle of the fourth century.

The "First Prayer of the Lord's Day" (19) runs as follows:

"We beseech thee, the Father of the Only-begotten, the Lord of the universe, the Artificer of created things, the Maker of things that have been made—pure hands do we stretch out, and our thoughts do we unfold to Thee, O Lord. We pray, have compassion, spare, benefit, improve, multiply (us) in virtue and faith and knowledge. Visit us, O Lord;[2] to Thee we present our own weaknesses. Be propitious and have pity on us all in common. Have mercy on this people; benefit it; make it gentle and temperate and pure; and send angelic powers, in order that all this Thy people may be holy and reverend. I beseech Thee, send holy Spirit into our mind and give us grace to learn with (ἀπὸ) holy Spirit the Divine Scriptures, and to interpret them purely and worthily, in order that all the lay-people present may be helped. Through Thine Only-begotten, Jesus Christ, in holy Spirit, through Whom to Thee (be) the glory and the might both now and to all the ages of the ages. Amen".

Here we note the emphasis on moral purity and progress—

---

[1] Justin, *Apol.* I. lxv, lxvii. 3–5, *Tryph.* xli, lxx.
[2] Cf. Psalm cv (Engl. cvi) 4.

both ideas characteristic of the whole collection of prayers—
and on purity and progress as fed by insight into the Divine
Scriptures, an insight dependent—alike in the preacher (the
bishop) and his hearers—on direct inspiration of God's holy
Spirit. Let us note further that it is "in (by) holy Spirit", in the
same sense, that acceptable worship is made possible, as
mediated by God's "Unique One" (μονογένους), Jesus Christ,
"through Whom" is ascribed to God "glory and might" (τὸ
κράτος, the root-word of "All-mighty" as a Divine epithet),
"both now and to all the ages of the ages". All these motifs
recur again and again throughout the prayer-book.

Then, after the Lessons and the Sermon, came a "Prayer
after rising up from the Sermon" (20): "God, the Saviour, God
of the universe, the Lord and Artificer of the world, the Be-
getter of the Only-begotten, Who hast begotten the living and
true expression (of Thyself),[1] Who didst send Him for the help
of the race of men, Who through Him didst call and make men
Thine own possession, we pray Thee on behalf of this people.
Send holy Spirit (on them), and let the Lord Jesus visit them;
let Him speak in the minds of all, and predispose their hearts
to faith. May He Himself draw their souls to Thee, O God of
mercies. Create a people even in this city; create a genuine
flock through Thine Only-begotten, Jesus Christ, in holy Spirit,
through Whom to Thee (be) the glory and the might both
now and to all the ages of the ages. Amen".

Here the idea of "the unique One", begotten of God as His
"living and real[2] expression" (as of a seal), is unfolded. Next,
the idea of His "visiting" God's people, as God Himself was in
the last prayer begged to visit them, through the effluence, as
it were, of His holy in-breathing, predisposing their hearts to
faith, and so drawing them to God, is made more explicit on
the other side from that referred to in the companion-prayer.
And in the thought of genuine spiritual likeness to God Himself
in His people, after the image of His reflection in His Unique
Son, the moral emphasis of that prayer recurs with fresh religious impressiveness.

After the Sermon, the Catechumens were dismissed with a
prayer (21) invoking God as their "emancipator", and asking
Him to continue His gracious work of enlightenment already
begun in them, until "by pure practical wisdom" (φρονήσει)

---

[1] Χαρακτῆρα : cf. Hebs. i. 3 (χαρακτὴρ τῆς ὑποστάσεως αὐτοῦ).
[2] Ἀληθινός—as in the Fourth Gospel.

they "advance so as to become worthy of the washing of regeneration and of the holy mysteries . . . ." There seems to have followed a laying-on of the bishop's hand, with prayer (28) that God's own "Divine and living hand" might accompany his action and "bless this people" unto knowledge, piety, and a share in God's "mysteries".

Passing over without comment the special prayers for the sick (22) and for fruitful fields (23), we come to the Church's intercessions proper for herself and for all men (24–27).

The first of these (24), styled a "Prayer concerning the Church", seems a general petition for such cleansing of the whole worshipping people as might qualify it to offer for itself acceptable praise. Specific intercession begins in the next prayer (25) or stage of one act of prayer; for all these intercessory prayers are really only paragraphs or stages of thought in the one great series of intercessions referred to by Justin Martyr. It analyses the local church and its needs in terms of its several component classes, official and otherwise. The prayer is in fact of the nature of a bidding prayer. And so we next reach the stage (26) at which the Church begins, on bended knee, to take up its function of priestly intercession, as a body of worshippers now becoming fitted by prayer itself to reach the full height of its privileged vocation, and to fulfil it in the next and final stage of intercession (27) for all sorts and conditions of men, both within the Church and outside it.

Before proceeding now to Serapion's eucharistic prayer itself, let us by the aid of Justin and Irenaeus, supplemented by the occasional references in the fathers and Church-Orders of the third century, try to reconstruct the order of the Lord's Supper, as it may have existed between the times of Irenaeus and Serapion. It must have been somewhat as follows:

I. Common intercessions for the Church and for all men.
   The kiss of peace or brotherhood.
   Offering of the people's gifts.
   Prelude—mutual benediction of minister and people:
      Sursum corda, etc.
II. The eucharistic or thank-offering prayer (anaphora):—
      Preface—adoration of God as Creator.
      The seraphic hymn (the Sanctus of Isaiah vi).
      Recital of the work of redemption.
      The narrative of the institution.
      The anamnesis ("In memory, then", etc.) and oblation.

Invocation on the worshippers or their oblation.

People's "Amen".

III. The Communion.

Post-communion thanksgiving and concluding prayer.

But what were the ideas under the influence of which the eucharistic prayer (or anaphora) had taken shape? Its essential idea was expressed in its very name. It was the "offering-up" of thanksgiving (εὐχαριστία) to God for all His benefits, in remembrance of His supreme gift, His Christ, in spiritual union with Whose perfect self-oblation the Church, as members of His mystical Body (inclusive of Him as Head), present the loaf and cup of wine, taken from and representative of all their gifts in kind. These samples, chosen from God's created things and brought to be devoted to His special uses, are solemnly but gladly offered up, to represent the offerers themselves as living sacrifices—unbloody, and so not of the non-Christian type, but belonging to the sphere of mind or spirit (that of λόγος or reason).[1] This aspect of the oblation (ἀναφορά), as one of communion with God, the Heavenly Sovereign and Father, through gifts of friendship exchanged, and as indicating homage on the part of the inferior, is first made clear by Irenaeus, though by his help it may then be read between the lines of Justin's references in his 'Dialogue with Trypho the Jew'. Irenaeus writes: "Therefore the Church's oblation . . . is reckoned with God a pure sacrifice and is acceptable unto Him.[2] Not that He is in need of a sacrifice from us, but because he who offers is himself glorified in that he offers, if his gift be accepted", that is, if he is treated as a friend by God, who deigns to accept a gift at his hands as a token of their friendship. "Therefore", continues Irenaeus later, "sacrifices do not sanctify a man, for God stands not in need of sacrifice; but the conscience of him who offers, being pure, sanctifies the sacrifice, and causes God to accept it as if from a friend".[3]

Irenaeus' doctrine of eucharistic worship is not only highly spiritual in idea, but it also implies a very-high type of Christian practice, if it is to correspond to the experience of the worshippers. For Irenaeus teaches that the Christian species of oblation, as distinct from the Jewish, is that appropriate to free

---

[1] Cf. Rom. xii. 1: . . . τὴν λογικὴν λατρείαν ὑμῶν—misleadingly translated in A.V. and R.V. "your reasonable service".

[2] A contrast with the unacceptable sacrifices denounced in Malachi i. 10 ff. (quoted in xvii. 5) seems intended.

[3] Iren. Adv. Haer. IV. xviii. 1, 3.

men rather than to those in bondage, meaning by bondage that to Law in religion, and to sin as not to be met by Law but only by grace. "Sacrifices, then, do not sanctify a man, for God stands not in need of sacrifice; but the conscience of him who offers, being pure, sanctifies the sacrifice, and causes God to accept it as if from a friend. Since, therefore", he goes on, "the Church offers (her oblation) with sincerity of mind" ("simplicitate", as contrasted with insincerity or inconsistency between inner and outer life), "her gift is justly accounted with God a pure sacrifice", like that of the Philippian church on the altar of Paul's service as God's servant.[1] It would not be surprising, then, if with an experience less conscious, on the average, of victory over sin, and so a diminishing sense of being God's moral free-men through Christ, Christians as time went on conformed their eucharistic doctrine to their changed practical experience. They came in fact to look to the eucharistic sacrifice —as the central act by which they sought fellowship with God and His life—for something that had not before been associated directly with it (except in so far as it brought to mind the atoning self-oblation of Christ), namely, cleansing and forgiveness of a bad conscience, the burden and bondage of actual sins.

At an earlier stage in the Church's life, normal forgiveness of a Christian man's sins, other than those recognized as so serious as to call for the Church's discipline, had been thought to be attainable by private repentance and confession to God in daily prayer, as well as by the Church's corporate prayer— prior to the eucharistic service—for forgiveness of sins. That worship, as we have seen in Irenaeus, itself presupposed such forgiveness, so that both the offerers themselves (and therefore their gifts also) might in that supreme act of adoration and self-committal be "pure", as being priests to God. But now, along with the growing dualism between the general and special priesthood of the Church—the rank and file on the one hand, and the sacrificing clergy on the other—the original idea, expressed in Irenaeus, was fading, and another idea was taking its place.

How do the eucharistic prayers of Serapion's day stand in relation to these two ideas of eucharistic worship and privilege, and to the transition from the earlier to the later perspective and conception? This brings us back to the question of the original order of the prayers and of the reason for the putting

---

[1] Iren. *Adv. Haer.* IV. xviii. 4. The reference is to Philippians iv. 18.

To these considerations another of great moment must be added, viz., the nature of the blessing asked for on behalf of the communicants. It is not forgiveness of sins, in virtue of the propitiatory sacrifice of the body and blood of Christ just offered, according to general Catholic theory from the fourth century onwards; but that "all who communicate may receive a medicine of life, for the healing of every sickness and for the strengthening of all progress and virtue", and again "health and wholeness and good courage and all progress, of soul and body, to this whole people". The reference here to the healthful bodily effect of the grace of the eucharist is a noteworthy aspect of ancient eucharistic theory generally, and of Serapion's prayers in particular. It connects itself with the whole thought of the ancient Church in most circles, from the period of Ignatius onwards, in proportion as Christians were influenced by modes of thought other than Jewish and Biblical on the nature and effects of sacramental rites. The same feature appears plainly in Serapion's prayers relating to the rite of baptism. This explains not only the fact that this Prayer-Book contains prayers for the special consecration of oil, bread, and water, for use by the sick as a medicine filled with spiritual or supernatural potency, but also the fact that after the Communion-Service proper it was open to worshippers to present oil and water to be consecrated with prayer on that occasion—when presumably it was thought that such prayer would be specially efficacious in securing the desired infusion of Divine power into the natural substance of the elements in question.

After this prayer of consecration (5) in the name of Christ, "the name of Him Who suffered, Who was crucified and rose again[1] and sitteth on the right hand of the Uncreated One", there follows the final prayer of benediction, described as the bishop's "laying on of hands after the blessing of the water and the oil" (6). Probably this act assumed a more-symbolic form than contact of the bishop's hands with the people's heads, and was in fact the same as the "stretching-forth" of the hands towards them, to which we have reference elsewhere in these prayers as an attitude of blessing alike in God and his representative. This brings us naturally to the prayers of consecration for the ministry of the Church, described by the same

---

[1] Compare Justin's reference to exorcism in the name of Jesus the Crucified [and Risen] One (*Apol.* II. vi. 6, *Tryph.* 30, 49, 76, [85]).

term, "laying-on-of-hands (or benediction)[1] of appointment" (χειροθεσία καταστάσεως). Of such prayers there are three only (12–14), a mark of the primitive conditions in vogue before the mode of appointment of the minor orders was thought worth recording. They are, by exception (in the East), in the ascending order of the stages by which the highest of them, the episcopate, was reached. The prayer over deacons is as follows (12):

"Father of the Only-begotten, Who didst send Thy Son and didst ordain the things on the earth, and hast given rules to the Church and orders for the profit and salvation of the flocks, Who didst choose out bishops, presbyters, and deacons for the ministry of Thy Catholic Church, Who didst choose through Thine Only-begotten the seven Deacons, and didst graciously give to them holy Spirit; make this man also a Deacon of Thy Catholic Church, and put in him 'a spirit of knowledge and discernment', that he may be able purely and unblameably to do service in this ministry in the midst of the holy People, through Thine Only-begotten, Jesus Christ, through Whom to Thee (be) the glory and the might, in holy Spirit, both now and to all the ages of the ages.[2] Amen".

This prayer is of interest chiefly for purposes of comparison with that in the Old Syrian Church-Order, suggesting as it does that the form in which the latter appears in the 'Canons of Hippolytus' has been influenced by Egyptian usage.

That over presbyters (13) is of greater moment, and calls for more careful study. It reads as follows:

"We stretch forth the hand, O Lord God of the heavens, Father of Thine Only-begotten, upon this man,[3] and beseech Thee that the Spirit of Truth may come to dwell upon him. Graciously give him prudence and knowledge and a good heart. Let a Divine Spirit come to be in him, that he may be able to be a steward of Thy people and an ambassador of Thy Divine oracles, and to reconcile Thy people to Thee, the un-created God, Who didst graciously confer (some) of the spirit of Moses upon the chosen ones, even holy Spirit. Give a portion

---

[1] Compare the use of the word "benedictio" in connexion with ordination in the ancient Roman Orders.

[2] This form of doxology, as regards the place of ἐν ἁγίῳ πνεύματι, seems to be characteristic of Serapion, modifying the earlier basis without δι' οὗ ... κράτος at all.

[3] [Dr. Bartlet notes in pencil that, unlike the deacon's and the bishop's, the presbyter's office is not named, and he is referred to by a different phrase—τὸν ἄνθρωπον τοῦτον, the bishop and the deacon being each designated by καὶ τόνδε. C.J.C.].

of holy Spirit to this man also, from the Spirit of the Only-begotten, for the grace of wisdom, knowledge, and right faith, that he may be able to serve Thee 'with a clean conscience' (1 Tim. iii. 9; 2 Tim. i. 3), through Thine only-begotten, Jesus Christ, through Whom to Thee (be) the glory and the might, in holy Spirit, both now and for all the ages of the ages. Amen".

Attention should be given to the way in which the Divine influence or inspiration, called in the ancient Church generally "holy Spirit", is here defined by the analogy between the communication of Spirit from Moses and from Christ respectively, the representatives of the old and new forms of God's covenant-relations with mankind. It also bears out, incidentally, the general impression, conveyed by the prayers as a whole, that their piety is conceived in essentially-Hebraic categories, touched and quickened to new and higher vitality and potency by the Diviner quality of Christ's personality, and so of the Divine Spirit of Grace mediated or set free by Him. More specifically, we observe that the functions of the presbyterate seem to relate mainly to the ministry of God's Word of Truth as contained in His "Divine oracles", and that its work of reconciling God's people to Him was carried on through this means. There is no reference to any sacramental ministry in the Eucharist. This becomes the more remarkable when we notice that the like is true of the ordination-prayer over a bishop (14):

"Thou Who didst send forth the Lord Jesus for the gain of the whole world, Who didst through Him choose the Apostles, Who dost generation by generation ordain holy bishops; make, O God of truth, this man also a living bishop, a holy bishop in the succession of the holy Apostles, and give to him grace and Divine Spirit, which Thou didst graciously give to all Thy true servants and prophets and patriarchs: make him to be worthy to shepherd Thy flock; and further, let him continue without blame and offence in the episcopate, through Thine Only-begotten, Jesus Christ", etc.

Here there is no reference to high-priesthood, or indeed to any sacramental act: instead of this the specific gifts of the chief pastor, as of his fellow-presbyters, are those of mental and moral insight, fitting for practical guardianship of the flock (cf. 25). When, then, we compare the conception of the episcopate in Serapion with that in the "Hippolytean" Church-Order, we find cause to doubt the latter's phrasing as fully typical even for the latter part of the third century. Some of its emphasis, in its present form at least, may in fact be local rather than typical at that date.

Serapion's prayer may strike us, in contrast to the fulness of that in the "Hippolytean" Church-Order and in other Orders dealing with both the presbyteral and with the episcopal offices, as somewhat brief, and possibly inadequate in the specific functions suggested. But may it not be that this is due to the fact that in Egypt the difference in idea between the two offices, or two grades of one order—that of the pastorate or special priesthood—was less than it was elsewhere in the fourth century? If so, we should take the two prayers together as representing, cumulatively, the full complement of episcopal functions, conferred in two stages on the man who was successively presbyter and bishop. Yet, even so, it remains noteworthy that nothing is said as to the function of conferring orders on others—a fact that becomes yet more significant when we recall the similar omission in the episcopal prayer of the old Syrian Church-Order in two of our authorities. It may well be, then, that the power to ordain was conceived not so much as a matter of Divine grace as of Church-order or expediency, as Jerome and Ambrosiaster seem to have regarded it.

Having now seen the conception of the Christian life, both as piety, and as corporate fellowship in the life of God through the medium of the "holy Spirit" or Divine influence energizing in soul and body, and so raising all to a higher power of life that is life indeed (which is the central conception of religion and religious salvation in these prayers), we are in a position to see the full significance of those prayers that deal with entrance into the membership of the Church through baptism.[1]

The realistic nature of its notion of the grace conveyed first to others through the baptismal water is most striking, and shows how far from Hebraic modes of thought as to the Spirit

[1] [Alike in the manuscript and in the typescript, this lecture or chapter is entitled "Serapion's Prayer Book and Cyril's Sacramental Lectures": and the following passage occurs in both as the sequel to the point here reached. C.J.C.]:
But this subject is developed with yet greater fulness in the *Addresses* of Cyril of Jerusalem to those who had just gone through the great and impressive experience of baptism, and so were ready to do justice to its full meaning, as understood in Jerusalem about the same time as that which Serapion's *Prayer-Book* represents for a typical church in Lower Egypt. Accordingly it will be best to deal here with the two witnesses together, for purposes of comparison — the more so that the results will furnish a good approach to the Church-Orders of the second half of the fourth century, to which we shall devote our next lecture [(last words altered in the typescript to "chapter").]

[This passage, however, is lined through in two out of the three extant typed

and its operation on the soul we have travelled. The order of
baptism in Serapion is as follows:

7. *"Sanctification of Waters.*

"King and Lord of all things and Artificer of the world, . . .
Thou Who didst redeem the creation that Thou didst fashion,
by the coming of Thine ineffable Word; see now from heaven
and look upon these waters, and fill them with holy Spirit.
Let Thine ineffable Word come to be in them and transform
their operation and cause them to be generative, being filled
with Thy grace, in order that the mystery which is now being
celebrated may not be found in vain in those that are being
regenerated, but may fill all those that descend (into them) and
are baptized with the Divine grace. . . . Form all that are being
regenerated (after) Thy Divine and ineffable form, in order
that, by means of having been formed and regenerated, they
may be able to be saved and to be counted worthy of Thy
Kingdom. And as Thine only-begotten Word coming down upon
the waters of the Jordan rendered them holy, so now also may
He descend in(to) these and make them holy and spiritual,
to the end that those who are being baptized may be no longer
flesh and blood, but spiritual, and able to worship, in holy
Spirit, Thee the uncreated Father through Jesus Christ, through
Whom to Thee (be) the glory and the might both now and to all
the ages of the ages. Amen".

8. *"Prayer on behalf of those being baptized.*

"We beseech Thee, O God of Truth, on behalf of this Thy
servant, and pray that Thou wouldst count him worthy of the
Divine mystery and of Thine ineffable regeneration. For unto
Thee, O Lover of men, is he now offered; to Thee do we dedicate
him. Graciously grant that he may share in this Divine regeneration, to the end that he may never again be led (away) by any
mischievous or evil being, but may serve Thee always and keep
Thine ordinances, Thine only-begotten Word guiding him, for
through Him to Thee (be) the glory and the might, in holy
Spirit, both now and to all the ages of the ages".

9. *"After the renunciation—a prayer.*

"O Lord almighty, seal the adhesion of this Thy servant

copies; and what has been printed above from this point to the end of the
chapter (incomplete as it seems to be) was apparently intended to take the
place of the promised joint treatment of Serapion and Cyril together. Furthermore, no discussion of Cyril's work—beyond the reference to him below on
p. 143 (n. 2) seems to be forthcoming in Dr. Bartlet's papers. I have therefore
altered the title of the chapter to suit its actual contents.   C.J.C.].

which has now been made to Thee, and continually keep his character and his manner (of life) unchangeable, ... to the end that he may be rendered perfect and genuinely Thine own, through", etc.[1]

10. *"After the acceptance[2]—a prayer.*

"O loving Benefactor, Saviour of all those who have turned to Thee, be gracious to this Thy servant. Guide him to the regeneration with Thy right hand. Let Thine only-begotten Word guide him to the bath. Let his regeneration be honoured; let it not be empty of Thy grace. Let Thy holy Word accompany him; let Thy holy Spirit be with him, scaring away and driving off every temptation: for through Thine Only-begotten, Jesus Christ", etc.

11. *"After he has been baptized and has come up—a prayer.*

"O God, the God of Truth, the Artificer of the universe, the Lord of all creation, bless this Thy servant with Thine own blessing. Make him pure by the regeneration; constitute him a partner with Thine angelic powers, in order that he may be called no longer flesh but spiritual, partaking of Thy Divine and

---

[1] [I append here no. 15, *Prayer relative to the anointing* (εἰς τὸ ἄλειμμα) *of those who are being baptized.* It is clearly a part of the baptismal ritual; but it does not appear in Dr. Bartlet's manuscript or typescript, possibly because its precise place, which is not indicated by the artificial arrangement of the oil-prayers in the original manuscript, is not certain. Brightman and Wordsworth both place it here, where it forms a suitable introduction to no. 10 (see below, n. 2 fin.). But it may possibly have stood originally before 9 or even before 7. It runs as follows:
["Kind and soul-loving Master, pitiful and merciful, God of truth, we call upon Thee, following out and obeying the promises of Thine Only-begotten, Who said,‖'Whosoever sins ye forgive, they are forgiven them' (John xx. 23); and we anoint with this unguent (τῷ ἀλείμματι τούτῳ) the men and women who come forward in this Divine re-birth, beseeching (Thee), so that our Lord Christ Jesus may exercise within them healing and strength-giving power, and may reveal by means of this anointing and cleanse away from their soul, body, (and) spirit every trace of sin and iniquity and Satanic guilt, and may by His own grace afford them forgiveness, 'in order that, having done with sin, they may live for righteousness' (1 Peter ii. 24), and that, being refashioned by means of this anointing (τῆς ἀλείψεως ταύτης), and being cleansed by means of the bath, and being renewed in the spirit, they may have strength to overcome in future the workings and deceits of this life which withstand and attack them, and may thus be bound and united to the flock of our Lord and Saviour Jesus Christ, and may inherit the promises along with the saints—for through Him (be) to Thee the glory and the might, in holy Spirit, for all the ages of the ages. Amen". C.J.C.].

[2] This word means "acceptance" or "adoption", i.e., adoption of the candidate by God as His child. It corresponds to the word used by Cyril of Jerusalem (*Catech. Myst.* i. 8) of the "adhesion" (σύνταξις) of the convert to Christ. "This was generally made by the recitation of a creed, to which, however, there is no distinct reference here" (J. Wordsworth, *Bishop Sarapion's Prayer Book* [1923], p. 71 n.). [It should, however, be observed that, on p. 129 above, Dr. Bartlet was disposed to accept as "convincing" Dr. Brightman's conjecture that we should read ἄλευψιν instead of ἀνάληψιν. C.J.C.].

universal Church" of God's planting.[1] Here the pseudo-Apostolic idea of Church-order, as having been given by Divine inspiration and authority to the Church in the Apostolic Age, attains its full-blown form—one on which the only possible advance of the imagination could be to assign the Church's whole institutional order to Christ Himself, a step actually taken in 'Testament (or final Will and Covenant) of our Lord', which must perhaps be dated a little later[2] and which belonged to another region. But while this was so, neither of these extravagant notions sprang suddenly to birth. They represented the gradual historical unfolding of the unhistoric idea that the order of the Church had been Divinely revealed and given from the first to and through the Apostles, in one way or another, instead of being a vital evolution under the pressure of God's Spirit, or the Spirit of Christ and His Gospel. It was the unfolding of the fact of the Church as the community of those who, through their acceptance of the Gospel of the Kingdom of God as begun on earth, had become possessed of and by the life of God as incarnate in Christ, the Head of a new type of humanity—a type realizing what had from the beginning been God's creative purpose. Certain important stages in the development of the naïve conception of the Apostolicity of the Church's actual order, of which conception the current notions of Apostolic Succession in its ministry were the expression and index, are represented in the various Church-Orders already passed in review. These prepared the way for its full-blown efflorescence, the 'Apostolic Constitutions', in the mind alike of its author and of the Church which, especially in the East, gave it such prompt and unquestioning acceptance.

The actual basis was laid for the compiler, and for the circle for which he wrote in the first instance, in the 'Didaskalia', written, as we have seen reason to believe, in the Antiochene region quite early in the third century. But the form of this work was itself suggested by the far earlier 'Didache', though the 'Apostolic Constitutions' add their own witness to the fact that this primitive work, so far from being (as some to-day argue) a hole-and-corner production, was in fact held even in early Catholic circles truly to represent the Apostolic beginnings.[3] For to the 'Didaskalia', itself the developed and exag-

---

[1] *Apost. Const.* I pref.
[2] [This is doubtful: see below, p. 151, n. 2.   C.J.C.].
[3] [See my note above, pp 54–56.   C.J.C.].

gerated fruit of the idea of the 'Didache' as Apostolic,[1] the compiler of the 'Apostolic Constitutions' adds his own expanded
version of the actual 'Didache',[2] as being too venerable a
product of the sub-Apostolic Age to be ignored. This version,
by the strong contrasts it affords when read side by side with
the original text, shows us in a flash the radical difference in
Church-feeling and Church-conceptions, which the intervening
three hundred years had wrought in the mentality of Christendom.

So far we have accounted for Books I–VI of the 'Apostolic
Constitutions' and for Book VII. i–xxxii. But what of the rest
of Book VII and the whole of Book VIII? Of these sections of
the work the former contains liturgical prayers, primarily of
thanksgiving, for the use of Church-members,[3] followed by
instruction for would-be members of "the holy Church", both
in the substance of the Christian faith and in the Church-order
by which their initiation into its life and corporate fellowship
was to be effected.[4] In these prayers, by the aid especially of
the parallels afforded by Serapion's Prayer-Book for a church
in Egypt about 350 A.D., we can recognize certain pre-anaphoral
prayers, probably those used in our compiler's own church
about A.D. 375, as forming the basis and substance of what we
find in the liturgical prayers just referred to. Similarly, the
instruction actually given to catechumens at the same place
and time is embodied in the immediate sequel. The chapter
which follows,[5] and ends with an Amen, dealing as it does with
the compiler's own chief interest, the office of the episcopate—
conceived as Apostolic in appointment and transmission—no
doubt came from his own hand, save for possible later additions
made for the sake of completeness by some early reader of the
work.[6] This being so, the domestic Christian prayers which
follow as a sort of Appendix,[7] viz., a morning- and an evening-
prayer, familiar to us as the "Gloria in Excelsis" and the "Te
decet Laus" of the Benedictine and other monastic Offices (into

---

[1] [Re-edited in *Apost. Const.* I–VI.   C.J.C.].
[2] [Re-edited in *Apost. Const.* VII. i–xxxii.   C.J.C.].
[3] *Apost. Const.* VII. xxxiii–xxxviii.
[4] *Apost. Const.* VII. xxxix–xlv.
[5] *Apost. Const.* VII. xlvi.
[6] The references to the obscure name "Marthones", a bishop of Tripolis in
Phoenicia, and to Aquila and Nicetes as bishops of "the parishes in Asia",
which come oddly in their present context, are perhaps due to the hand of
someone familiar with the pseudo-Clementine romance.
[7] *Apost. Const.* VII. xlvii–xlix.

which it finally found its way), and a blessing over daily food, were probably added by another hand.

Furnished with these analogies, we are able easily to account for the long eucharistic liturgy distinctive of the eighth Book.[1] This appears to be a part of the service connected with the rites for the appointment of a bishop (now conceived as a pontiff or chief-priest). It again is, no doubt, the local use, partly re-written by our compiler in terms of his own special theology. That theology we can now identify fairly well, by the aid of comparison with the theology of the interpolator of the Ignatian Epistles. The latter belong to much the same circle[2] and date, though perhaps he wrote a few years earlier, if what he used was not the 'Apostolic Constitutions' themselves, but the expanded 'Didaskalia' called 'Diataxeis', which Epiphanius also seems to quote. The theology in question was of the same type as that adopted by Eusebius of Caesarea,[3] especially in his work against Marcellus, who minimized in a Sabellian direction the dis-tinction between Father and Son. While not rejecting the Nicene theory of Christ's pre-existent and incarnate person, Eusebius and the compiler of the 'Apostolic Constitutions' dwelt on the subordination of the Son, in both of these states, to the unorig-inated and self-existent or absolute being of God His Father. But this aspect of the 'Apostolic Constitutions' concerns us here only in so far as it enables us to recognize and eliminate what in the compiler's text is due to his own revising hand rather than to his sources.

This brings us to the question of the second main written basis of his work, besides the 'Didaskalia'. The question has only recently been cleared up by the identification of the "Hippo-lytean" Church-Order as the common basis not only of large sections of the eighth Book of the 'Apostolic Constitutions',[4] but also of a wide-spread group of documents, some earlier than this compilation and some later in their present form. Of the former class one may name the latter portion of a volume of Church-Orders in Latin contained in the ancient Verona-manuscript, and in the Egyptian form of the same work (com-

---

[1] *Apost. Const.* VIII. vi–xv.

[2] His actual locality may have been that of Castabala, to the north-west of Antioch.

[3] Whose *Ecclesiastical History* is the main source of the compiler's historical allusions.

[4] *Apost. Const.* VIII. i–v, xvi–xxvi, xxix–xxxii—and less-directly most of what follows down to xlvi, though this is actually based on the usage of his own church.

monly, though misleadingly, called the 'Egyptian Church-Order') in its earliest traceable text. Of the latter class, we possess: (1) the so-called 'Epitome', based for the most part on the 'Apostolic Constitutions', but going back in the prayers for the ordination of a bishop and a reader (and also in minor touches elsewhere) to the so-called "Hippolytean" Church-Order, in a fairly-early text; (2) the 'Testament of our Lord'; and (3) the 'Canons of Hippolytus', which, while precious as representing an early line of the text of the Church-Order of Hippolytus independent of that underlying the 'Egyptian Church-Order', yet has much later matter, picked up during its history as a document in Egypt, down to the time when it was translated into Arabic. Where it agrees with the 'Testament of our Lord' (which represents a region widely removed from itself), it is of the greatest weight in fixing the primitive form of this so-called "Hippolytean" source. This latter we shall hereafter call, in keeping with our argument in a former lecture,[1] the 'Old-Syrian Order'; it probably belonged to the same region to which the other sources used in the 'Apostolic Constitutions' belonged. The points at which, and the way in which, the later compilation modifies this fundamental and most-representative Old-Syrian source, are most important for the definition of the compiler's ideal of Church-order and that of his time and place, and so for the rate and direction of the changes passing over northern Syrian Christianity in the century which probably lay between that source and the compiler himself. To the changes relating to the office of the ministry we shall have to return later.

To return now to our literary and historical analysis of the 'Apostolic Constitutions'—besides the local oral tradition of the compiler's own region, to which may be referred the substance of all in the eighth Book which does not go back to the Old-Syrian Church-Order, there was perhaps one other body of Church-rules which lay before him. It might have contained the first fifty (those recorded by Dionysius Exiguus) of the eighty-five so-called 'Apostolic Canons' which conclude the work,[2] save for its closing peroration. The latter,[3] like the chapter on "Good Order" ($\epsilon\vec{v}\tau a\xi i a$) in the Church, and especially among its graded hierarchy,[4] which immediately precedes those Canons, and out of which they seem to grow organically (as also verbally

---

[1] See above, pp. 105 ff.
[2] *Apost. Const.* VIII. xlvii.
[3] *Apost. Const.* VIII. xlviii.
[4] *Apost. Const.* VIII. xlvi.

by the "Well, then" [τοίνυν], which introduces them), shows our
author's own favourite motifs, and no doubt comes from his
pen. It is addressed, like the end of the eighty-fifth Canon,
directly to the bishops of the Church at large, and urges upon
them the observance of the foregoing Divine pattern of Church-
order, as the condition of salvation and especially of peace
between them, the prime guardians of peace in the Church
generally. The opening clause of the closing benediction is very
characteristic. "And God, the sole Unbegotten, and Maker
through Christ of the universe, shall in (virtue of) holy Spirit
unite you all by means of peace, (and) perfect you unto every
good work. . . .".[1]

In the above-outlined analysis of the literary structure of the
'Apostolic Constitutions', one is on fairly-safe ground for the
most part, save for the still-disputed matter of the "Hippolytean" Church-Order, the nucleus of which many are content to
trace to a Roman Church-Order contained in a work of Hippolytus, whether that 'On Grace-gifts' (περὶ χαρισμάτων) or rather
one entitled 'Apostolic Tradition'. Otherwise, the Verona Latin
fragments of a volume of Church-Orders, published in 1900,[2]
have given us the framework ready to hand of a compilation
such as our 'Apostolic Constitutions'. For it contains the
'Didaskalia', the 'Apostolic Church-Order' (in its final Egyptian
form), and the Syrian Church-Order, which came, by virtue of
some Hippolytean basis (smaller or larger), to be current as a
body of "Apostolic tradition" regarding the Church's constitution "through the medium of Hippolytus". But while the
compiler's idea of writing up his more-unified body of 'Apostolic
Constitutions' no doubt came to him from some such volume,
in which earlier Orders, Apostolic in one sense or another,
followed each other within the limits of a single manuscript,
it was probably not a volume of exactly the same contents as
that of our Latin manuscript that lay before him: in any case,
even if it were so, he did not adopt it entirely, as it stood, as the
framework of his organic construction. For, unlike the 'Testament of our Lord' (which belongs to another region, probably
bordering on Cappadocia), he ignores the 'Apostolic Church-
Order', and uses instead the 'Didache'. Nor is it to be assumed
that the text in which the so-called "Hippolytean" or Old-
Syrian Church-Order lay before him was the same as that
preserved in our Latin version. It probably still included the

---

[1] *Apost. Const.* VIII. xlviii. 3.   [2] See above, p. 107, n. 2.

first section, 'On Grace-gifts', which our Latin version pre-
supposes, but does not give. The text implied elsewhere, e.g.,
in his prayer over a bishop, is not verbally identical. This being
so, it is natural to ask whether or no there are indications that
his other chief source, the 'Didaskalia', was in exactly the same
form as that in which it is preserved in our Latin and Syriac
versions. The answer seems to be in the negative. Not only have
we traces of the 'Didaskalia', especially in citations from
Epiphanius (about 375 A.D.), as current under the title 'Ordin-
ances ($\Delta\iota\alpha\tau\acute{\alpha}\xi\epsilon\iota\varsigma$) of the Apostles'—a title very similar to, if not
identical with, the original form of the title prefixed to the
'Apostolic Constitutions' ($\delta\iota\alpha\tau\acute{\alpha}\xi\epsilon\iota\varsigma$ or $\delta\iota\alpha\tau\alpha\gamma\alpha\acute{\iota}$); but internal
evidence also seems to point strongly in the same direction.
That is, an intermediate form of the 'Didaskalia' came into
being, in order to bring things up to date, at some date between
the first half of the third century and the latter part of the
fourth, very much as we saw to be the case with other Apostolic
Church-Orders.[1]

The[2] fact that the 'Apostolic Constitutions' purported to be
given to the Church through the medium of Clement, the
disciple of Peter, makes the work an outgrowth of the pseudo-
Petrine variety of the genus pseudo-Apostolic. But there was
another famous reputed disciple of Apostles—one belonging to
Antioch, the very centre of the pseudo-Petrine tradition. This
was Ignatius, the first and most famous of Antiochian bishops,
and one whose writings actually survived to the end of the
fourth century. It was natural, then, that another member of
the same school of thought and Church-ideals as the author of
the 'Apostolic Constitutions' should take Ignatius' Epistles as
the basis for his propaganda in the interests of a graded hier-
archic system of Church-order, with the episcopate as its centre
and pivot, and should do so in an even-more emphatic and
thorough-going spirit than his rather-earlier colleague. The
Pseudo-Ignatian Epistles, which long stood in the way of the
identification and general recognition of the genuine seven

---

[1] See above, pp. 93–96.

[2] [It seems clear that this section of the lectures, at least as represented in the
extant typescript, is not complete. Not only the general wording of the title,
but a pencil note alongside of it in the manuscript, suggests that Dr. Bartlet
intended to deal also with *The Testament of our Lord*, a Cilician Church-Order
of about 350–360 A.D. The manuscript contains at this point a host of pencil
notes: but there is nothing that could be suitably printed as a conclusion of the
chapter, except the passage which follows from this point on. C.J.C.].

(though, in the light of the later development, we must be ready, if needful, to recognize occasional interpolated words or clauses even in them), were the result. They differ from the system of the 'Apostolic Constitutions' only in details, such as the order of the second and third traditional Roman bishops, viz., Anencletus and Clement, and . . . ? one or two of the minor orders.

Besides the comprehensive compilations we have already dealt with, which attained a sort of organic unity by the hand of an individual author, we have finally to note the existence of collections more of the type represented by the Verona Latin version. That is, the component parts are hardly more than placed in succession in a manuscript, and so meant to be read together as mutually supplementary: they are loosely connected by literary links, to the extent at least of cross-references between the several units, in keeping with the general idea that they are all writings of the Apostles themselves as a corporate body. That this was the case in the original form of the Greek collection underlying the Verona-manuscript is hardly likely in view of the fact that, at the close of its "Hippolytean" Church-Order, the first person singular of Hippolytus's own address to his readers in commending to them some kind of 'Apostolic Tradition' is allowed to survive. On the other hand, in the prefaces to the ordination-prayers for presbyters and deacons, the pseudo-Apostolic form of address seems to have crept in, and in the latter case a back-reference to the 'Apostolic Church-Order' as a supplemental authority apparently occurs. There may be secondary touches in this manuscript; but the process seems to have gone somewhat further in the Egyptian 'Statutes of the Apostles', that part of the Egyptian Octateuch, or yet-more-comprehensive corpus of pseudo-Apostolic Church-law. To the genesis of this larger whole there went also the 'Testament of our Lord', as the final authority lying at the foundation of all. And the case was much the same with the corresponding Octateuch of the Syrian Church.

CHAPTER IX

REVIEW AND CONCLUSIONS[1]

WE have now to try to review the general effect of our survey of Church-life and Church-order down to the close of the fourth century. In so doing we are first struck by the varying nature of our evidence at different stages of the story. To remember and allow for this becomes thus the first duty of the historian of the institutions of the early Church, on pain of constructing otherwise an artificial mosaic rather than a reflexion of the real past. If the first and last law of the historical interpretation of a single document is the law of context, including not only the nearer context of its words but also the wider context of the whole writing (i.e., its place in its writer's whole outlook and interests in writing), surely the same law applies no less to the necessity of reading a document or a series of documents in relation to the total context of Church-life and Church-usage which can be shown to have any relevance to it or them. This is the case particularly with the occurrence of the same terms, which at different times and places may bear somewhat varying senses.

But in order to apply this great canon of historical context-judgment successfully, we must not only be on our guard against using loosely and inexactly data from different writers whose time and place are known to us, but also take even more pains to locate and date, as far as possible, anonymous documents like Church-Orders.

There is further difficulty in connexion with the accurate use of them as historical evidence for processes of change in practice and in the ideas behind such change. For not one of those Church-Orders which we have to handle is strictly speaking a unit: they all include different historic strata side by side, whether by way of simple accretion by means of additions or interpolations, or in virtue of the working-up of earlier historical units into some fresh organic synthesis, due to a single moulding

---

[1] [I have taken the liberty of restoring to their places in the text of this chapter certain passages which Dr. Bartlet had—perhaps for reasons of brevity— square-bracketed in his manuscript and omitted from his typescript. Such passages as I have included seemed to me too good to lose: but in order to avoid all possible risk of misrepresenting his meaning, I have placed them within double round brackets (( )). C.J.C.].

mind, like the author of the 'Apostolic Constitutions', our chief specimen of that type.

If these chapters contain any fresh contribution to their subject, it will be partly in the direction just indicated, as suggesting the essential conditions of a sound method in the handling of our evidence, and partly in the form of a steady effort to treat Church-order as relative to and conditioned by the kind of Church-life which it expresses, and on which in turn it reacts not a little as time goes on. The specific nature of Christian life, whether individual or corporate, turns mainly upon emphasis on certain ideas and usages in preference to others, within the total faith and practice of the Church, whether local or general, at the time in question. And with this vital matter of distinctive emphasis we begin our present review.

What, we asked in our first chapter, was the genius of genuinely-primitive Church-life and Church-order, both in the Apostolic Age and in so much at least of the Sub-Apostolic Age as was really determined by Apostolic teaching and practice? Apostolic Church-life was essentially the outcome of a new experience, which first came to birth on the Day of Pentecost, and which was reproduced in every part of the expanding Church in its early days. It was an experience of overpowering Divine inspiration, called "holy Spirit", and viewed as the characteristic possession and mark of Christians, both collectively and individually, as distinct from all outside the Church. It was in virtue of such inspiration that Christians felt themselves to be "holy", or marked out with the consecrating touch of God Himself as members of His holy People or Church, and set apart from all else for His special possession. This consciousness of Divine energy working God's will within, as if by God's own animating breath (the root idea of "spirit"— $\pi\nu\epsilon\hat{\nu}\mu\alpha$—in the Bible), gave rise to a wonderful spontaneity of inward impulse towards the expression of the first Diviner vision of the meaning and end of human life. It was essentially joint-life with God. The natural issue of such a consciousness of sharing a common privilege and interest, in virtue of so sacred and inherent a bond of Divine origin, was an intense sense of "fellowship", of social solidarity raised to its highest power. The primitive Christian Church, then, in its religious essence, may be defined in terms of the Apostolic benediction (2 Cor. xiii. 14). It was the fellowship, both subjectively and objectively, of the love of God, revealed and shed abroad in human hearts, through the grace of Jesus Christ, as realized in and by holy or Divine inspiration.[1] This fellowship took effect alike in the inner and in the outer spheres of human life, in the soul and in the body, and in all that concerned the good of either. Primitive maxims like the following express this vividly: (("Never rejoice, save when ye have looked on your brother in love";[2] or even more boldly and impressively)), "Thou hast seen thy brother: thou hast seen thy God".[3] And again, "If ye are sharers in that which is immortal, how much more (should ye be) in things mortal".[4] In such a perspective and atmosphere the great ideal of religion as love to God and one's neighbour attained a new meaning and possibility of fulfilment. Thus in emphasis and in characteristic genius Apostolic Christianity was a religion of inspiration, mediated through the historic revelation in Jesus the Lord's Anointed, God manifest in manhood. As such it was a religion animated by a spirit of power, free—so long as it was true to its historical basis in Christ—to create an order of corporate or Church-life akin to its own nature. But, it may be asked, is not this very idea of an inspired community, drawing its life so largely from within its own consciousness, ((even though it have an objective norm or test of true development in the historic personality and teaching of its Founder and abiding spiritual Head)), very hard to harmonize in practice with any notion of "order", as an element of coherence and effective unity? ((How can the forms of organized life which it finds and fashions at one stage fail to become a new sort of Law, hampering and in the end arresting by the weight of prescriptive authority the continuous free initiative which seems an indispensable principle of the liberty of the Spirit, as it was enjoyed by the Church of the first age?)). How real this difficulty of harmonizing the two actually is, is illustrated by the fact that our survey has shown emerging more and

---

[1] This idea, which made the Church in an experimental sense the Spirit-moved body of Christ, in all its members severally and in their corporate action, together with the consequences which flowed from this faith taken seriously in practice, has been set forth with much insight and competent scholarship by Dr. C. Anderson Scott in his book entitled *The Fellowship of the Spirit* (London, 1921).

[2] [A non-canonical supposed saying of Jesus preserved by Jerome (*Comm. in Ephes.* v. 4). C.J.C.].

[3] [A non-canonical supposed saying of Jesus, preserved by Clement of Alexandria (*Stromateis*, I. xix. 94, II. xv. 70) and Tertullian (*De Oratione*, 26). C.J.C.].

[4] *Didache*, iv. 8.

more, particularly in the Church-Orders of the third and fourth
centuries, the theory of an original constitution or binding order
imposed by Divine authority upon the Church, ((the docile
acceptance of which came to be regarded as the very water-
mark and proof of the fact that the Divine Spirit was present
in an individual or in a group of Christians smaller or larger)).
This binding constitution was sometimes conceived as a body
of definite usages forming what can be called a "Catholic", i.e.,
a universally-valid, order; and sometimes it was thought of, as
in modern times is most frequently the case, as a matter of only
one or two constitutive principles, such as Apostolic Succession,
and the Catholic type of episcopate associated therewith, as
its concrete, historic medium of transmitted authority. But in
any case, the end of the process in ancient Catholicism was
certainly a new system of Law for the Church, wholly analogous
in nature and similar in its effects to the Law in Judaism.
Over against this may be placed the judgment of Dr. Hort, who
speaks of "the futility of endeavouring to make the Apostolic
history into a set of authoritative precedents",[1] (resting on a
supposed constitutional commission covering their action in the
region of Church-order and guaranteeing certain elements in
it as permanently binding on faith), precedents "to be rigorously
copied without regard to time and place, thus turning the
Gospel into a second Levitical Code.[2] The Apostolic Age is full
of embodiments of purposes and principles of the most instructive kind: but the responsibility of choosing the means was left
for ever to the Ecclesia itself, and to each Ecclesia, guided by
ancient precedent on the one hand and adaptation to present
and future needs on the other. The lesson-book of the Ecclesia,
and of every Ecclesia, is not a law but a history".[3] Such a judgment is warranted by the distinctive nature of Christianity as a
religion mediated under the form, not of a law, but of a unique
historic personality. ((For that personality not only is embodied,
as regards its historic manifestation, in an abiding written form,
but also works in the Spirit communicated to the society or
Church which was created by the action of the same Spirit.

---

[1] F. J. A. Hort, *The Christian Ecclesia*, p. 232.

[2] How true a description this sentence of Hort's is of what happened in
certain circles as early as the third century may be seen from Cyprian (as cited,
for example, in Lightfoot's essay on 'The Christian Ministry' in his *Philippians*,
pp. 240 ff., 258 f.), from *Didaskalia* II, and even more from the corresponding
part of *Apost. Const.* at the end of the fourth century.

[3] F. J. A. Hort, *The Christian Ecclesia*, pp. 232 f.

Thus the controlling Spirit of Christ continues to live as an interpretative power in the Church, enlightening it as to the true meaning alike of its Founder's life and teaching, and of its own tradition of life and order to which these have given birth)).

It is this lesson-book of an age-long history that we have been studying in these chapters. And what we have now to notice is not so much its legal rather than evangelic spirit, in the sense of the above passage, as the gradualness of the stages by which Christians ceased to be aware of the many past adaptations of Apostolic principles to new conditions, which lay between the Apostles' own thoughts and practices and those which in their own day were coming to lay almost-exclusive claim to Apostolic authority. ((The paradox of the whole story is, in fact, the degree to which the Church-order which came finally to claim such sacrosanct fixity had itself grown up gradually by the free plastic movement of the Church's common mind under the consciousness of a guiding spirit of Divine life within it, albeit increasingly denying to minorities a like freedom to adhere to forms of order previously recognized as fit expressions and vehicles of the Spirit's action, and much more so a freedom to obey what seemed to them amid changing conditions to be the leading of the Spirit then and there.

((Here we may see an excessive zeal for a positive principle of good, namely, the Christian principle of unity in action, as flowing from a love which "looks also on the things of others" (Phil. ii. 4), a zeal which thus caused the principle in question to pass into the loveless spirit of coercive intolerance, in the interests of the seeming short-cut to unity through uniformity —which is the method of Law, not of the Spirit. "Corruptio optimi pessima".

((But it is good at the same time to realize for how long a time the instinct of the Church as the "fellowship of the Spirit"— that Spirit of Christ, the fruit of which is "love, joy, peace, longsuffering, kindness, generosity, trustworthiness, gentleness, self-control" (Gal. v. 22 f.), in contrast with strife, wrath, faction, division, as states of the soul, whether in minorities or majorities—lived on and arrested the growth of externally-imposed uniformity, such as was tending to repress the free spirit of Christian prophecy and the impulse to exercise the grace-gifts of the Spirit for the common good.

((In so saying, we are not at the moment thinking primarily

of the traces of the Spirit's free energy in those groups of Christians who passed, whether mainly as a result of their own infirmities of temper, or as a result of those of the official leaders of the majority, outside the communion of what came to call itself—over against those whom it had excluded—the "Universal" or "Catholic Church")).[1] The story of Montanism has its lessons of warning to all, if especially to those who try to be true to the Spirit by adhering to past forms, as if these were God's last word.

But for the present we are concerned more with the traces of the persistence of the free and prophetic Spirit under forms of order which appealed to the Church at large as safer and yet not inconsistent with free, if more-ordered, illumination. These forms were of the official type, and show growing conformity to existing varieties of order, proper to contemporary thought and usage. This process of assimilation went on for the most part unconsciously, by a natural instinct due to racial mentality and training. No doubt, too, the Church felt herself free to use such existing forms as were untainted by idolatry and at the same time congenial to herself. In its first stage, when under the leadership of Jews like the Apostles, most of her usages were of the Hebraic type, having been taken over from Judaism. At this basal stage of Church-order, any elements taken over from other sources (as Christianity passed into the wider life of the Roman Empire—with its cosmopolitan though largely Greek culture) were but secondary, and remained secondary for a century or more. And even thereafter the process of naturalization in terms of Greek, Oriental, and Roman culture, went on with very varying degrees of rapidity and thoroughness. Thus in northern Syria, to which along with Egypt most of our early Church-Orders happen to belong, the Jewish tradition was especially strong and influential. Here we find that the great changes in emphasis mostly come only in the third century; and even so, in its second rather than its first half. During the second century the non-Jewish mentality of the Church was constantly increasing in volume, and was gradually reading its own thoughts, both theological and sacramental, into the Church's Biblical language and symbolic rites, and was

---

[1] [The sequence of thought at this point is not very clear. Dr. Bartlet apparently has in mind certain manifestations of spiritual freedom even within the "Catholic Church" itself. But the sad fact was that such freedom usually led to excommunication by the majority, as was the case with the Montanists. Hence the point of the immediately ensuing reference to them. C.J.C.].

likewise grafting its own usages and forms upon the fundament-
ally-Jewish basis of Church-order.[1]

Local conditions as affecting Church-order fall under two
main heads, external and internal. An instance of the former is
afforded by the separation of the social and human side of the
fellowship of the Spirit, in the primitive Lord's Supper, from its
aspect of Divine worship, represented at first by the eucharistic
hallowing of the meal of brotherly love (agape) by words of
solemn blessing or thanksgiving addressed to God in prayer. As
Roman administration looked askance at such social gatherings
(when not legally sanctioned) as possible centres of sedition, this
fact told strongly for the separation in question, especially as
the growth of numbers made the old type of the corporate
Church-Supper inconvenient in any case. Thus even if, as is
probable, agapae on one scale or another,[2] private or semi-
private, continued to be held as occasion favoured, the corporate
eucharist or solemn thanksgiving over bread and wine would
largely escape suspicion by becoming attached to the ordinary
Sunday-worship, on the lines of Jewish worship in the synagogue. This was a most momentous change, leading as it did to
new associations of ideas and new ritual developments in
keeping therewith. Thus had the eucharistic prayer remained,
as in the 'Didache'[3] and in the breaking of bread in Acts (ii. 42,
46, xx. 7, 11), as also in Pauline usage (cf. 1 Cor. x f.), connected
with a social meal, it would hardly have developed the awe-
inspiring meaning which "the awful mysteries" of late fourth-
century writers came to connote.

But there was, I suspect, another factor, internal to Church-
life itself, making for this same separation, viz., the desire to
avoid the risk of factious sectional eucharistic groups arising
within a local church, and so tending to destroy its corporate
unity—a danger against which, as we see from Ignatius, the
bishop was felt to be the great rallying-point and safeguard.
This danger would be the greater as numbers increased.

But such local increase had other far-reaching effects upon

[1] [The following note is written in Dr. Bartlet's hand on the back of a letter
dated 11th March 1926. C. J. C.]: *Birkbeck Lectures.* Preface or epilogue—dwelling
on the Jewish or rather Hebraic type of the life and order in the early Church,
and the gradual fading of this before the incoming of the Hellenistic type: the
symbolic theory of outer forms replaced by the more realistic.

[2] On this subject, as on all relating to the history of the Christian love-feasts,
see Dr. J. F. Keating's *The Agapé and the Eucharist in the Early Church*
(Methuen, 1901).

[3] *Didache,* ix f.

Church-order, in the way of a more-elaborately specialized ministry. The classic instance of this is afforded by the church in Rome, revealed to us in a letter written by its bishop Cornelius to Fabius, bishop of Antioch, about 252 A.D.[1] This furnishes a landmark in our knowledge of developing Church-order. Its special interest for us here is that it illustrates the expansion of the ministry, by subdivision of labour among a larger number of offices, as due to the increase of numbers; that in fact what we call the minor orders, those below deacons, were due mainly to this cause, since in the account of public worship in the 'Didaskalia', of somewhat earlier date, the deacons alone suffice for its purposes. In Rome, however, the large body of presbyters, forty-six, points to there being already many Chapels-of-Ease, as it were, besides the central congregation, where was the bishop's official chair and where he usually led the worship. Further, while the deacons were limited even at Rome, by the characteristically-Roman instinct to adhere to strict precedent in matters of official form, to the number seven—found in the Church's book of ecclesiastical laws and precedents, the Acts of the Apostles (vi. 3)—the needed practical relief was obtained, again characteristically, by a sort of legal device, the appointment of secondary or subordinate deacons, one to assist each of the seven. There were also forty-two acolytes or attendants, six of these, as well as a subdeacon, being under the immediate direction of each deacon;[2] and all these offices would come into operation in public worship largely in connexion with the localized duties of certain of the presbyters implied above. This anticipation of the future elaboration of Church-order was, we repeat, closely connected with the contingent factor of growth in numbers, in the first instance mainly in certain great cities.

Next we come to consider another and most important factor in the different forms under which Church-order existed at the same period in different parts of the Roman Empire. This is the local factor in its psychological aspect, that due to racial and cultural varieties of mentality and custom. It worked largely by a process of natural selection upon the fundamental or Jewish genius and forms of primitive Christianity, causing some principles and elements to persist and develop along the

---

[1] Quoted in Eusebius, *Church-History*, VI. xliii. 11. See above, p. 120.
[2] So W. H. Frere, in *Essays on the Early History of the Church and the Ministry*, p. 302.

line of their original and proper spirit, and some to be modified
or replaced by other principles and forms of Church-order.
Much depended, then, upon the degree of affinity or otherwise
between this or that local cultural type underlying the superficial Graeco-Roman uniformity of the Roman Empire, and the
Hebraic genius and forms of Apostolic and even early sub-
Apostolic Church-life. In this respect the affinity was greatest
in northern Syria and Egypt, in those circles where Christianity
at first took root, in virtue of the large Jewish settlements in
them and the strong Jewish tradition diffused around them; and
the like is equally true, to judge from Clement and Hermas, of
Rome in the West, where there was also a psychological affinity
in the legal cast of mind in religion proper to both. Thus Latin
minds would naturally fix upon those aspects and forms of
Church-order which lent themselves most easily to a legal
interpretation and development, while it would tend, first
merely to tolerate, and then to modify and set aside, those
elements, such as the "charismatic" and particularly the prophetic, which did not readily accord with their native sense of
the fitness of things. ((We see the impatience of this type of
mentality with variety of forms, rather than uniformity, in the
controversy which took place in the latter part of the second
century about the proper time for the observance of Easter,
wherein the spirit of the Roman bishop Victor contrasts with
the larger and more-comprehensive attitude of the Greek
Irenaeus, who urged that the convergence in idea of independent methods of expression did but confirm the essential truth
behind both forms of manifesting the Easter-faith)). As it
happens, however, nearly, if not quite, all of our earliest
existing Church-Orders (as distinct from incidental references
to Church-order) belong to the East, and in the first instance to
a region centring in Antioch and at no point very far removed
from it and its type of Christianity. That is, northern Syria
and the borders of Cilicia and Cappadocia adjacent to it, where
a certain blending of Asian racial culture would also be found,
seem to cover the whole area represented by every one of our
third-century Church-Orders in their original forms.[1]

Church-order being, like Church-life, an expression of the
spiritual under the concrete, visible, and material forms of

[1] [It was at this point that the matter I have reproduced above, on pp. 119–
124, originally stood in Dr. Bartlet's typescript: see p. 119, n. 2. C.J.C.].

time and space, we should naturally expect that this aspect of things, namely the symbolic or sacramental, would have a profound influence on its development. And such in fact was the case. Accordingly our study of the whole subject would be incomplete and misleading, if we passed over this factor in total silence, even in such a brief survey as this.

The sacramental principle is that of spiritual suggestiveness, outward and sensible things or acts being regarded as signs of inward and spiritual realities. Now the essential spiritual reality of Church-life was fellowship in the Spirit, or spiritual oneness in and through love, at once Divine and human, the human being seen as akin to the Divine in its true idea and inmost nature. This profound truth appears in Old-Testament foreshadowings in the idea of Messiah, God really and fully present as man with men; and in the New Testament it was realized in Jesus the Christ, in Whose personality the Word of God, the "Good News" or Gospel, was incarnate and so objectively expressed. Thus the primary Christian sacrament is the incarnate Christ. Once realized in this supreme form, however, the Gospel-fact and -message could again be expressed to sense in a secondary and more-purely symbolic way, by forms addressed directly to the senses and not only indirectly, through the remoter conventional symbolism of human language. Thus sacraments, as Augustine put it, are "visible words" ("visibilia verba"), and make an appeal to the intuitive insight and receptivity of the whole man or personality, below the partial and limiting conceptions of the reflective intellect, which varies so greatly in men, at this or that stage of mental development. In that respect, viz., as intuitive rather than reflectively intellectual, the experience mediated by the Spirit through outward sacrament is analogous to the insight or vision lying at the root of "prophecy" rather than doctrine. Hence they appeal directly to the spiritual feelings, to that side of our rational or ideal nature which is in immediate and vital alliance with the emotions. In a word, they speak to the heart in the sense in which the heart, in the sphere of religion, is, as intuitive, larger than, indeed potentially inclusive of, the head or analytical understanding. Sacraments, then, may be regarded as specially-appropriate media of mystical or implicit, rather than rationalized or explicit, spiritual experience, if only the accent here falls, not on the vague aspect of the mystical, but on the suggestive aspect—suggestive of ideal truths larger and deeper than we have as yet ability to think out into clearness of perception. In this sense not only is the personality of the historic Jesus the supreme sacrament, "God manifest in the flesh", the Divine dwelling completely in the human, with all the limitations of bodily existence (Col. ii. 9); but the Cross also, as Paul preached it, viz., as setting forth to the heart Christ as crucified, is a sacrament. So too with the Lord's Supper, as reproducing the Passion and its significance in its ultimate aspect, viz., that of communion with God and with our fellow-men, as conditioned by Christ in His most-essential aspect, love to the uttermost self-giving.

Now at the heart of all the spiritual suggestiveness of such a sacrament lies the idea of unity, unity with God, but no less unity with men as co-heirs of the Divine love and grace. All then in the ordering of this great sacrament—the one most distinctive of Christ's Church—that may tend to obscure the aspect of unity must be avoided; while all that by its very form tends to further its realization should, as heightening the central suggestions of the sacrament, be welcomed and utilized. This consideration was a chief factor making for the unification of the ministry of the eucharist as regards human agency. It lay behind the preference for man, rather than woman, as the actor in this most representative of corporate Church-acts—man being more typical of mankind as a whole.[1]

The eucharist was par excellence the sacrament of oneness, of communion in all spiritual relations, human as well as divine: any breach of love, as profaning the quality of the sacrifice of thanksgiving by the brethren acting as united to and in Christ, their Head and High-priest in Heaven, was guarded against by the symbolic kiss of peace before they began their eucharist, by lifting their hearts above, to the heavenly sphere ("Sursum corda"), where in spirit all that followed was enacted and took effect. The worship proceeded in the form of a symbolic representation on earth, by means of bread and wine (as the antitypes of spiritual realities), of the heavenly worship—earth and heaven, human and Divine, being essentially united in the spirit, "in holy Spirit in the holy Church", as it was expressed in the

---

[1] With the question of expediency to-day, as compared with earlier centuries, we are not here concerned. It may now be important to qualify the symbolism of unity in the interests of avoiding the suggestion of dualism between man and woman, even "in Christ". For the symbolism, even if originally meant in its inclusive aspect, *may* be viewed rather in its exclusive aspect, and so obscure to many minds the vital truth of spiritual equality before God.

The hypothesis therefore of confusion through misinformation, which some scholars have recently advanced is no longer tenable.[1]

As one looks back on the whole development of the ministry of the Divine Spirit in and to the Church, from its widely-different and spontaneous forms in the Apostolic Age to its highly-concentrated and regulated forms in the persons of a specialized clergy—forming a sacred class marked off from the general body of Christians by the sharp dividing-line of ordination—one cannot but be struck by the greatness of the contrast in form and order. To all outward appearance there is a shrinkage in the relative numbers of those exercising, or feeling any call to exercise, Spirit-gifts for the good of the whole brotherhood. In a word, the conception of Church-life and -ministry implied in St. Paul's words in Romans xii (to say nothing of 1 Cor. xii–xiv) had become well-nigh unintelligible, so great was the change, not only in practice, but also in thought and standpoint.

What, then, of the inner spirit and ethos behind the changed forms? How far was there an underlying identity of type? Had the admitted historical continuity of the development, scrupulously safeguarded—so far as concerned outward order—through the transmission of the regular ministry by ordination, availed to conserve the original type in the very soul of the Church? What of its sense of "holy Spirit" from God as the life of life in its whole membership, severally as well as corporately?

These are grave questions, to which there are no easy answers, and to which it is hard even to essay in a brief space any answers that shall not run the risk of being misleading. Yet some sort of an attempt at appraising the nature and meaning of the changes in question, which affect all Church-life down to our own day, must be made ere we close our study of it.

What is clear is the immense change in form. The element of fixity in the modes under which Church-life had come to express itself corporately, as compared with the striking freedom and

1927), pp. 39–95: he enumerates the various theories that have been propounded, without himself fixing finally on any. But it may be added that Dom Morin himself, in *Revue Bénédictine*, vol. xlv, pp. 251–255 (July 1928), abandoned his proposed identification of Ambrosiaster with Evagrius, and tentatively advocated the claims of Nummius Aemilianus Dexter, son of Pacianus, the Spanish bishop of Barcelona, and a friend of Jerome. C.J.C.].

[1] [See below, p. 171, n. 1.   C.J.C.].

variety of the ways of doing this in the Apostolic Age, must be our first and dominant impression, as we look back from the end of the fourth century. The element of "order" is not only more in evidence, but is also more rigid and dominant. In fact it now leaves little or no room for the liberty of the Spirit, as directly related to personal (in distinction from official) inspiration in such a way as to be available for the common good in worship, teaching, or counsel. Prophecy—in the original Christian sense of fresh insight vouchsafed to individuals by God's own free action, to which it was the Church's part to give recognition and opportunity of utterance—was practically a thing of the past. In so far as it entered into the Church's mind at all, it was assumed to have become confined to certain official channels, those of the primary order of formally and ritually consecrated "priests", i.e., the presbyterate and its official head the bishop. It was no longer recognizable, in any normal or practical way, outside those humanly-imposed limits.

Further,[1] "the holy Church" is no longer spoken of, possibly not even conceived of, as itself "a royal priesthood", "kings and priests unto God": and herein we feel already[2] one of those changes, at first of emphasis, but later of more than emphasis, which—when taken together—mark off pretty sharply the genius of Catholic Christianity in the fourth century from that of primitive or Apostolic Christianity, and even of the so-called Apostolic Fathers as a whole.

The sole exception[3] was one which rather proves the rule that the Church as such had no longer any use for free Christian prophecy in its midst, as of old. For it was only in non-churchly persons, like hermits and others who retreated almost as much from ordinary Church-fellowship as they did from the world, that fourth-century Christians were able to recognize and find a place for the free prophetic function of the Spirit in unordained members of Christ's Body.

In this way, as in others, the monastic movement among Christian ascetics, i.e., among those "in training" for the fully-

---

[1] [I insert at this point a paragraph which originally stood in Dr. Bartlet's first draft for Chapter V, but which he noted as to be used in Chapter IX. It hangs together well enough with the context. C.J.C.].

[2] [This word was originally intended to refer to the language of the *Didaskalia*; but it is still more in place as referring to the fourth century. C.J.C.].

[3] [I.e., to the general discontinuance of the exercise of personal Grace-gifts on the part of the laity. I here begin to transcribe a fresh and separate section of Dr. Bartlet's untyped manuscript, which however looks as if it was meant as the sequel to what precedes my last paragraph. C.J.C.].

holy life, was a vent for elements in the spirit of primitive Christianity which, under the actual Catholic order which supervened, had otherwise no longer any place or honour in the Church. Thus monasticism became the severest of criticisms of fourth-century Christianity and its Church-order. True, its adherents were not—like those of Montanism in its widest sense[1] (including not only a Tertullian, but also the author of the 'Apostolic Tradition on Grace-gifts' underlying the first part of the eighth Book of the 'Apostolic Constitutions')— excommunicated by the official Church for their prophetic attitude to the practical standards of the majority of their day. On the other hand, the movement withdrew Christians from ordinary Church-fellowship, this last being now no adequate sphere in which to nurture and express the truly-devoted or holy life of the Christ-type. There were various reasons, doubtless, for the relative failure of Church-life implied by this pessimistic and aloof attitude of many of the most earnest Christians of the fourth century.[2] Yet it may be doubted if one of the chief inherent or religious causes, alike of that failure and of the attitude of the ascetic puritans of the fourth century, was not the fact that Church-order, having gradually developed in the way we have traced, had failed to stimulate and foster the full resources of corporate Church-life and -fellowship, particularly by way of mutual edification on the part of lay-Christians and the stirring-up of each other to their common vocation as a light and a leaven among men. "Prophecy" had in fact, owing no doubt to various abuses, been "despised", and "the Spirit"— as the Spirit of prophecy—had been "quenched" (1 Thess. v. 19 f.). Thus the fruits of the Spirit, which—as Irenaeus had said in his day—needed to be "watered" by "the prophetic grace",[3] had been restrained from full growth, and the Church made thereby less "serviceable to God". Owing to fear of abuses, which meant only half-faith, the use of the full potential life of grace, latent in the Spirit's power in unordained members of Christ's Body, was discouraged and gradually atrophied.

Thus a spiritual dualism arose between the exclusive ministry

---

[1] [The context should make it clear that Dr. Bartlet is here using the word "Montanism" in an unusual and entirely-untechnical sense. C.J.C.].

[2] Such reasons as may have been connected with the enormous difficulties presented to the Church by its new relations to society generally in and after Constantine's day, are set forth in outline in the *C.O.P.E.C. Commission Report*, vol. xii, 'Historical Illustrations of the Social Effects of Christianity'.

[3] See the passage quoted above, p. 52, n. 1.

and the religious orders on the one hand, and on the other the laity, for whose Grace-gifts in the ministry of the Word no sphere of exercise was any longer conceded. It was a dualism totally alien to the spirit of the primitive Church. The preaching of Origen in the presence and at the request of the bishops of Jerusalem and Caesarea—which was condemned by his own bishop, Demetrius of Alexandria—was one of the last-known survivals of the older order of thought and usage. Such growing rigidity, as the confinement of the normal ministry in things spiritual to the ordained, made the Church a less-richly and less-comprehensively organized body than it had been at the beginning, and so reduced its spiritual quality from a more-vital level (where personality has fuller scope) to a more-purely institutional or semi-mechanical one. To that extent it was less truly "organized". For, as Dr. Hort has said, "there is indeed a certain ambiguity in the word 'organisation' " as applied to the Church. For while a maturer stage of organisation than that of the Apostolic churches "must of necessity involve the creation of more special organs of the community", i.e., a regular or ordained ministry, "Still the very origin and fundamental nature of the Ecclesia as a community of disciples", who themselves (rather than the episcopate, as Cyprian and others after him conceived) were "the primary body, and, it would seem, even the primary authority", "renders it impossible that the principle" (of the sovereignty of the brotherhood as such) "should rightly become obsolete. In a word we cannot properly speak of an organisation of a community from which the greater part of its members are excluded . . . . so that the offices of an Ecclesia at any period are only a part of its organisation, unless indeed it unhappily has no other element of organisation".[1]

Now a primary "element of organisation" in the Apostolic and sub-Apostolic Church consisted in that part of its order which expressed the consciousness of being animated throughout by the grace of "holy Spirit" for the common profit, including informal public prayer and thanksgiving and exposition of

---

[1] F. J. A. Hort, *The Christian Ecclesia*, pp. 229 f. [Dr. Bartlet refers several times to Dr. Hort and his work—see above, pp. 1, 26, 125, 156 f. —and evidently felt that the latter's picture of the early Church gave strong support to his own views. Yet Hort was personally a High-Churchman and a sacerdotalist: and Dr. L. Elliott-Binns says, ". . . it is a little strange to find a Nonconformist writer [C. Silvester Horne] saying that 'Dr. Hort surprised Free Churchmen by proving to them their own principles'. I think that the surprise would have been mutual" (*Religion in the Victorian Era*, p. 303). C.J.C.].

the Word. That all scope for Church-exercise of such diffused "prophetic" functions of the Spirit, beyond the specialized ministries recognized and authorized by ordination, should be ruled out as unallowable, even in the absence of the more-qualified regular ministers in question, was a development of Church-order which implied a less-perfect organization of the Church's total spiritual life. For to restrict the pre-existing larger liberty of utilizing all the actual Grace-gifts of the community must surely have meant the atrophy of those gifts through lack of the educative effect of their exercise, and a diminution of the sense of co-operation on the part of the rank and file in the whole vocation of the Church. This absolute rather than relative dualism of spiritual functions, and consequently of spiritual qualifications and responsibilities, was bound to mean a less-potent impact of Christians, both in word and also in life (for in life also did the duality of standards operate) on society outside.

This restriction of the "prophetic" side of Christian life had come about by quite-natural psychological processes and stages. Here the primary fact was that as time went on prophetic insight assumed, by a natural and healthy psychological law, less enthusiastic and ecstatic forms, as reflexion developed in association with a growing body of traditional teaching—itself the product in the first place of inspired insight. Thus, under normal conditions of developing Church-life, there existed at first no necessary antithesis between the prophet and the pastor; and men of the greatest prophetic gifts frequently became presbyters and overseers of the churches. There were bishops who, like Ignatius and Polycarp, were felt to be "prophetic" in the quality of their personal insight into the inner meaning or soul of Apostolic and other traditional truth. It was only when all prophetic grace came (chiefly as a result of antipathy to certain types of prophecy which challenged comparison with the established type of teaching) to be treated in practice as confined to the official ministers of the Word, in particular the bishops, that the decisive step was taken; and prophecy outside the regular ministry was virtually regarded as a thing of the past—much as it was in the Jewish Church for centuries prior to the coming of John the Baptist.

But whatever the precise cause and manner of the change may have been, the upshot was that St. Paul's ideal that all Christians, as such, might "prophesy" (1 Cor. xiv. 1, 3, 5), and that some at least apart from representative or elective Church-office should exercise this charisma (1 Cor. xi. 4, xiv. 26; Rom. xii. 6 ff.), would at the end of the fourth century have ranked as heresy and lawless disorder. That there was gain as well as loss in the development which led to this result need not be denied, even by those who hold it to have been an impoverishment that this gain should have been at the cost of the liberty of the Spirit.[1]

Thus the spirit, rather than the letter, of the Catholic idea of Church-order, emerges with fresh meaning from recent research, with not a little fresh evidence before it. It is a form of Catholicism which includes, and no longer excludes, the great ideas connected with the freedom of the Spirit, which are rooted in primitive Christianity, and which the Protestant Reformation has helped us in modern times to recover. We are thus encouraged and enabled to take in hand that larger, more many-sided, more-elastic, and more-vital synthesis of different aspects of the full spiritual reality of Church-life. For that reality has never yet been fully and consciously embodied and lived out in the order of any past age of the Church, since Apostolic days. "Quod semper, quod ubique, quod ab omnibus", is still-less applicable as an historical test of Catholic order than it is of Catholic doctrine. It is only in the depths of the religious consciousness, as shown in the fruits of true Christian piety and obedience to conscience, that it has any validity in the realm of experience or of coherent theory.

APPENDICES[2]

1. THE AUTHORITY OF CHRIST AS RELATED TO CHURCH-ORDER

Church-life and -order must always be closely related to the Church-idea itself. This idea had, at the beginning, two aspects

---

[1] [It is at this point that we reach the close of what Dr. Bartlet left in manuscript. I doubt whether he intended it to be the real conclusion of the whole. I have inserted, therefore, as the most fitting terminus-ultra-quem-non for our printed version a paragraph transferred from an earlier point in the manuscript (see p. 166, n. 1), which looks like the close of at least one draft of what was probably drafted more than once. C.J.C.].

[2] [I have put here in the form of appendices a transcript of other manuscript bits left by Dr. Bartlet in a very rough form, clearly relevant to the subject of his lectures and explicitly destined by him to be used for his last lecture, but incapable of being now incorporated in the text thereof, without unduly breaking the continuity of thought. C.J.C.].

—a fact which, while often overlooked, is yet of great moment for a truly-historical view of our subject. One aspect was related to the past—the tradition of the Jewish People as the special People of God, out of which the Church emerged, and with which it was largely, though in decreasing measure, continuous. The other aspect was related rather to the future, in so far as that future was the outcome of its distinctively-Christian character, due to the new thing which its Founder brought with Him into the world, as Irenaeus says, in His own personality.[1] Hence the idea of the Church in the Apostolic Age has two aspects, according as we think of it as determined on the one hand, in form, by the Jewish Messianic hope of the Kingdom of God on earth, and on the other, in spirit, by the religious emphasis visible in the life and teaching of its Founder. This emphasis lay in His claim to have fulfilled the Divine idea hitherto adumbrated in Israel, only by transcending its past forms and particularly by giving to its religion a new centre through His own Messianic consciousness and life as God's Anointed King for all mankind.

The question of questions, then, which is often ignored—or rather, an answer to which is tacitly assumed—is how far Jesus the Messiah, the Church's Founder and Head, Himself laid down a new Church-order corresponding to the new spirit of life which He knew Himself to have brought from God to those prepared to receive it both within Israel and outside it.

In answering this question, hardly any scholars to-day, to whatever school of thought they may belong, hold to the old assumption that Jesus foreknew the future course of the Church's actual history, and so instituted its complete ecclesiastical constitution for all time as the heavenly pattern supernaturally revealed by anticipation to the Apostles on earth. Yet this was the assumption working in the minds of those who defended the developed Church-order from the third and fourth centuries onwards; and this powerfully affected their estimate of its sacrosanct character and authority.

Nevertheless, not a few scholars still think they can, along with fidelity to the newer or frankly-historical standpoint as to

---

[1] [I do not know what *particular* passage, if any, in Irenaeus Dr. Bartlet here had in mind. There are many Christological expressions in his works of which the above might be regarded as a rough paraphrase or summary: see, e.g., *Adv. Haer.* III. xix, IV. ix–xi, xxvi. 1, V. xxi, and *Demonstr. of the Apost. Preaching,* 89; cf. also F. M. Hitchcock, *Irenaeus of Lugdunum,* pp. 127–157. C.J.C.].

Christ's foundation of the Church in germ as a society possessed by His own Spirit and left to its progressive guidance, claim that along with this foundation in germ the Christ laid down certain definite constitutional principles, so to speak, meant to be binding on the Divine Society's self-organization for all time. Among these principles—beyond those strictly-spiritual ones which are organic to the Church's type of life, such as Faith, Hope, Love—the chief is that of governmental authority, in relation to all branches of Church-order and -worship, as bestowed immediately on the Apostles alone and only mediately, through formal commission from them, upon other ministers in the Christian Society. This is what the doctrine of Apostolic Succession still means for many to-day.

To others it seems that this notion is absolutely excluded, as a pure anachronism, hardly less so than the old conception of a full-blown constitution for the Church imparted during the forty days before the Ascension. It is excluded by the fact that the Apostles obviously expected the Messiah's Return at almost any time, and originally long before the end of their own lives. While this perspective alone explains their surprise at the extension of the Kingdom to the Gentiles, it leaves no room for the idea of a ministry to be continued by formal commission from themselves to a second generation, let alone an indefinite number of generations.

Whilst holding, then, that Jesus the Christ did *reconstitute* the Israel of God on a Messianic basis at the Last Supper in the Upper Room—when already He was sure that the Kingdom was not to come with first intention, but only through a process beyond His own earthly life, on the basis of the great redemptive act of His own self-sacrifice, with a view to change men's unready hearts, I cannot see any real historical evidence that He did more than appoint the Twelve as the prime missionaries of a missionary-society of disciples of the new movement for the repentance of Israel pending His own early Return in some form not clear to Himself, but reserved by the Father in His own counsel. This is what St. Peter expects in his speech on the Day of Pentecost. This perspective determines all the Apostolic thought and action in Acts. The survival of the protective husk of Jewish forms of thought continued almost unchanged till 70. . . .[1]

[1] [I have had to abandon the attempt to decipher the last few words of the passage: but its drift is clear. C.J.C.].

2. THE NEW-TESTAMENT WRITINGS AND CHURCH-ORDER

The New-Testament body of writings—literature would be a misleading word to use—is the precipitate of a life inspired and prophetic in quality and origin. Even where it has most taken the form of definite order, this is so. And it is rightly viewed only when read in the light of the process or life-history by which the Christian spirit clothed itself in fixed forms of self-expression for practical purposes. To take it rigidly or in a legal spirit, and with legal methods of application, belies its original and real meaning. In St. Paul's language, it then ceases to be spirit and life, and becomes a deadening letter. The real accent or emphasis of all order in the expression of such a pulsating life as is reflected in the New-Testament writings was and still is spirit and not letter, liberty and not law (in an external, coercive, or repressive sense). Its intention was essentially positive, namely, to supply the best direction or channel of free, unimpeded expression for the spirit of loyal love to God and man, as approved by actual experience within the loving and beloved community. Beyond this there was at first no thought of going, especially as all was felt to be provisional, pending the near end of the existing order of life at the Return of Christ in visible power.

3. HERESY AND SCHISM—THEN AND NOW

. . . Here we note that the great danger to Christianity is heresy, even more than schism—heresy, that is, of a fundamental kind, touching the idea of God. This sensitiveness is specially typical of the East as compared with the West, where the emphasis is reversed, and right attitude to Church-order tends to count for more than matters of theology. It is true that, on the points of unorthodoxy here in view, East and West were alike in their sense of the gravity of the issue: but in actual practice, such points emerged more clearly and frequently in the East, as springing more easily out of the Greek and Oriental mentality than out of the Latin. On the other hand, the latter felt more strongly about organized unity, and regarded schism as more deadly.

We see the difference already in the attitude of Hippolytus of Rome early in the third century, as compared with that of the bulk of the Roman Church in supporting Callistus, the duly-appointed bishop. To the more-Greek mentality of Hippolytus,

Callistus was guilty of a fundamentally-untrue theology of the Incarnation and of the Godhead as implied in it, as well as of laxity in failing to insist on the Christian ideal of living. To him, then, those who were true to a fully-Christian theology, as defined by Scripture interpreted in the light of the best tradition of the Church as a whole, were the true guardians of the Gospel of Christ entrusted to the Church as its appointed witness, and were therefore—because fulfilling the Church's proper function—the real Church, even though they were a minority in numbers and were in protest against the bishop whose sole claim rested on formal correctness of appointment. That is, while claiming to be the true Church for the time being in Rome, since the majority by adherence to Callistus put themselves in a false position as regards the deposit of the Apostolic faith, Hippolytus and his circle made orthodoxy determinative of true ecclesiastical order, and braved the appearance of schism from the merely-empirical point of view, that of regular Church-order.

The perspective of the 'Didaskalia' is the same, when it says: "Before all things beware of all hateful, evil, and unlawful heresies, and fly from them and from those who draw near to them, as from a blazing fire". Its next words about schism are expanded in the 'Apostolic Constitutions' as follows: "And flee schisms also: for it is not lawful (θεμιτόν) either to turn the mind aside to impious heresies, or to separate from those like-minded (to oneself) through love of power (φιλαρχίαν)".[1] Here we have a very just statement of the matter. Separation due to a wrong personal motive, a moral defect, is impious, an act of high-handed rejection of the Divine Will, though known. But where likemindedness on vital matters of Christian truth is lacking, it may be otherwise.

That is a principle to which all Christians may well assent in general terms: it is its application to particular cases, especially as regards what is vital Christian truth for the purpose in hand, that has ever been the real difficulty between two types of mind and ethos in the Church, the Catholic and the Puritan, the zealot for Church-order and the zealot for Gospel-truth, each with his own understanding of the Gospel of Christ in and for the Church.

In regard to the application made in the 'Didaskalia' (as distinct from that made by Hippolytus), namely, to a dualist view of God and the world, there is no difference among

[1] *Didask.* VI. i. 1 (Connolly, p. 194); *Apost. Const.* VI. i. 1.

Christians to-day, though there was bonâ-fide conscientious difference at the time. This fact may give us ground for hope that a gradual movement of all sincere Christian men towards agreement may take place: but it should also encourage us to hope for a more-patient charity on both sides during the process than was shown in past days, while Christians were yet learning by painful experience that full unity of faith means a unity of concrete and not merely abstract belief. For such faith realizes by actual insight the variety implicit in a great idea, which must needs reveal itself first more on one side than another to the diverse types of humanity which we men, in the Divine providence, possess by nature. Reverence for conscience as the core of personality, such as shrinks from all coercive methods in dealing with conscientious differences, is one of the greatest achievements of the Divine education of our race, and belongs to the spirit rather than the letter of Christ's own teaching. Hence we need not wonder that it has been learned only very slowly by Christians, pari-passu with the true idea of God as above all the Father.

Here, in the correlation of orthodox faith and right conduct, the Christian's view of God and the Christian's duty to his fellows, we have a certain justification of the close connexion, which the Church kept in ancient times and long after, between schism and heresy. Both are related to the kind of faith—in that more vital and religious sense in which it was demanded for God and His Gospel by Christ Himself—which animates the soul's personal life and experience, its response to the Spirit of God within. But in the third and fourth centuries this faith was more and more assumed to be infallibly tested by the individual's attitude to the orthodox definition of doctrine, the formulated creed. The equivalence of "the faith" objectively regarded (fides quae creditur) and as subjectively appropriated (fides qua creditur) is, indeed, much greater in the corporate form of both than in the individual: and so far the Catholic assumption had a certain validity, apart from the question as to the adequacy of the current creed as an expression of the truth of the Gospel. But even so, its method of enforcing this assumption on individuals and communities by coercive means, first moral and then physical, was and remained a sub-Christian element in early Church-order; and as such it reflected also on the adequacy of that order as regards both its Christian ideal and its practical Christian value.

BIBLIOGRAPHY

OF DR. J. VERNON BARTLET'S PRINTED WORKS

THE ideal bibliography should not be only accurate but exhaustive. Whatever lapses from accuracy may lurk in the ensuing list owe their origin to the regrettable frailty of the compiler; but certain lapses from completeness are due to the difficulties attending his task. Dr. Bartlet appears to have kept no complete record of what he published; and there is no practical means of discovering *all* the articles and letters he produced. Search, however, has been made, so far as time and opportunity allowed; and the results are incorporated in the following pages. But the omission of some items (possibly even some substantial articles) has had to be sorrowfully accepted as a practical necessity. Information regarding any of these will be welcomed by the Editor even after this book is published. It is hoped there are not many of them.

Titles of articles, letters, and addresses are printed in roman type within single inverted commas. Titles of series are printed in roman type within double inverted commas. Titles of books and periodicals are printed in italics.

1890

Short replies on 'Lightfoot's *S. Ignatius*' and 'Origen's *Treatise on Prayer*', in *Expository Times*, vol. i, p. 232 (July—under "Requests and Replies").

Preparatory editorial work on Edwin Hatch's *The Influence of Greek Ideas and Usages upon the Christian Church* (Hibbert Lectures, 1888), edited by A. M. Fairbairn, D.D. (see above, p. xix, and pp. viii f. of Dr. Fairbairn's preface).

1891

Review of James Iverach's *St. Paul: His Life and Times*, in *Critical Review*, vol. i, pp. 104–106 (Jan.).

Review of Emil Schürer's *History of the Jewish People in the Time of Jesus Christ*, Div. I, vols. i and ii, in *Critical Review*, vol. i, pp. 164–170 (April).

'Early Church Organization with some reference to the beginnings of Ecclesiastical Canons'—a paper read to the Oxford Society of Historical Theology at its inaugural meeting on 5th May (see above, p. xix), and summarized in its *Abstract of Proceedings for the Year 1891–1892*, pp. 14–18.

Reviews of W. Lefroy's *The Christian Ministry* and W. D. Killen's *The Framework of the Church*, in *Critical Review*, vol. i, pp. 292–296 (July).

Review of Rendel Harris's and J. Armitage Robinson's *The Apology of Aristides* (i.e. "Texts and Studies", vol. I, pt. i), in *Critical Review*, vol. i, pp. 415–419 (Oct.).

1892

Review of A. C. McGiffert's *Eusebius: Church History*, etc. and of *Socrates, Sozomen: Church Histories* (i.e., vols. i and ii of "Nicene and Post-Nicene Fathers"), in *Critical Review*, vol. ii, pp. 64–70 (Jan.).

Review of A. Harnack's *Pistis Sophia* and *Brot und Wasser* and of E. Schwartz's *Athenagorae libellus pro Christianis*, etc. (i.e., "Texte und Untersuchungen", vol. VII. ii and vol. IV. ii), in *Critical Review*, vol. ii, pp. 191–195 (April).

'Fides Divina et Fides Humana; or, Faith according to Christ', in *Expositor*, Series IV, vol. v, pp. 401–417 (June).

Review of W. Wrede's *Untersuchungen zum Ersten Klemensbriefe*, in *Critical Review*, vol. ii, pp. 280–283 (July).

Review of A. Harnack's *Die griechische Uebersetzung des Apologeticus Tertullians* and *Medizinisches aus der ältesten Kirchengeschichte* (i.e., "Texte und Untersuchungen", vol. VIII. iv), in *Critical Review*, vol. ii, pp. 387–390 (Oct.).

Review of W. T. Slater's *An Introduction to Church History*, in *Critical Review*, vol. ii, pp. 390–395 (Oct.).

'Christ's Use of the Term "The Son of Man" ', in *Expositor*, Series IV, vol. vi, pp. 427–443 (Dec.).

1893

'Philippians i. 22', in *Expository Times*, vol. iv, p. 177 (Jan.).

Review of M. R. James's *The Testament of Abraham*, etc. (i.e., "Texts and Studies", vol. II, pt. ii), in *Critical Review*, vol. iii, pp. 80–85 (Jan.).

'Newman Smyth's "Christian Ethics" ' in *Expository Times*, vol. iv, pp. 269–272 (Mar.).

'Didaché, Ch. xvi.: to what stratum does it belong?'—a paper read to the Oxford Society of Historical Theology on 25th May, and summarized in its *Abstract of Proceedings for the Year 1892–1893*, pp. 65–68.

'Christ's Use of "the Son of Man" ', in *Expository Times*, vol. iv, p. 403 (June—under "Contributions and Comments").

Review of L. Hallier's *Die edessenische Chronik* and of R. Raabe's *Die Apologie des Aristides* (i.e., "Texte und Untersuchungen", vol. IX. i), in *Critical Review*, vol. iii, pp. 301–307 (July).

'Alexander Vinet: a Pioneer of the Nineteenth Century', in *Expository Times*, vol. v, pp. 15–20 (Oct.).

' "The Son of Man": a Rejoinder', in *Expository Times*, vol. v, pp. 41 f. (Oct.—under "Contributions and Comments").

1894

Reviews of H. von Schubert's *Die Composition des Pseudopetrinischen Evangelienfragments*, E. von Dobschütz's *Das Kerygma Petri*, and F. Loofs' *Studien über die dem Johannes von Damaskus zugeschriebenen Parallelen*, in *Critical Review*, vol. iv, pp. 65–68 (Jan.).

Early Church History: a Sketch of the first four Centuries. In "Present Day Primers". London (Religious Tract Society). (April). See also above, pp. xx f., and below, under Feb. 1897, Oct. 1905, Mar. 1911, and Sept. 1925.

'The Development of the Historic Episcopate', in *Contemporary Review*, vol. lxv, pp. 795–817 (June).

Review of F. C. Conybeare's *The Apology and Acts of Apollonius*, in *Critical Review*, vol. iv, pp. 268–274 (July).

'Is Joel a Unity?', in *Expository Times*, vol. v, pp. 567 f. (Sept.— under "Contributions and Comments").

Reviews of K. J. Neumann's *Der römische Staat und die allgemeine Kirche*, and E. G. Hardy's *Christianity and the Roman Government*, in *Critical Review*, vol. iv, pp. 371–379 (Oct.).

1895

Review of F. J. A. Hort's *Judaistic Christianity*, in *Critical Review*, vol. v, pp. 18–23 (Jan.).

1896

Review of Jean Réville's *Les Origines de l'Épiscopat*, in *Critical Review*, vol. vi, pp. 31–37 (Jan.).

'William Sanday', in *Expository Times*, vol. vii, pp. 216–219, 271–275 (Feb. and Mar.).

Review of E. Klostermann's *Ignatius von Antiochien* and J. Führer's *Ein Beitrag zur Lösung der Felicitas-Frage* and *Zur Felicitas-Frage*, in *Critical Review*, vol. vi, pp. 154–157 (Apl.).

Review of E. Noeldechen's *Tertullian's 'Gegen die Juden'*, and Paul Pape's *Die Predigt u. das Brieffragment des Aristides*, also of E. Rolffs' *Urkunden aus dem antimontanistischen Kampfe des Abendlandes* and A. Harnack's *Zur Abercius-Inschrift* (i.e., "Texte und Untersuchungen", vol. XII. ii and iv), in *Critical Review*, vol. vi, pp. 158–163 (Apl.).

1897

Early Church History, etc. reprinted (Feb.). See above, under Apl. 1894.

'The Lambeth Conference and the Historic Episcopate', in *Contemporary Review*, vol. lxxii, pp. 68–85 (July).

Review of F. E. Brightman's *Liturgies, Eastern and Western*, vol. i, in *Critical Review*, vol. vii, pp. 282–286 (July).

Review of A. C. McGiffert's *A History of Christianity in the Apostolic Age*, in *Critical Review*, vol. vii, pp. 463–470 (Oct.).

1898

'Epistle' in Jas. Hastings' *A Dictionary of the Bible*, vol. i, pp. 729–731.

'Some Points in Pauline History and Chronology'—a paper read to the Oxford Society of Historical Theology on 10th Feb., and summarized in its *Abstract of Proceedings for the Year 1897–1898*, pp. 35–38. See below, under Oct. 1899.

'Apostolical Succession', in *Contemporary Review*, vol. lxxiv, pp. 247–269 (Aug.—written jointly with A. J. Carlyle).

Review of F. C. Conybeare's *The Key of Truth: a Manual of the Paulician Church of Armenia*, in *Critical Review*, vol. viii, pp. 383–389 (Oct.).

1899

The Apostolic Age: its Life, Doctrine, Worship and Polity. In "Ten Epochs of Church History", alias "Eras of the Christian Church". Edinburgh (T. and T. Clark) and New York (Scribner). (June). Dates of reprints unknown. See above, p. xxii.

'Helps', and 'Heresy', in Jas. Hastings' *A Dictionary of the Bible*, vol. ii, pp. 347 f. and 351.

'Only let us be mindful of the Poor. Galatians II. 10', in *Expositor*, Series V, vol. ix, pp. 218–225 (Mar.).

'The Living Christ'—an address delivered on 28th Sept. at Boston, U.S.A., and printed in *Volume of Proceedings of the Second International Congregational Council*, Boston, 1900, pp. 474–476. See above, p. xxiv.

'Some Points in Pauline History and Chronology', in *Expositor*, Series V, vol. x, pp. 263–280 (Oct.). See above, under Feb. 1898.

'Impressions of the Boston Council', in *Mansfield College Magazine*, vol. ii, pp. 103–107 (Dec.).

1900

'Matthew, Apostle', and 'Matthew, Gospel of', in Jas. Hastings' *A Dictionary of the Bible*, vol. iii, pp. 295 f. and 296–305.

Review of *The Expositor's Greek Testament*, vol. ii (Acts, Rom., and 1 Cor.), in *Critical Review*, vol. x, pp. 434–445 (Sept.).

1901

The Acts. Introduction, Authorized Version, Revised Version with Notes, Index, and Map. In "The Century Bible". Edinburgh and London (T. C. and E. C. Jack—now Nelson and Sons). Frequently reprinted, but apparently never revised.

'The Two Forms of the Word "Jerusalem" in the Lucan Writings' —a paper read to the Oxford Society of Historical Theology on 23rd May, and summarized in its *Abstract of Proceedings for the Year 1900–1901*, pp. 68 f. See below, under Jan. 1902.

1902

The Earlier Pauline Epistles: Corinthians, Galatians, and Thessa-lonians. In "The Temple Bible". London (Dent), and Philadelphia (Lippincott).

'Regeneration', 'Saint', and 'Sanctification', in Jas. Hastings' *A Dictionary of the Bible*, vol. iv, pp. 214–221, 352 f., and 391–395.

'The Twofold Use of "Jerusalem" in the Lucan Writings', in *Expository Times*, vol. xiii, pp. 157 f. (Jan.). See above, under May 1901.

Review of John Wordsworth's *The Ministry of Grace*, in *Critical Review*, vol. xii, pp. 40–49 (Jan.).

Review of G. T. Purves's *Christianity in the Apostolic Age*, in *Critical Review*, vol. xii, pp. 120–123 (Mar.).

'Barnabas and the Epistle to the Hebrews'—a paper read to the Oxford Society of Historical Theology on 6th March, and summarized in its *Abstract of Proceedings for the Year 1901–1902*, pp. 51–58. See below, under June and July 1902, and Nov. 1903.

'Non-Episcopal Churches', in *Contemporary Review*, vol. lxxxi, pp. 530-543 (Apl.).

'Barnabas and his genuine Epistle', in *Expositor*, Series VI, vol. v, pp. 409–427 (June), and vol. vi, pp. 28–30 (July).

Mission from God: A Meditation on Conscience (i.e., "The Broad Plain House Papers", No. IV). A paper read at the Broad Plain House Conference (Bristol) on 2nd Oct.

'Two Notes on the Fourth Gospel' (John ii. 13–25 and John iv. 43–45), in *Expository Times*, vol. xiv, pp. 118–121 (Dec.).

1903

' Note on Acts xii 25', in *Journal of Theological Studies*, vol. iv, pp. 438–440 (Apl.).

'Primitive Christianity', in *Expository Times*, vol. xiv, pp. 324–326, (under "Recent Foreign Theology")—a review of F. G. Heinrici's *Das Urchristentum*.

Review of T. M. Lindsay's *The Church and the Ministry in the Early Centuries*, in *Hibbert Journal*, vol. ii, pp. 173–177 (Oct.).

'The Epistle to Hebrews as the work of Barnabas', in *Expositor*, Series VI, vol. viii, pp. 381–396 (Nov.).

1904

Review of F. X. Funk's *Patres Apostolici*, vol. i, in *Critical Review*, vol. xiv, pp. 41–44 (Jan.).

Review of A. Stahl's *Patristische Untersuchungen*, in *Critical Review*, vol. xiv, pp. 113–115 (Mar.).

Review of O. Bardenhewer's *Geschichte der altkirchl. Literatur*, vols. i and ii, in *Critical Review*, vol. xiv, pp. 207–215 (May).

'Mark the "curt-fingered" Evangelist', in *Journal of Theological Studies*, vol. vi, pp. 121–124 (Oct.).

1905

'The Epistle of Barnabas' and (for the Gospels) 'II Clement', in *The New Testament in the Apostolic Fathers*. Oxford (Clarendon Press). Pp. 1–23, and 130–136.

How and Why the Gospel Won Europe (i.e., "The Atonement of Christ and other Lectures delivered in the Central Hall, Manchester", no. III [pp. 55–80]). London (Kelly). Printed also the same year in *What is Christianity? A Series of Lectures delivered in the Central Hall, Manchester*, vol. ii, pp. 102–127 (no. 26), as well as separately. London (Kelly).

'The Historial Setting of the Second and Third Epistles of St John', in *Journal of Theological Studies*, vol. vi, pp. 204–216 (Jan.).

'The Oxyrhynchus "Sayings of Jesus" ', in *Contemporary Review*, vol. lxxxvii, pp. 116–125 (Jan.).

'The Alexandrine Origin of 2 Clement'—a paper read to the Oxford Society of Historical Theology on 9th Feb., and summarized in its *Abstract of Proceedings for the Year 1904–1905*, pp. 21–27. See below under 1906.

' Recent Johannine Literature', in *Expository Times*, vol. xvi, pp. 205–208 (Feb.—Reviews of W. M. Ramsay's *The Letters to the Seven Churches* and Jas. Drummond's *The Character and Authorship of the Fourth Gospel*).

'Ambrosiaster', in *Mansfield College Magazine*, vol. iv, pp. 154 f. (Mar.).

'Review of H. Achelis' and J. Flemming's *Die Syrische Didaskalia* (i.e. "Texte und Untersuchungen", N.F. vol. X. ii), in *Hibbert Journal*, vol. iii, pp. 632–635 (Apl.).

'Thoughts on the Welsh Revival', in *British Weekly*, vol. xxxiii, p. 30 (Supplement to issue of 13th Apl.).

'More Words on the Epistle to Hebrews', in *Expositor*, Series VI, vol. xi, pp. 431–440 (June).

Review of C. Taylor's *The Oxyrhynchus Sayings of Jesus*, in *Review of Theology and Philosophy*, vol. i, pp. 11–18 (July).

Review of J. Warschauer's *Jesus Saith: Studies in some 'New Sayings' of Christ*, in *Review of Theology and Philosophy*, vol. i, pp. 170 f. (Sept.).

Early Church History, etc., reprinted. (Oct.). See above, under Apl. 1894.

1906

'The origin and date of 2 Clement', in *Zeitschrift für die neutestamentliche Wissenschaft*, vol. vii, pp. 123–135. See also above, under Feb. 1905.

Review of A. Harnack's *The Expansion of Christianity in the First Three Centuries*, translated by Jas. Moffatt, in *Review of Theology and Philosophy*, vol. i, pp. 542-552 (Feb.).

Review of *Zeitschrift für die neutest. Wissenschaft.* 1906. *Heft* 2, in *Review of Theology and Philosophy*, vol. ii, pp. 66 f. (July).

'Melito the Author of the Muratorian Canon', in *Expositor*, Series VII, vol. ii, pp. 210–224 (Sept.).

1907

'Mr. Campbell's Book: What his "New Theology" stands for', in *Christian World* for 21st March (p. 4).

'Early Church History and Literature', in *Review of Theology and Philosophy*, vol. ii, pp. 675–685 (May—reviewing several recent works).

'The late Gaston Frommel and his Writings', in *Expository Times*, vol. xviii, pp. 477 f. (July—under "Contributions and Comments").

1908

'Is the Congregational Ministry Apostolic?'—an address delivered on 3rd July at Edinburgh, and printed in *Volume of Proceedings of the Third International Congregational Council*, London, 1908, pp. 213–220. See above, p. xxiv.

'The Eucharistic Congress'—a letter on religious liberty, published in *The Times* for 14th Sept. (p. 8).

'The Eucharist in the Early Church'—a paper read to the Oxford Society of Historical Theology on 26th Nov., and summarized in its *Abstract of Proceedings for the year 1908–1909*, pp. 32–36. See below under 1909.

1909

'The Eucharist in the Early Church', in *Mansfield College Essays presented to the Reverend Andrew Martin Fairbairn, D.D. on the occasion of his seventieth birthday November 4, 1908*, pp. 43–68. See above, under Nov. 1908.

'Didache', in Jas. Hastings' *A Dictionary of the Bible*, extra vol., pp. 438–451.

'Papias', and 'Teaching of Jesus', in Jas. Hastings' *A Dictionary of Christ and the Gospels*, vol. ii, pp. 309–312 and 699–706.

'Baptism (New Testament)', in Jas. Hastings' *Encyclopaedia of Religion and Ethics*, vol. ii, pp. 375–379.

'Acts of the Apostles' in *A Standard Bible Dictionary*, edited by M. W. Jacobus, E. E. Nourse, and A. C. Zenos. New York and London (Funk and Wagnall). Pp. 7–11. See also below, under 1926 and 1936.

Review of Jean Réville's *Origines de l'Eucharistie*, in *Review of Theology and Philosophy*, vol. iv, pp. 566–573 (Mar.).

'Gaston Frommel and his contribution to modern religious thought', in *Homiletic Review*, vol. lvii, pp. 406–410 (June).

'Christian Baptism', in "Occasional Paper" No. 5 of the Swanwick Free Church Fellowship (Feb.), pp. 22–32. Later reprinted, along with a reply by J. E. Roberts and an appendix by J. H. Rushbrooke, in a private and confidential pamphlet entitled *Christian Baptism* (pp. 3–16), published jointly by the Swanwick Free Church Fellowship and the Baptist Fellowship.

'Two New Testament Problems', in *Expositor*, Series VIII, vol. v, pp. 464–467 (May—on 'St. Paul's Fate at Rome'), and pp. 548–551 (June—on 'The Riddle of the Epistle to the Hebrews').

'The Moral Aspect of Disendowment'—an address delivered on 11th or 12th Nov. under the auspices of The Liberation Society, and printed in *Disendowment: Its Legal and Moral Aspects*, pp. 23–31, along with an address by T. Bennett on 'The Legal Aspect of Disendowment'. London (The Liberation Society). See above, p. xxvii and below, under 1914.

1914

'The Moral Aspect of Disendowment', as above, under Nov. 1913, reprinted (date uncertain, but probably before August).

'The Right to a Living Wage', in *Contemporary Review*, vol. cvi, pp. 203–208 (Aug.).

Review of W. Bousset's *Kyrios Christos*, in *Review of Theology and Philosophy*, vol. x, pp. 313–332 (Dec.).

1915

Nil.

1916

'The Ordination Prayers in the Ancient Church Order', in *Journal of Theological Studies*, vol. xvii, pp. 248–256 (Apl.).

'The Validity of the Congregational Ministry'—a paper read on 11th May at the Annual Assembly of the Congregational Union of England and Wales, and published as a booklet under that title, along with addresses by J. D. Jones and P. T. Forsyth. London (Congregational Union of England and Wales). Pp. 3–19.

'John Brown Paton: An all-round Christian', in *Mansfield College Magazine*, vol. ix, pp. 138–141 (June—a review of Paton's *Life* by his son, J. L. Paton).

1917

Christianity in History. A Study of Religious Development, Parts I and II, Part III ch. vi, Part IV chs. ii and iii, Part V chs. iv and v (the rest being the work of A. J. Carlyle). London (Macmillan). See also above, pp. xxviii f., xli, xlvi, xlix, and below, under 1935.

'Reservation of the Sacrament'—a letter published in *The Guardian* for 8th Mar. (p. 188).

'Titus the Friend of Luke, and other related questions', in *Expositor*, Series VIII, vol. xiii, pp. 367–375 (May).

'The Irish Convention'—a letter published in *The Times* for 21st June (p. 9).

'The Religion of Mr. Wells', in *Mansfield College Magazine*, vol. ix, pp. 179–183 (July—a review of H. G. Wells's *God the Invisible King*).

'A Fresh Labour of Professor Souter's', in *Mansfield College Magazine*, vol. ix, pp. 183 f. (July—a review of A. Souter's edition of *Tertulliani Apologeticus*).

'Fragments of the *Didascalia Apostolorum* in Greek', in *Journal of Theological Studies*, vol. xviii, pp. 301–309 (July).

'A new fifth-sixth century fragment of 1 Timothy', in *Journal of Theological Studies*, vol. xviii, pp. 309–311 (July).

'Some Aspects of Baptism in Early Christianity'—a paper read to the Oxford Society of Historical Theology on 29th Nov., and summarized in its *Abstract of Proceedings for the Year 1917–1918*, pp. 29–37.

1918

'Reunion: the Present Outlook', in *Contemporary Review*, vol. cxiv, pp. 427–435 (Oct.).

'Unity, Orders, Sacraments', in *Interpreter*, vol. xv, pp. 19–27 (Oct.).

'A Recent Visit to France and French Protestants', in *British Weekly*, vol. lxv, p. 148 (5th Dec.). See above, p. xxviii.

1919

'The Religious Background of the New Testament Writings', in the one-volume *Commentary on the Bible*, edited by A. S. Peake. London (T. C. and E. C. Jack). Pp. 636–644.

' Corporate Authority', in *Towards Reunion: being contributions to mutual understanding by Church of England and Free Church Writers*. London (Macmillan). Pp. 193–223.

'Among the French Protestants', in *Mansfield College Magazine*, vol. x, pp. 263–266 (Apl.).

Review of the first edition of *Essays on the Early History of the Church and the Ministry*, edited by H. B. Swete, in *Journal of Theological Studies*, vol. xx, pp. 357–370 (July). This review was replied to by C. H. Turner in the preface to the second edition of the *Essays* (1921), pp. xxiii ff.

1925

'Peace among Nations. 1925 and after'—a letter published in *The Times* for 1st Jan. (p. 8).

'The present position of research on the Gospels'—a paper read to the Oxford Society of Historical Theology on 12th March, and mentioned in its *Abstract of Proceedings for the Years 1923–1925*, p. 35, but apparently never more fully reported.

Early Church History: A Sketch of its first four Centuries. See above, under Apl. 1894. Revised Edition (Sept.).

'The late Dr. I. Abrahams'—a letter published in the fourth edition of *The Times* for 12th Oct. (p. 10).

'John Massie, 1843–1925', in *Mansfield College Magazine*, vol. xii, pp. 219–225 (Dec.).

1926

'Acts of the Apostles, The', in *A New Standard Bible Dictionary*, edited by M. W. Jacobus, E. E. Nourse, and A. C. Zenos. Completely revised and enlarged. See above, under 1909, and below under 1936. New York and London (Funk and Wagnall). Pp. 21–25.

Also the following articles in the same work:

'Apollos', pp. 56 f.

'Apostle', p. 57.

'Baptism, Baptize', pp. 93–95.

'Barnabas', pp. 95 f.

Also the revision of J. Denney's earlier article on 'Church Life and Organization' (pp. 132–137), and Sir R. A. Falconer's earlier articles on 'Timothy' (pp. 908 f.), 'Timothy, Epistles to' (pp. 909–912), 'Titus' (p. 913), and 'Titus, Epistle to' (pp. 913 f.).

'Liberal Evangelicalism. A Critical Examination of Dr. Orchard's "Foundations of Faith" ', in *Christian World* for 27th May (p. 10—portrait on p. 3).

'The Spirit of St. Francis. Some Applications to Modern Life'—a letter published in *The Times* for 7th Oct. (p. 8).

'The Congregational Ministers' Campaign against War', letters published in *Christian World* for 14th Oct. (p. 7), 4th Nov. (p. 7), 18th Nov. (p. 7), and 9th Dec. (p. 9).

'Church Congress. A Nonconformist's Reflections'—a letter published in *The Times* for 16th Oct. (p. 8).

' "Back to the Coal Report" '—a letter published in *The Times* for 25th Oct. (p. 12).

1927

Review of V. Taylor's *Behind the Third Gospel: a Study of the Proto-Luke Hypothesis*, in *Congregational Quarterly*, vol. v, pp. 103 f. (Jan.).

Review of H. Bulcock's *The Passing and the Permanent in St. Paul: Studies in Pauline origins, development and values*, in *Congregational Quarterly*, vol. v, pp. 104 f. (Jan.).

'The Consecration Prayer'—a letter on the new Prayer-Book, published in *The Times* for 4th March (p. 10).

'The Theory of Consecration'—a letter on the new Prayer-Book, published in *The Times* for 25th March (p. 10).

Address on Dullness delivered on 7th July (Speech Day) at Silcoates School, near Wakefield, and summarized in *The Silcoatian*, New Series, Number 1 (Dec.), pp. 3 f.   See above, p. xxxv.

Contributions to the World Conference on Faith and Order, reported in *Faith and Order. Proceedings of the World Conference, Lausanne, August 3–21, 1927* (edited by H. N. Bate), pp. 206 f. (address on the Creeds), 290–301 (address on the Sacraments— see also *The Times* for 15th Aug. [p. 12] and *Christian World* for 18th Aug. [p. 10]), 422, 429. For the reports of Commissions on which Dr. Bartlet served, see the same volume, pp. 213, 368, 389–391, 423, 428 f., 466 f., 472 f. Alternative reports of Dr. Bartlet's two main addresses are provided in Canon E. S. Woods' book, *Lausanne 1927*, pp. 78–80 and 107–111: also (*ibid.* pp. 160–166) a memorandum summarizing Dr. Bartlet's resultant impressions of the Conference as a whole. See above, p. xxxi.

'The Oath in Ireland'—a letter published in *The Times* for 30th Sept. (p. 15).

'The Sacraments of Baptism and the Lord's Supper', in *Review of the Churches*, vol. iv, pp. 489–496 (Oct.).

Contribution to 'An Unreported Lausanne Conversation on the Eucharist', edited by Sir Henry Lunn, in *Review of the Churches*, vol. iv, p. 512 (Oct.).

1928

Foreword to C. J. Cadoux's *Catholicism and Christianity*. London (Allen and Unwin). Pp. vii–xii.

'The Bishops and Reservation'—a letter on the new Prayer-Book, published in *The Times* for 10th Jan. (p. 10).

'The Prayer-Book'—a letter to *The Guardian* for 2nd Mar. (pp. 131 f.).

The Psychology of the Christian Faith: being Selections from the Writings of the late Gaston Frommel. London (S.C.M.). The translation was by J. Macartney Wilson, the introduction (pp. vii–xxii), selection, revision and editing by J. V. Bartlet. (Apl.).

'The Congregational Council and the Revised Prayer-Book', a letter published in *Christian World* for 19th April (p. 7).

'The Practical Issue—Free Churchmen and Bishops'—a letter on the new Prayer Book, published in *The Times* for 29th May (p. 13 —jointly with W. B. Selbie). This letter is fully quoted in *Oxford Chronicle* for 1st June (p. 7).

'The Prayer-Book'—a letter published in *The Times* for 9th June (p. 10—jointly with W. B. Selbie).

'The Derivation of "Religion" '—a letter published in *The Times* for 22nd Sept. (p. 11).

'The Bible as Authority'—a paper read on 11th July at the Congregational Theological Conference at Oxford, and printed in *Congregational Quarterly*, vol. vi, pp. 537–541 (Oct.). See also *Christian World* for 19th July (p. 12).

'A New Year of Endeavour—The Truest Homage', a letter on Armistice-Day, published in *The Times* for 10th Nov. (p. 13).

'Science and the Poets—a new Outlook on the World'—a letter published in *The Times* for 13th Dec. (p. 10).

1929

A Reasonable Faith, in Section I (God in the Modern World) of Benn's shilling series of "Affirmations".

'Acts of the Apostles', in The *Encyclopaedia Britannica*, fourteenth edition, vol. i, pp. 142–145.

Also the following articles in the same work:

'Apostle', vol. ii, pp. 119–121.

'Barnabas' vol. iii, p. 118.

'Barnabas, Epistle of', vol. iii, pp. 118 f.

'Frommel, Gaston', vol. ix, p. 864.

'Hebrews, Epistle to the', vol. xi, pp. 371–373.

'Luke', vol. xiv, p. 475.

'Mark, St.', vol. xiv, p. 909.

'Paul', vol. xvii, pp. 385–394.

'Stephen', vol. xxi, pp. 383 f.

'Vinet, Alexandre Rodolphe', vol. xxiii, p. 173.

See above, under 1910 and 1911. Speaking generally, all Dr. Bartlet's 1910–11 articles reproduced in the 1929-edition are considerably abbreviated in the latter; those on 'Apostolic Fathers', 'Clementine Literature', 'Congregationalism', 'Hermas, Shepherd of', and 'Papias', are also rendered anonymous, and that on 'Matthew, St.' is replaced by an article contributed by another author.

'The Life and Work of Paul', in *The Abingdon Bible Commentary*, edited by F. C. Eiselen, E. Lewis, and D. G. Downey. London (Epworth Press), and New York (Abingdon Press). Pp. 931–943.

Review of H. Bulcock's *Religion and its New Testament Expression*, in *Congregational Quarterly*, vol. vii, pp. 109 f. (Jan.).

Review of H. J. Bayliss' *Minucius Felix and his Place Among the Early Fathers of the Latin Church*, in *Congregational Quarterly*, vol. vii, p. 110 (Jan.).

Review of F. M. Powicke's *Stephen Langton*, in *Congregational Quarterly*, vol. vii, pp. 110 f. (Jan.).

'Bishops and the Prayer-Book. A Nonconformist Appeal'—a letter published in *The Times* for 15 Feb. (p. 10).

'The Prayer-Book'—a letter published in *The Times* for 5th Mar. (p. 12).

Review of H. J. Lawlor's and J. E. L. Oulton's *Eusebius' Ecclesiastical History*, in *Congregational Quarterly*, vol. vii, pp. 249 f. (Apl.).

'The Meaning and Task of Christology', 'The Earlier Christologies', and 'The Later Christologies', in *The Lord of Life: a Fresh Approach to the Incarnation*. London (S.C.M.). (May). Pp. 115–136 (ch. v), 137–166 (ch. vi.), 167–189 (ch. vii). See above, pp. xxxvi, xli, xlvi, xlix f.

'A Significant Life: A. S. Peake, 1865–1929', in *British Weekly*, vol. lxxxvi, p. 457 (29th August).

'Roman Catholicism and Education'—a letter published in *The Times* for 24th Oct. (p. 12).

'The Churches at Unity'—a letter on South India published in *The Times* for 19th Nov. (p. 12—jointly with three others).

'Dr. Garvie on Church Unity'—a letter published in *British Weekly*, vol. lxxxvii, p. 190 (28th Nov.).

1930

Foreword to Eleanor McDougall's *St Augustine: A Study in his personal Religion*. London (S.C.M. Press). Pp. 5–8. (Jan.).

'The South Indian Church Union Scheme: a Genuine Concordat', in *South India United Church Herald*, vol. xxi, pp. 287–290 (Mar.). Apparently reproduced in large part in *Madras Guardian* a little later. See above, pp. xxix f.

Review of *The Abingdon Bible Commentary*, in *Congregational Quarterly*, vol. viii, pp. 221 f. (Apl.).

Review of Dom. R. H. Connolly's *Didascalia Apostolorum*, in *Congregational Quarterly*, vol. viii, pp. 222 f. (Apl.).

Review of R. B. Tollinton's *Selections from the Commentaries and Homilies of Origen*, in *Congregational Quarterly*, vol. viii, p. 223 (Apl.).

Review of H. J. Schonfield's *The Lost 'Book of the Nativity of John'*, in *Congregational Quarterly*, vol. viii, pp. 244 f. (Apl.).

'The Living Church: Its unity'—an address delivered on 5th July at Bournemouth, and printed in *Proceedings of the Fifth International Congregational Council*, London, 1930, pp. 153–159. Also a comment on 7th July in the discussion on Christianity and War, *op. cit.*, p. 201. See above, p. xxiv.

Review of H. M. Foston's *Man and the Image of God*, in *Congregational Quarterly*, vol. viii, pp. 525 f. (Oct.).

'Nonconformists and Lambeth. Approaches to Reunion'—a letter published in *The Times* for 14th Oct. (p. 10).

'The Christian Ministry. Loyalty and Obedience'—a letter on Reunion published in *The Times* for 23rd Oct. (p. 10).

'Professor Bartlet and Dr. Norwood'—a letter on Anglicanism, published in *Christian World* for 30th Oct. (p. 9).

'Let us at least understand one another'—a letter on Anglicanism, published in *Christian World* for 6th Nov. (p. 9).

'Reunion and how to approach it'—a letter published in *Christian World* for 20th Nov. (p. 9).

1931

Review of J. G. Machen's *The Virgin Birth of Christ*, in *Congregational Quarterly*, vol. ix, pp. 224–227 (Apl.).

'The Theology of the Group Movement', in *Christian World*, for 16th Apl. (p. 9) and 23rd Apl. (p. 7).

Review of A. S. Pringle-Pattison's *Studies in the Philosophy of Religion*, in *Congregational Quarterly*, vol. ix, pp. 354 f. (July).

Review of S. P. T. Prideaux's *Man and his Religion*, in *Congregational Quarterly*, vol. ix, pp. 355 f. (July).

'Congregationalism, Essential and Relative', in *Essays Congregational and Catholic, issued in commemoration of the Centenary of the Congregational Union of England and Wales*. Edited by Dr. Albert Peel. London (Congregational Union). Pp. 35–52 (Oct.).

1932

'The Doctrine of Grace to-day: an attempted dogmatic Eirenicon', in *The Doctrine of Grace*, edited by W. T. Whitley. London (S.C.M. Press). Pp. 355–372 (ch. XI (*d*)). See above, p. xxxii.

'Papias' *Exposition* and its Evidences as to the Gospels'—a paper read to the Oxford Society of Historical Theology on 25th Feb., and mentioned in its *Abstract of Proceedings for the Year 1932*, p. 24, and probably reproduced in *Amicitiae Corolla*: see below under 1933.

'St. Patrick'—a letter published in *The Times* for 19th Mar. (p. 8).

'Charles Gore: a personal appreciation', in *Hibbert Journal*, vol. xxx, pp. 459-467 (Apl.).

'The Doctrine of "Particular Guidance". With special reference to the Group Movement', in *Expository Times*, vol. xliii, pp. 317–319 (Apl.).

' "Catholic" Principles in the S(outh) I(ndia) Union', in *Church Union: News and Views*, vol. ii, p. 230 (May). See above, pp. xxix f.

'The Value of Episcopacy in the Twentieth Century', in *Church Union: News and Views*, vol. iii, pp. 21–23 (July). See above, pp. xxix f.

'The Gambling Industry'—a letter published in *The Times* for 24th Oct. (p. 15).

1933

'Papias's "Exposition": its Date and Contents', in *Amicitiae Corolla. A Volume of Essays Presented to James Rendel Harris, D.Litt. on the occasion of His Eightieth Birthday*. Edited by H. G. Wood. London (University of London Press). Pp. 15-44.

Review of A. V. Williams Jackson's *Researches in Manichaeism*, in *Congregational Quarterly*, vol. xi, pp. 101–103 (Jan.).

'Christian Pacifism'—letters published in *Christian World* for 22nd June (p. 2), 6th July (p. 5), 3rd Aug. (p. 5), and 17th Aug. (p. 9).

'Christian Pacifism', in *Christian World* for 31st Aug. (p. 9).

'Further Thoughts on the Scheme' (for Church-Union in South India), 'and Amendments thereto', in *Church Union : News and Views*, vol. iv, pp. 49–52 (Sept.). See above, pp. xxix f.

1934

(Part-author with A. E. Garvie). A footnote on the episcopate, in *Convictions. A Selection from the Responses of the Churches to the Report of the World Conference on Faith and Order, held at Lausanne in 1927*. Edited by L. Hodgson. London (S.C.M. Press). P. 52. See above, p. xxxii.

1935

Christianity in History, etc. Cheap reprint. See above, under 1917.

'Prophesying Doom. Human Personality'—a letter published in *The Times* for 1st Jan. (p. 10).

'Prophets of Doom'—a letter published in *The Times* for 14th Jan. (p. 8).

'A New Gospel'—a letter on the newly-discovered fragment, published in *The Times* for 31st Jan. (p. 10).

'Historical Progress in Religion, as seen in the Bible'—a paper read as the Presidential Address to the Oxford Society of Historical Theology on Feb. 7th, and noticed in its *Abstract of Proceedings for the Years 1934–1937*, p. 4, but never printed in extenso.

'The Abyssinian "Impasse". A League Protectorate. Preferential Rights for Italy'—a letter published in *The Times* for 3rd Sept. (p. 13).

1936

'Acts of the Apostles, The', in *A New Standard Bible Dictionary*, edited by M. W. Jacobus, E. C. Lane, and A. C. Zenos. Third Revised Edition (see above, under 1909 and 1926). New York and London (Funk and Wagnall). Pp. 21–25.

Also the following articles in the same work:

'Apollos', pp. 56 f.

'Apostle', p. 57 (with M. W. Jacobus).

'Baptism, Baptize', pp. 93–95.

'Barnabas', pp. 95 f.

Also the revision of J. Denney's earlier article on 'Church Life and Organization' (pp. 132–137), and Sir R. A. Falconer's earlier articles on 'Timothy' (pp. 908 f.), 'Timothy, Epistles to' (pp. 909–912), Titus' (p. 913), and 'Titus, Epistle to' (pp. 913 f.).

'Christian Worship as reflected in Ancient Liturgies', in *Christian Worship: Studies in its History and Meaning*. By Members of Mansfield College. Edited by N. Micklem, and dedicated to W. B. Selbie. Oxford (Clarendon Press). Pp. 83–99.

'The Fourth Gospel'—a letter on Dr. R. Eisler's views, published in *The Times* for 10th Feb. (p. 8).

'Air-pollution'—a letter published in *The Times* for 10th Mar. (p. 17).

'The German Claim'—a letter on Locarno, published in *The Times* for 30th Mar. (p. 13).

'Baptism in the Early Church', in *Christian World* for 23rd Apl. (p. 8).

'Pre-War Mansfield', in *Mansfield College Magazine*, vol. xiv, pp. 403–408 (June).

'Infant Baptism', in *Christian World* for 18th June (p. 7—replying to criticism).

'A Personal Explanation'—a letter on Infant Baptism in *Christian World* for 2nd July (p. 5).

'Name for No. 552'—a letter suggesting a name for the sister-ship to the 'Queen Mary', published in *The Times* for 15th Dec. (p. 17).

1937

'The Primate's Appeal. Religion and Modern Thought. The Line of Approach'—a letter published in *The Times* for 6th Jan. (p. 13).

'Unity in Diversity', in *Christian World* for 29th July (p. 16).

'Alcohol and Health'—a letter published in *Oxford Times* for 26th Nov. (p. 6).

'Doctors and Drink'—a letter published in *Oxford Times* for 10th Dec. (p. 6).

1938

(Part-author with R. H. Lord). 'Thomas Arthur Wolfendale, 1886–1938', in *Mansfield College Magazine*, vol. xiv, pp. 530 f. (July).

'Need for "Air-planning" '—a letter published in *The Times* for 2nd August (p. 11).

'Czechoslovakia. Racial and National Rights. A Distinction ignored'—a letter published in *The Times* for 8th Sept. (p. 13).

Review of C. J. Cadoux's *Ancient Smyrna*, in *Mansfield College Magazine*, vol. xiv, pp. 560–563 (Dec.).

1939

'Robert Harley Lord, 1887–1939', in *Mansfield College Magazine*, vol. xiv, pp. 583 f. (July).

'Fresh Approaches to Christian Theology', in *Christian World* for 13th July (p. 9) and 20th July (p. 13).

' "Hitler's War" '—a letter published in *The Times* for 11th Sept. (p. 4).

'Some Personal Aspects', in *Expository Times*, vol. li, pp. 110 f. (Nov.—under "Entre Nous").

1940

'German Propaganda'—a letter published in *The Times* for 6th Jan. (p. 4).

'Religion and the Nation'—a letter on religious education, published in *The Times* for 2nd Mar. (p. 6).

'Why Nonconformity?'—a letter published in *Christian World* for 14th Mar. (p. 5).

'South Indian Unity'—a letter published in *Christian World* for 11th Apl. (p. 8).

'The Propriety of "Infant Baptism" '—a letter published in *Christian World* for 11th July (p. 5).

A supplementary paragraph to the obituary notice of J. T. Davies, in *Mansfield College Magazine*, vol. xiv, p. 627 (Oct.).

1942

Church-Life and Church-Order in the First Four Centuries (Birkbeck Lectures, 1924), edited by C. J. Cadoux. Oxford (Blackwell).

C. J. C.

SUBJECT-INDEX

The reader should bear in mind that all references to parts of Scripture and to early Christian writers and writings are included in the other two Indices.

In certain cases the page-numbers specified in this Index represent places where the indexed item is referred to under some other term.

INDEX OF PARTS OF SCRIPTURE QUOTED OR REFERRED TO

204

INDEX OF EARLY CHRISTIAN WRITERS AND WRITINGS QUOTED OR REFERRED TO